Spiritual INNOVATORS

Spiritual INNOVATORS

Seventy-Five Extraordinary People Who Changed the World in the Past Century

Edited by Ira Rifkin
and the Editors at SkyLight Paths

Foreword by Dr. Robert Coles,
winner of the Pulitzer Prize

Walking Together, Finding the Way
SKYLIGHT PATHS® Publishing
Woodstock, Vermont

Spiritual Innovators:
Seventy-Five Extraordinary People Who Changed the World in the Past Century

Library of Congress Cataloging-in-Publication Data
Spiritual innovators : 75 extraordinary people who changed the world in the past century / edited by Ira Rifkin and the editors at SkyLight Paths.
p. cm.
Includes bibliographical references and index.
ISBN 1-893361-43-8 (hardcover)—ISBN 1-893361-50-0 (paperback)
1. Spiritual biography. I. Rifkin, Ira. II. SkyLight Paths Publishing.
BL72 .S69 2002
200'.92'2—dc21 2001007688

10 9 8 7 6 5 4 3 2 1

Manufactured in Canada

Walking Together, Finding the Way
Published by SkyLight Paths Publishing
A Division of LongHill Partners, Inc.
Sunset Farm Offices, Route 4, P.O. Box 237
Woodstock, VT 05091
Tel: (802) 457-4000 Fax: (802) 457-4004
www.skylightpaths.com

Contents

Foreword

by Dr. Robert Coles

As I read the pages that follow I couldn't help but remember the remarks that theologian Paul Tillich offered those of us who were lucky then, in 1958, to be members of his seminar—a class meant to consider what this book has summoned for its readers. "Spiritual energy is sometimes reduced rather than enhanced by formal religious observance," our Harvard professor told us, and there we were yet again, silently considering the import of spoken words, their ironic thrust not easily understood by most of us.

As if aware of our response and anxious to make himself as clear as possible, our professor repeated himself. He then went into an extended soliloquy of sorts, during which he reminded us that the prophets Jeremiah and Isaiah were insistently critical of the status quo, even as Jesus of Nazareth was restlessly original-minded, ready to take on various principalities and powers directly or by implication. By the time Tillich finished, we were all still eager to return to the safety of talk about books and about our interpretations of a particular reading assignment. But Tillich had one more comment, which would last and last in our thinking, and which came to my mind as I went through this book: "The Bible's prophets were not theologians—they were storytellers, determined to give us all much pause." He went on to contrast abstract analysis with the concrete narrative presentations of various storytellers, in whose direction he urged us to travel. I think of him today when I encounter them: Flannery O'Connor, for instance, who urged on us, "Where feeling for a story is absent, theory will not supply it." At another point she wryly observed, "The task of the novelist is to deepen mystery, and mystery is a great embarrassment to the modern mind."

In a sense, this book offers dozens of "extraordinary people" who dared in their various ways to carry forth the kind of searching, unconventional spiritual explorations of mind, heart, and soul that Tillich favored, and O'Connor as well. Those of us who meet the seventy-five individuals in these pages will be given a lucky chance to think of their respective messages, keep them very close to ourselves as we try to figure out life's meaning and purpose—the spiritual direction we aim to pursue and our reasons. Even as Tillich wanted us to keep in mind his thoughts (not to mention those of the great prophets of Israel he called upon), even as Flannery O'Connor wanted to unnerve us a bit in her fiction and jolt us every now and then in her essays, these seventy-five spiritual innovators confront us with their words and deeds, their brave willingness to say and do what they believed to be both necessary and spiritually befitting. Here are individuals who affirmed in their daily lives what truly matters; thereby, they touch us, inspire us, stir us to take stock of this earthly existence given us. Collectively, a large gift, indeed, from them to so many, the readers of this book included.

A Note from the Editors

An adventure—that's what developing *Spiritual Innovators: Seventy-Five Extraordinary People Who Changed the World in the Past Century* has been for us.

Two years ago, as the new century dawned, members of our editorial team in Vermont were musing about the incredible century of religion that had just passed. We discussed the unprecedented exposure of East to West that has happened in the past century, the steps taken toward equalizing roles available to women and minorities, the armed conflicts that have been inspired by religious hatred and misunderstanding, the growth of pluralism—not just tolerance—as a concept, and the refreshing cross-pollination that has happened across spiritual and religious traditions.

Our conversation eventually turned to people. People. Who, we asked each other, were the most extraordinary spiritual and religious people of the past century?

One of us mentioned the remarkable spiritual leaders we have seen (for instance, Maha Ghosananda, Martin Luther King, Jr., and Daniel Berrigan). Another said that the spiritual leader as celebrity was a twentieth-century phenomenon (such as H. H. the Dalai Lama, Mother Teresa, and Billy Graham).

We left the room that afternoon with a mission. We would canvas the world's spiritual and religious leaders, as well as experts in leading universities and seminaries, asking: "Draw up your list of the ten most important spiritual/religious innovators of the twentieth century. Tell us those people who, in your opinion, brought the most change, excitement, innovation, creativity, and vitality to the religious and spiritual lives of people throughout the world."

We asked representatives of nearly every religious tradition and spiritual persuasion. We tallied their results, added a few of our own opinions and our analysis, and drew up the final list of seventy-five.

You will no doubt find someone dear to you and your spiritual life missing. We apologize for that. If we had room, we no doubt would have included, for instance, Jean Vanier, John A. T. Robinson, Krister Stendahl, Bernie Glassman, John Shelby Spong, Joan Halifax, M. Basil Pennington, Louise Hay, Karl Rahner, William Sloane Coffin, Alan Watts, Gershom Scholem, and many many others.

We commissioned religion journalists, authors, book editors, and other experts to write each of the seventy-five profiles of these extraordinary people. Ira Rifkin, award-winning religion journalist, brought them all together into a book.

Chögyam Trungpa, Pope John XXIII, Aimee Semple McPherson, and D. T. Suzuki ranked numbers 2–5 in our survey. Our greatest surprise in the process? The top vote-getter was none other than "Dr. Bob," the cofounder of Alcoholics Anonymous. AA may just be the most important spiritual organization founded in the past century.

JON M. SWEENEY
Editor in Chief

Acknowledgments

My sincerest thanks to the talented writers who crafted the profiles contained in this book. Their names are listed elsewhere, but their work is this book's core. Thank you as well to SkyLight Paths, particularly Stuart, Jon, Emily, and Maura.

Most of all, I wish to thank my personal guides: my wife, Ruth, and sons, Brady and Jesse.

—I. R.

INTRODUCTION

by Ira Rifkin

On a blustery Sunday evening in November 1997, the Orthodox Christian Ecumenical Patriarch Bartholomew I came to Johnstown, Pennsylvania, and the faithful, more than a thousand of them, packed Christ the Saviour Cathedral for this once-in-a-lifetime religious experience. Among them was a local family with a severely disabled son. The youth, his body contorted by cerebral palsy, appeared to be a teenager but at twenty was really more a young man. He sat in a wheelchair, his body jerking uncontrollably. Saliva dripped down his jaw, and family members took turns wiping it away. As did everybody, the family stayed in place for hours in advance of the late-arriving patriarch, who was wrapping up a long tour across the United States.

A history of devastating floods has brought Johnstown a measure of notoriety. But Orthodox Christians are familiar with Johnstown for a more gratifying reason; it has one of the most devout and varied Orthodox communities of any small American city. In the mid-twentieth century, immigrants from Eastern Europe and the Balkans flocked to the town, founded more than a century earlier by Joseph Johns, to work in the area's then-thriving steel mills and coal mines. They brought with them the multiple ethnic strains of Orthodoxy that had nurtured their ancestors for centuries.

Even today, Johnstown remains tied to its ethnic religious roots and is still home to seven Orthodox churches, serving some fifteen hundred congregants out of the town's total population of about twenty thousand. There is one Greek, two Serbian, one Ukrainian, one Russian, one Antiochian, and one Carpatho-Russian congregation. Christ the Saviour Cathedral—with its tan-and-brown brick exterior and three cupolas, the onion domes that give Orthodox churches their distinctiveness—is Carpatho-Russian, and it is the mother church of the American Carpatho-Russian Orthodox Diocese of the USA.

The temperature that night was below freezing, and a light snow fell. But it was stifling inside the cathedral. Its walls, ceiling, and icon screen that divided the congregation from the altar were resplendently covered with the Byzantine-style paintings of Jesus, Mary, and the saints so venerated by Orthodoxy's theology of the image. The young man and his family sat in the first row of the nave, placed there to make it easy for the patriarch to bestow his blessings upon them. I had been traveling with the patriarch as a reporter, a non-Christian observer trying to make sense of a tradition I knew little about. Johnstown began for me as just one more stop in the patriarch's overcrowded schedule, an evening that would warrant no more than a paragraph or two in the wrap-up story on his trip I was to file the next day.

I made my way to the front of the church to await Bartholomew as well, and as I did I noticed the wheelchair-bound youth and his family. The father wept openly, and his body language spoke of the burden he must carry with him every day of his life. At first the father's pain was my entire focus, and I imagined how I would feel if I were in his place. Then my attention shifted to an appreciation of the lavish communal and spiritual support the family received from the congregation and its patriarch. Later I learned that the father was not Orthodox. He was Protestant and had married into the Orthodox embrace. But his religious identity did not prevent him from reaching out for divine help in whatever form it presented itself.

The patriarch eventually showed up, and after concluding the doxology, or noneucharistic prayer service, he moved toward the youth. Bartholomew—believed by the Orthodox to be the 270th successor in an unbroken line to the apostle Andrew, and looking every bit the part with his gold crown, long white beard, and red-and-white outer vestments—placed his hands upon the young man's head and briefly stroked it, as the father wept even more. Tears also began to flow from the other family members, as fellow congregants seated nearby touched and hugged them in an outpouring of compassion and understanding. I cried as well. So much for maintaining a professional demeanor.

I remember noticing what looked to be a smile on the youth's face, but whether it was in fact a smile I could not tell. I do know that

I found the experience spiritually meaningful in an extraordinary way. I have since come to understand that the night in Johnstown—its mingling of millennia-old tradition, its universal themes of human frailty and otherworldly longing, the crossing of once rigid sectarian barriers—also spoke volumes about religion and spirituality in the twentieth century.

Pope John Paul II called the twentieth century the most violent in history, and surely it would be tough to counter that assessment. But the hundred-year period was also a time of remarkable material progress that, to varying degrees certainly, benefited much of the world's population. Dramatic technological advances lowered the barriers of time and distance, allowing events and ideas that reflected both the best and the worst of humanity to become global experiences.

The realm of the spirit was no less transformed. Time is a continuum, of course, and in many ways the twentieth century was a mere continuation of events and processes that can be traced back hundreds of years, to the Enlightenment and the philosophical, social, and economic changes that flowed from it, and even further into the recesses of human history. Yet the implications of the changes unfolding over time seemed to come together more quickly in the twentieth century than ever before.

Suddenly, it seemed, religions and their underlying spiritual philosophies were free to break their cultural constraints, giving rise to unprecedented interfaith exchanges. Secularism and consumerism became dominant traits of Western culture, leaving traditional faiths scrambling to adjust and in danger of being left behind. Eastern forms moved westward to fill the resulting spiritual voids, even as Western culture spread eastward to undermine the very same Eastern ideologies being embraced half a world away. New religious movements developed; some were the offspring of established faiths, some were the free-form creations of charismatic individuals, and some represented the reemergence of paths long neglected. The atmosphere of greater freedom, greater choice, and greater openness led to the Second Vatican Council, the ordination of women in many Protestant denominations and within Judaism, and the involvement of religious leaders in political and social liberation movements in the United States and elsewhere.

By the end of a century that endured fascism, communism, the threat of atomic annihilation, and the excesses of capitalism, the world seemed in need of spiritual succor, and religious revival blossomed. In the West, studies repeatedly stressed that the so-called baby-boomer generation was engaged in a frenetic search for a faith to call home. New Age and exotic Eastern faiths were sampled widely and incorporated into the spiritual worldviews of many. More and more young people, particularly in urban areas, abandoned family religious ties for new ones of their own choosing.

Traditional faith was, for a time, relegated by some to the dustbin of history. Witness the now ludicrous-seeming mid-1960s *Time* magazine cover that arrogantly asked, "Is God Dead?" Not only is God or, more precisely, faith in God alive and well, but traditional religion and its pious spirituality seemed the most robust of faiths at the century's conclusion, even as bitter and sometimes violent disputes raged over whose definition of God should prevail. Conservative Evangelical and Pentecostal churches grew faster than their liberal kin in the West as well as in Latin America and Christian areas of Africa. Traditional interpretations also came to dominate in Hindu India and across the Islamic world. The end of the twentieth century saw the human desire for understanding of its place in the world as unquenchable as ever, if not even more confusing.

What, then, is a "spiritual innovator" in an age of nonstop transformation? Let's begin by trying to define *spiritual.* We can start by opening a dictionary or two. There you will find references to sensitivity or attachment to religious values, or the quality or state of being spiritual, or an encounter with transcendent reality—dry definitions that fail to impart the sense of poetic mystery associated with the true spiritual state. I think the Jewish philosopher Martin Buber probably came closer. Spirituality, he said, is recognizable in those "moments of silent depth in which you look upon the world-order fully present."

But what if you have never recognized such a moment? Perhaps it is easier to understand the sublime by turning to an example from the profane. In the American political debate over what constitutes hard-core pornography, the late Supreme Court Justice Potter Stewart commented that even if he could not define the offending material, "I know it when I see it." What cannot be articulated is readily apparent to the eye. The same may be said for spirituality, as opposite an experience to pornography as there is. Using words to describe spirituality is ultimately as dissatisfying as looking at a map to understand the grandeur of California's Big Sur coast or Nepal's Mount Everest; all it can do is point the way. Spirituality, then, is about an inner feeling of connection, no matter how brief, with the mystery of creation—that Higher Power spoken of in Alcoholics Anonymous and understood so very differently by Buddhist, Muslim, and tribal shaman.

Defining the term *innovator* is far easier. *Merriam-Webster's Collegiate Dictionary* defines it thus: "to introduce as or as if new . . . to make changes, do something in a new way." And a spiritual innovator? Sure he or she introduces or does something in a new way within the realm of ultimate truth. But, here again, words do not convey the important quality that elevates an individual to the level of true spiritual innovator. The noted American journalist Garry Wills put his finger on that quality in writing about Dorothy Day, founder of the Catholic Worker community. She was the sort of inspirational leader, said Wills, "who makes you say, after meeting them, 'I've got to be better than I am.'"

Seventy-five such individuals are profiled in this book. Why seventy-five? Because it is a number large enough to provide a broad sweep of the century's diverse spiritual innovators, yet small enough to force us to limit this volume to those whose contributions, at this stage, appear the most far-reaching. Our choices were made with the help of experts from different traditions, and we sought to be inclusive of varying and sometimes conflicting viewpoints, and to include representative figures from around the world. Militant atheists are included with devout monotheists, strict sectarians as well as universalists, overt proselytizers and those who preferred quiet witness, some with saintly personalities and others critics might dismiss as charlatans or as having political agendas. Still, we recognize that not everyone will agree with our choices. Frankly, that is the nature of spiritual questions: one person's heaven is another's hell. But we make no claim to omniscience, and any oversights are our responsibility.

We also recognize that innovations come in many forms, and in response we sought to categorize those profiled according to their primary contributions. This classification is obviously inexact. The very nature of innovation seems to defy clear categorization. Moreover, the century's advances in communications and travel further blurred the lines that divide. How else can you explain the Dalai Lama, Tibetan Buddhist monk and pop culture phenomenon at the same time?

It is appropriate, then, to open this book with a chapter titled "They Shook Things Up." If nothing else, the spiritual status quo was unrelentingly challenged during the twentieth century. It is equally appropriate to end the book with a chapter titled "They Spoke from the Power of Silence," for silence, say the mystics, is at the core of spiritual transformation. In between, we profile those who died or otherwise suffered greatly for their spirituality and in doing so profoundly affected the world around them; and those who became larger-than-life figures in the way that only the twentieth century's enveloping mass media could make them. We also devote chapters to innovators whose main contributions were their extraordinary intellects, and to those whose writings on spirituality seized the intellects of readers. Additional chapters focus on individuals who turned their inner convictions into mass public demonstrations of love for others, and those who were able to see beyond sectarian visions by fostering common understandings.

Regardless of their contributions, the innovators profiled here affected the world in a grand manner. For the rest of us, the inner process unfolds in a less dramatic fashion, moments of insight that build, often imperceptibly, on those that came before. Johnstown, Pennsylvania, was one such moment for me. A glimpse of the spirituality inherent in a religious tradition I had previously regarded as exotic, and even threatening to my own, unexpectedly but incrementally altered my worldview. And is that not spiritual innovation in its most basic and common form?

A cautionary note: This book is meant as an introduction. Our goal is to inspire readers and motivate them to seek out more information on those spiritual innovators to whom they feel drawn. But nothing here is meant to be a substitute for spiritual experience. That, as the term implies, can only be gained experientially. The only way to truly glimpse the understandings that motivated this book's collection of spiritual innovators to act as they did is to seek out the experiences that shaped who they became. Step into the emptiness of the holy of holies for yourself.

1

THEY **SHOOK** THINGS UP

In his 1941 message to the United States Congress, President Franklin Delano Roosevelt spoke of four "essential" human freedoms: freedom of expression, freedom from want, freedom from fear, and freedom of worship. Taken together, they say much about the twentieth century.

The last century of the second Christian millennium was a time of extraordinary upheaval. Empires came and went, traditional beliefs were reconsidered, cultural barriers broke down, and social and personal liberation took flight. Unprecedented material comfort was accompanied by the rapid spread of revolutionary ideas. And freedom, or at least its promise, was the prevailing zeitgeist. It was no less so for spiritual and religious innovators.

In the United States, William J. Seymour and Aimee Semple McPherson challenged the Protestant establishment and in doing so helped make Pentecostalism the world's fastest-growing Christian movement in the late twentieth century. Mary Baker Eddy, meanwhile, founded the Church of Christ, Scientist, commonly called Christian Science. Not only did this trio upset the applecart of accepted Christian "truths" but they also shattered race, gender, and social boundaries within the church world. Meanwhile, Bhaktivedanta Prabuphada forced the Western religious establishment to take notice of his Hare Krishna movement, a 1960s spiritual touchstone.

At different times during the century, three men may be said to have personified the period's emphasis on freedom of expression and worship. They are Shirdi Sai Baba, a legendary Indian fakir (wandering ascetic) with a penchant for shocking others; G. I. Gurdjieff, a rogue figure who charmed many of Europe's artistic and intellectual elite; and Chögyam Trungpa, a Tibetan lama who took delight in dashing monastic tradition. Each transcended conventional notions of how a spiritual teacher is expected to act. In doing so, all appealed to an unprecedented individualism adopted by many, and particularly in the West, as the twentieth century moved toward closure.

The iconoclasms of Bertrand Russell, Robert Funk, and Mary Daly also fall within the century's recurring intellectual theme. Russell, a Nobel Prize winner in literature, employed his prodigious talents on behalf of reasoned atheism and broad antimilitarism. He coauthored a famous call for a halt to nuclear weapons development—at the height of cold war fervor for just such weapons. Funk, founder of the Jesus Seminar, employed twentieth-century marketing techniques to make academic reworking of Christianity's most basic beliefs a public and media sport—angering traditionalists to no end. A product of the feminist movement, Daly not only questioned the Roman Catholic Church's patriarchal hierarchy but also sought to rewrite its language—even if doing so meant creating idiosyncratic terminology of her own to make the point. Her radicalism forced sharp public conflict with the ecclesiastical establishment even as she inspired many another feminist theologian. Russell, Funk, and Daly—freethinkers all.

Freedom is also very much what Elijah Muhammad and Desmond Tutu are about. Both challenged the prevailing power structures of their homelands in efforts to lift their people out of degrading and debilitating economic, social, and political straits—although they certainly went about it in different ways. Muhammad, leader of the Nation of Islam, adopted a controversial message of preferred religious and racial separateness, keeping his followers as societal outsiders while laying the groundwork for the large-scale African-American move toward Islam that marked the century's final decades. Tutu was a mirror opposite. An Anglican archbishop, he worked from within the South African establishment to dismantle the system of racial separation known as apartheid, becoming a global symbol of nonviolent struggle for freedom and reconciliation between former enemies, for which he was awarded the Nobel Peace Prize.

Zalman Schachter-Shalomi and Starhawk, meanwhile, represent another perspective on freedom, one uniquely late twentieth century. Schachter-Shalomi came from a highly traditional Hasidic Jewish background, yet ended up teaching at a Buddhist university after becoming the guiding light of the spiritually oriented Jewish Renewal movement. Starhawk, a feminist "ecospiritual" writer-activist, is a leading figure within the Goddess and Wicca movements. Hers is an anticapitalist, politically oriented, earth-based spirituality drawn from pre-Christian pagan paths—an in-your-face worldview that one might think unlikely to draw serious attention from more establishment religionists.

Yet it often does. And that says volumes about contemporary attitudes toward Roosevelt's four freedoms.

CHÖGYAM TRUNGPA
(1940–1987)

An important teacher of the Kagyü and Nyingma lineages of Tibetan Buddhism, known for their emphasis on meditation practice and learning, Chögyam Trungpa was one of the most influential forces in spreading Buddhism to the West. Particularly attracting young people, he had an unusual talent for communicating with Westerners in their own idiom, speaking in terms of their own culture rather than Tibetan tradition, and linking Buddhist concepts with those of modern psychology. His uncompromising, nontheistic message about the dangers of "spiritual materialism" sounded an alarm amid the chaotic spiritual supermarket of the 1970s.

Chögyam Trungpa founded a network of meditation centers around the world as well as the Naropa Institute (now Naropa University) in Boulder, Colorado. He also developed an original teaching called Shambhala Training, named after a legendary Himalayan kingdom said to represent the ideal enlightened society, as well as the inner state of enlightenment latent within everyone. This teaching is unique in its emphasis on a secular rather than a religious approach to spiritual practice. Other secular studies he fostered among his students include calligraphy, flower arranging, Japanese archery, tea ceremony, dance, theater, health care, psychotherapy, poetry, elocution, and translation.

Chögyam Trungpa had an unusual talent for communicating with Westerners in their own idiom, linking Buddhist concepts with those of modern psychology.

He was born in eastern Tibet into the Mukpo clan, descended from King Gesar of Ling. Following his identification as the eleventh descendant in the line of Trungpa *tülkus* (incarnations of teachers), he was addressed by the title Chögyam Trungpa Rinpoche.

(Chögyam is a contraction of Chökyi Gyatso, which was part of his novice monk name. *Rinpoche* means "teacher." Currently he is referred to as the Vidyadhara, "wisdom holder.") Having already been enthroned as the abbot of the Surmang monasteries, Chögyam Trungpa fled to India at the age of nineteen when the Chinese invaded his homeland in 1959. Subsequently he went to Great Britain, where he studied at Oxford University in the mid-1960s and founded Samye Ling, the first Tibetan Buddhist practice center in the West, in Scotland in 1967.

After a car accident that left him partially paralyzed on his left side, he broke with tradition by abandoning his monastic vows and marrying an Englishwoman in 1969. The following year they moved to the United States, where he established meditation and study centers in Vermont and Colorado. In 1986 the center of his activities was moved from Boulder to Halifax, Nova Scotia, where he died the following year. Today Shambhala International, the umbrella organization connected with his work, is under the leadership of his eldest son, Sakyong Mipham Rinpoche. Chögyam Trungpa is honored by several commemorative shrines *(stupas)* containing his physical remains; the principal one, known as the Great Stupa of Dharmakaya, was consecrated at Rocky Mountain Shambhala Center in 2001.

His Words

The genuine heart of sadness comes from feeling that your nonexistent heart is full. You would like to spill your heart's blood, give your heart to others. For the warrior, this experience of sad and tender heart is what gives birth to fearlessness. Conventionally, being fearless means that you are not afraid or that, if someone hits you, you will hit him back. However, we are not talking about that street-fighter level of fearlessness. Real fearlessness is the product of tenderness. It comes from letting the world tickle your heart, your raw and beautiful heart. You are willing to open up, without resistance or shyness, and face the world. You are willing to share your heart with others.
—*Shambhala,* p. 46

Books by Chögyam Trungpa

Born in Tibet. 1966. 4th ed. Boston: Shambhala Publications, 2000.
Crazy Wisdom. Boston: Shambhala Publications, 1991.

Cutting through Spiritual Materialism. 1973. Reprint, Boston: Shambhala Publications, 1987.

The Essential Chögyam Trungpa. Edited by Carolyn Rose Gimian. Boston: Shambhala Publications, 1999.

The Heart of the Buddha. Boston: Shambhala Publications, 1991.

Illusion's Game: The Life and Teaching of Naropa. Boston: Shambhala Publications, 1994.

Meditation in Action. 1969. Reprint, Boston: Shambhala Publications, 1996.

The Myth of Freedom and the Way of Meditation. 1976. Reprint, Boston: Shambhala Publications, 1988.

Shambhala: The Sacred Path of the Warrior. 1984. Reprint, Boston: Shambhala Publications, 1995.

Training the Mind and Cultivating Loving Kindness. Boston: Shambhala Publications, 1993.

Organization

Shambhala International, 1084 Tower Rd., Halifax, NS B3H 2Y5, Canada; phone: 902-425-4275, ext. 10; e-mail: info@shambhala.org; web site: www.shambhala.org.

Other Resources

Audiotapes and videotapes: Kalapa Recordings, 1084 Tower Rd., Halifax, NS B3H 2Y5, Canada; phone: 902-420-1118, ext. 19; e-mail: recordings@shambhala.org; web site: www.shambhalashop.com/recordings/vctrbio.html. More than one hundred tapes are available.

School: Naropa University, 2130 Arapahoe Ave., Boulder, CO 80302; phone: 303-444-0202; e-mail: info@naropa.edu; web site: www.naropa.edu.

Retreat centers: Karmê Chöling Buddhist Meditation Center, 369 Patneaude Ln., Barnet, VT 05821; phone: 802-633-2384; e-mail: karmecholing@shambhala.org; web site: www.kcl.shambhala.org. Rocky Mountain Shambhala Center, 4921 County Rd. 68C, Red Feather Lakes, CO 80545; phone: 970-881-2184; e-mail: rmsc@shambhala.org; web site: www.rmsc.shambhala.org. Meditation retreats, educational programs, and contemplative conferences.

"Real fearlessness is the product of tenderness."

MARY DALY
(1928–)

Reborn in the tumult of the feminist movement of the 1960s and 1970s, Mary Daly refines and redefines theological language to give new meanings and understandings to the Christian establishment she views as being in ruins.

Not only a feminist in the extreme, Mary Daly is also a scholar of theology and the author of several controversial but well-received books and papers. She holds three Ph.D. degrees—the first in religion from Saint Mary's College in Notre Dame, Indiana. Wanting to continue her education but unable to find a graduate school in the United States that admitted women into its theology programs, she studied at the University of Fribourg in Switzerland, where she was the first woman to earn a Ph.D. in sacred theology. Her third Ph.D., also from Fribourg, is in philosophy.

Her reconstruction of Christian, primarily Catholic, theology led to constant struggle with the administration of Boston College, where she taught for twenty-five years until her forced retirement. The conflict began when she published *The Church and the Second Sex* in 1969. While her book received wide national acclaim, the college tried to fire her because of her unorthodox theological position and her attack on the Catholic Church. Following protests from students around the country, Boston College reinstated her with tenure. The pressures prompted her to shine ever brighter, as she published more radical books and lectured around the world. But in 1999 a male student to whom she had denied access to her class filed a discrimination suit, prompting the college to cancel her courses and to maintain that she voluntarily resigned—a claim she contests.

As one of the founding mothers of feminist theology, Daly claimed that "as long as God was male, then male was God."

As one of the founding mothers of feminist theology, Daly claimed that "as long as God was male, then male was God." In her second book, *Beyond God the Father,* she named and claimed that God is a verb. This radical shift in conceptualizing God fueled other feminist writers to uncover and denounce the impact of the church and the church's language in keeping women subservient. She has made it her mission to identify how organized religion, primarily the institutional Catholic Church, gave birth to and perpetuates the oppression of women.

She lectures widely and continues to write in a unique style, changing spelling, capitalization, and hyphenation to shed new light on old words. As self-defined in *Websters' First New Intergalactic Wickedary of the English Language,* she is a "Positively Revolting Hag—a stunning, beauteous Crone; one who inspires positive revulsion from phallic institutions and morality, inciting others to Acts of Pure Lust."

Her Words

Why indeed must "God" be a noun? Why not a verb—the most active and dynamic of all? Hasn't the naming of "God" as a noun been an act of murdering that dynamic Verb? And isn't the Verb intimately more personal than a mere static noun? The anthropomorphic symbols for God may be intended to convey personality, but they fail to convey that God is Be-ing. Women who now are experiencing the shock of nonbeing and the surge of self-affirmation against this are inclined to perceive transcendence as a Verb in which we participate—live, move, and have our being.
—*Beyond God the Father,* pp. 33–34

Gyn/Ecology *n* 1: knowledge enabling Crones to expose connections among the institutions, ideologies, and atrocities of the foreground; habit of Dis-covering threads of connections hidden by man-made mazes and mysteries; practical wisdom concerning the complex web of relationships among Spinsters and all Elemental beings.
—*Websters' First New Intergalactic Wickedary of the English Language,* p. 77

Hag *n* : a Witch, Fury, Harpy who haunts the Hedges/Boundaries of patriarchy, frightening fools and summoning Weird Wandering Women into the Wild.
—*Websters' First New Intergalactic Wickedary of the English Language*, p. 137

Books by Mary Daly

Beyond God the Father: Toward a Philosophy of Women's Liberation. 1973. Reprint, Boston: Beacon Press, 1985.
The Church and the Second Sex. 1969. Reprint, Boston: Beacon Press, 1985.
Gyn/Ecology, the Metaethics of Radical Feminism. 1978. Reprint, Boston: Beacon Press, 1990.
Outercourse: The Bedazzling Voyage Containing Recollections from My Logbook of a Radical Feminist Philosopher. San Francisco: HarperSanFrancisco, 1992.
Pure Lust: Elemental Feminist Philosophy. San Francisco: HarperSanFrancisco, 1992.
Quintessence—Realizing the Outrageous Contagious Courage of Women: A Radical Elemental Feminist Manifesto. Boston: Beacon Press, 1998.
Websters' First New Intergalactic Wickedary of the English Language. With Jane Caputi and Sudie Rakusin. 1987. Reprint, San Francisco: HarperSanFrancisco, 1992.

"Why indeed must 'God' be a noun? Why not a verb—the most active and dynamic of all?"

MARY BAKER EDDY
(1821–1910)

Few women have started religious movements, and few religions—whether started by men or women—have been launched successfully in America, but Mary Baker Eddy and the Church of Christ, Scientist she founded are exceptions. Mary Baker Eddy's *Science and Health,* and her longtime leadership of the new church, resulted in a movement whose influence extends far beyond its membership rolls, evidenced in part by the wide readership of the venerable newspaper the *Christian Science Monitor* and by the explosion of interest among many in spiritual healing.

Raised on a New Hampshire farm, Eddy suffered from frequent bouts of nervous and spinal ailments. Ill health kept her largely out of school, but by her early teens she was writing poetry that reflected on issues such as death and immortality. Her health continued to deteriorate through two marriages—the first ended after six months with her husband's death, the second lasted twenty years. A decade into her second marriage, she met Phineas Parkhurst Quimby, a healer who believed sickness was a problem of the mind. Under his care, she recovered some of her strength, and she studied with him for several years.

Eddy herself dated the birth of Christian Science to an incident soon after Quimby's death in 1866, when she injured her back falling on ice. Three days later, having read the gospel accounts of Jesus' healing, she rose from bed and declared herself healed. By 1875 she had bought a home in Lynn, Massachusetts, which served as a meeting place for students. She held the first Christian Science

Sin and illness, in Eddy's view, emanate from humans' estrangement from God, and spiritual healing is considered a rediscovery of a key element of Jesus' ministry.

service and soon after published her monumental *Science and Health with Key to the Scriptures.* A year later the Christian Science Association was formed, and in 1879 the Church of Christ, Scientist formally came into being. Eddy soon moved the church to Boston, where its headquarters remain, and in 1877 she married Asa Gilbert Eddy, her third husband. In 1889 a Christian Science college opened; there Mary Baker Eddy planted the seeds for her mostly female students to open churches around the nation.

Science and Health was, essentially, a biblical commentary, in which Eddy expounded on the underlying message of healing in the text. Sin and illness, in her view, emanate from humans' estrangement from God, and spiritual healing is considered a rediscovery of a key element of Jesus' ministry. In addition to publishing several new editions of *Science and Health,* she founded the daily *Christian Science Monitor* and the weekly *Christian Science Sentinel,* publications based on core Christian values. By the time of her death, *Science and Health* had sold 400,000 copies.

In the 1880s Eddy appeared less often in public, even as the church continued to grow. She rarely visited Boston, even for the dedication of the "Mother Church" in 1895. She continued to work at her New Hampshire home until her death in 1910.

Her Words

The prayer that reforms the sinner and heals the sick is an absolute faith that all things are possible to God—a spiritual understanding of Him, an unselfed love. Regardless of what another may say or think on this subject, I speak from experience. Prayer, watching, and working, combined with self-immolation, are God's gracious means for accomplishing whatever has been successfully done for the Christianization and health of mankind.
—*Science and Health,* p. 1

In Christian Science mere opinion is valueless. Proof is essential to a due estimate of this subject. Sneers at the application of the word *Science* to Christianity cannot prevent that from being scientific which is based on divine Principle, demonstrated according to a divine given rule, and subjected to proof. The facts are so absolute and numerous in

support of Christian Science, that misrepresentation and denunciation cannot overthrow it.
—*Science and Health,* p. 342

"All my work, all my efforts, all my prayers and tears are for humanity, and the spread of peace and love among mankind."
—*New York American* interview, 1907

Books by Mary Baker Eddy

Manual of the Mother Church. Rev. ed. Boston: Christian Science Publishing Society, 1897.
Science and Health with Key to the Scriptures. 1875. Reprint, Boston: rev. ed., 1891. Writings of Mary Baker Eddy, 2000.

Books about Mary Baker Eddy

Gill, Gillian. *Mary Baker Eddy.* Reading, Mass.: Perseus Books, 1998.
Nenneman, Richard. *Persistent Pilgrim: The Life of Mary Baker Eddy.* Etna, N.H.: Nebbadoon Press, 1997.
Smith, Louise A. *Mary Baker Eddy: Discoverer and Founder of Christian Science.* Boston: Christian Science Publishing Society, 1991.

Organization

First Church of Christ, Scientist, 175 Huntington Ave., Boston, MA 02115; phone: 617-450-2000.

Other Resources

Web site: www.tfccs.com. Official web site of the Christian Science Church.
Library: The Mary Baker Eddy Library for the Betterment of Humanity is slated to open in 2002 on the Mother Church grounds. www.marybakereddylibrary.org.

"The prayer that reforms the sinner and heals the sick is an absolute faith that all things are possible to God."

ROBERT FUNK
(1926–)

As founder of the Jesus Seminar, the tradition-challenging group of Bible scholars, Robert Funk helped spark a new and intense late-twentieth-century wave of interest in the historical Jesus and the historicity of the Christian Gospel stories. His scholarship advocates for a rationalist approach to Christianity that recognizes the human hands—and their agendas—that shaped the Bible.

As a teenager Funk led revival meetings; today he says he is laying the groundwork for a new Reformation. After biblical studies at Vanderbilt University, he taught at Texas Christian, Harvard, and Emory Universities. Funk became a leader in the Society of Biblical Literature, an organization of Bible scholars, but broke with it in 1980 over frustration with what he viewed as members' inability to bridge the gap between academic inquiry and what was taught in most churches.

He founded the Jesus Seminar in 1985. At its meetings Bible scholars use textual analysis and other scholarly methods to decide by vote issues such as the extent to which specific Bible passages represent Jesus' actual words. Using colored beads, scholars vote in public meetings on whether Jesus undoubtedly said a particular statement (red); most likely said it (pink); probably did not say it though it represents ideas close to his own (gray); or definitely did not say it (black). These votes resulted in *The Five Gospels,* a translation of the four canonical Gospels and the Gnostic Gospel of Thomas, color-coded according to scholarly consensus.

Funk hopes to see emerge a new Christianity that is suited for a rationalist age.

The seminar's public displays of academic consensus have drawn widespread media attention and constitute as radical an assault on the cloistered world of New Testament scholarship as they do on official church teachings. Seminar scholars have developed a portrait of Jesus that likens him to an iconoclastic sage, healer, and social activist. Many of the most familiar of Jesus' sayings, including the Lord's Prayer, Jesus' words from the cross, and any of his claims to being divine or the Messiah, are among those that Funk and his colleagues have dismissed as nonhistorical. Remaining are many of Jesus' parables, his oft-enunciated concern for the poor and marginalized, and his disdain for social divisions. From this effort, Funk hopes to see emerge a new Christianity that is suited for a rationalist age and incorporates the latest scholarship. In addition to the Jesus Seminar, he founded Polebridge Press, which publishes seminar scholars' works, and the Westar Institute, a research center in California.

His Words

The plot early Christians invented for a divine redeemer figure is as archaic as the mythology in which it is framed. A Jesus who drops down out of heaven, performs some magical act that frees human beings from the power of sin, rises from the dead, and returns to heaven is simply no longer credible. The notion that he will return at the end of time and sit in cosmic judgment is equally incredible. We must find a new plot for a more credible Jesus.
—"Twenty-one Theses," in *The Fourth R,* July–August 1998

In the minds of many, especially those who claim Christianity or Judaism as their heritage, Jesus is inseparably connected with the topic of institutionalized religion. When the name Jesus is mentioned, "religion" is assumed to be the subject. But, in fact, the Jesus of whom we catch glimpses in the Gospels may be said to have been irreligious, irreverent, and impious. The first word he said, as Paul Tillich once remarked, was a word against religion in its habituated form; because he was indifferent to the formal practice of religion, he is said to have profaned the temple, the Sabbath, and breached the purity regulations of his own legacy; most important of all, he spoke of the kingdom of God in profane terms—that is, non-religiously.
—*Honest to Jesus,* p. 303

Books by Robert Funk

The Acts of Jesus: The Search for the Authentic Deeds of Jesus. San Francisco: HarperSanFrancisco, 1998.

The Five Gospels: The Search for the Authentic Words of Jesus. San Francisco: HarperSanFrancisco, 1993.

Honest to Jesus: Jesus for a New Millennium. San Francisco: HarperSanFrancisco, 1996.

New Gospel Parallels: The Gospel of Mark. San Francisco: HarperSanFrancisco, 1995.

For a more complete list of books by Robert Funk, see *The Acts of Jesus.*

Organization

Westar Institute and the Jesus Seminar, P.O. Box 6144, Santa Rosa, CA 95406; phone: 707-523-1323; fax 707-523-1350.

Other Resources

Web site: www.westarinstitute.org/Jesus_Seminar/jesus_seminar.html. Official web site of the Jesus Seminar.

Videotape: *The Search for Jesus,* ABC News special report by Peter Jennings, aired in June 2000 and relied heavily on Jesus Seminar scholarship; available at www.abcnewsstore.com/jesus.html.

"The plot early Christians invented for a divine redeemer figure is as archaic as the mythology in which it is framed."

G. I. GURDJIEFF
(c. 1877–1949)

G. I. Gurdjieff adapted Eastern mystical teachings to create a spiritual path suitable for modern life in the West. An enigmatic figure characterized as a "rogue teacher" or a master of "crazy wisdom," he often used shock tactics to awaken his pupils to the truth about themselves. He emphasized spiritual work in groups, rather than the guru-disciple relationship, as essential for Westerners.

Georges Ivanovich Gurdjieff taught that most human beings lead a life of "waking sleep" and are slaves to mechanical habit. Fully identified with every passing thought, desire, and negative emotion, they are but a collection of "I's" while having the illusion of a unified self. To remedy this condition, he created methods of working on the intellect, emotions, and physical body; his techniques included self-remembering and self-observation, "objective movements," and sacred dance. Other important aspects of Gurdjieff's teaching were the ray of creation, the law of the octave, the law of three forces, and the enneagram, a nine-pointed diagram that expresses relationships in symbols.

Gurdjieff was born of Greek and Armenian parents in Alexandropol (now Gumri), Armenia. According to his memoir, *Meetings with Remarkable Men,* he studied in monasteries and esoteric schools in remote parts of Central Asia and the Middle East. He began to teach in Russia around 1912 and was soon joined by the philosopher P. D. Ouspensky and the composer Thomas de Hartmann, who later collaborated with Gurdjieff in creating musical works.

Gurdjieff emphasized spiritual work in groups, rather than the guru-disciple relationship, as essential for Westerners.

At the outbreak of the Russian Revolution in 1917, Gurdjieff went to the city of Essentuki in the Caucasus, and in 1919 he established the Institute for the Harmonious Development of Man in Tiflis (now Tbilisi), Georgia. There he was joined by the artist and theatrical designer Alexandre de Salzmann and his wife, Jeanne de Salzmann, a teacher of rhythmic dance. In 1922 he settled in France, near Fontainebleau, and in 1924 suffered a near-fatal automobile accident. In 1933 he moved to Paris, where he met with pupils, wrote, and taught his system, known as "the Work," until his death.

Many well-known individuals in the arts were attracted to Gurdjieff, and numerous teachers and heirs of the Work split into various submovements. Study continues today in groups throughout the world, the major schools being in Paris, New York, and London. Gurdjieff's writings are often difficult to read; he said that he deliberately made them demanding so that readers would have to make the effort. Works written by his pupils, especially Ouspensky's *In Search of the Miraculous,* are more accessible.

His Words

Although to be either masters or slaves in a collective existence among children, like ourselves, of the COMMON FATHER, is unworthy of man, yet thanks at the present time to the conditions existing which have already been thoroughly fixed in the process of the collective life of people, the source of which lies in remote antiquity, we must be reconciled to it and accept a compromise that, according to impartial reasoning, should correspond both to our own personal welfare, and also at the same time not be contrary to the commandments specially issuing to us people from the "Prime-Source-of-Everything-Existing." Such a compromise, I think, is possible if certain people consciously set themselves, as the chief aim of their existence, to acquire in their presences all the corresponding data to become masters among those around them similar to themselves.
—*Beelzebub's Tales to His Grandson,* p. 1235

Remember you come here having already understood the necessity of struggling with yourself—only with yourself. Therefore thank everyone who gives you the opportunity.—Inscribed by Gurdjieff above the walls of the Study House at his Institute in Prieuré near Paris.
—*Views from the Real World,* p. 273

Books by G. I. Gurdjieff

Beelzebub's Tales to His Grandson: An Objectively Impartial Criticism of the Life of Man. All and Everything, ser. 1. New York: Penguin Books, 1999.

The Herald of Coming Good. Edmonds, Wash.: Holmes Publishing Group, 1987.

Life Is Real Only Then, When I Am. All and Everything, ser. 3. New York: Penguin Books, 1999.

Meetings with Remarkable Men. All and Everything, ser. 2. New York: E. P. Dutton, 1991.

Views from the Real World: Early Talks in Moscow, Essentuki, Tiflis, Berlin, London, Paris, New York, and Chicago. New York: Penguin Arkana, 1984.

Books about G. I. Gurdjieff

Hartmann, Thomas, and Olga de Hartmann. *Our Life with Mr. Gurdjieff.* Rev. ed. London: Arkana, 1992.

Hulme, Kathryn. *Undiscovered Country: A Spiritual Adventure.* Boston: Little, Brown, 1997.

Moore, James. *Gurdjieff: The Anatomy of a Myth.* Rockport, Mass.: Element Books, 1991.

Ouspensky, P. D. *In Search of the Miraculous: Fragments of an Unknown Teaching.* New York: Vintage Books, 1974.

Peters, Fritz. *Boyhood with Gurdjieff.* New York: E. P. Dutton, 1964.

Organization

Gurdjieff Society, London; e-mail: enquiry@gurdjieff.com.

Other Resources

Periodical: *Gurdjieff International Review:* web site: www.gurdjieff.org.

Film/Videotape: *Meetings with Remarkable Men,* directed by Peter Brook. 1979.

CD: *The Complete Piano Music of Georges I. Gurdjieff and Thomas de Hartmann,* performed by Cecil Lytle, 3 vols.

"Conscious faith is freedom. Emotional faith is slavery. Mechanical faith is foolishness."

AIMEE SEMPLE McPHERSON
(1890–1944)

Among the earliest widely popular women Christian evangelists, Aimee Semple McPherson was the first to use modern culture to convey the Pentecostal Christian message through pageants, plays, and a popular radio broadcast of her sermons that brought her a nationwide following and, eventually, a new Christian denomination.

Sister Aimee, as her followers called her, arrived in Los Angeles in 1918 and began preaching a form of Christian Pentecostalism that emphasized a positive message about salvation. In the Pentecostal movement—with its fiery message of personal repentance and the coming Apocalypse—she was the first to establish a leading role for the woman evangelist. By 1925 she had a following of tens of thousands and built the 5,300-seat Angelus Temple, complete with an orchestra pit and a radio studio that carried her sermons far beyond Southern California.

She traveled widely, too, preaching in tent revivals from San Francisco to Philadelphia and New York. Her sermons were full of fire and brimstone and were often delivered in elaborate costumes, as she adapted her message to dramatic interpretations of Bible stories and morality plays she wrote. Her example influenced other Pentecostal women preachers, from Lucy Farrow to Tammy Faye Bakker.

McPherson was one of the first white Pentecostal preachers to cross the color line, often worshiping with and preaching to African Americans. The coming together of the races, she believed, was one of the surest signs that the "end times" promised by God

McPherson was one of the first white Pentecostal preachers to cross the color line, often worshiping with and preaching to African Americans.

were at hand. In 1936 she and a number of leading African-American preachers celebrated the thirtieth anniversary of the Pentecostal movement's birth among black laborers worshiping at an Azusa Street mission.

Scandal followed McPherson throughout her career. A third marriage ended in divorce, and in 1926 she reportedly drowned—only to turn up in Mexico several days later saying she had been kidnapped. The kidnapping story was disputed by those who claimed that she had been on a romantic getaway with a married engineer from her own radio station. She was charged with conspiracy to produce false testimony but the case never came to trial due to insufficient evidence. She died of an accidental prescription drug overdose in 1944.

Eventually, Angelus Temple spawned the International Church of the Foursquare Gospel, a Pentecostal denomination that, at the time of McPherson's death, numbered 29,000 followers. It now claims some 3.5 million adherents worldwide.

Her Words

Sometimes when laboring in certain portions of the Master's vineyard, we have felt that we were reaching many, but when, under the burden of prayer, the Lord catches us up in the Spirit, and with clarified vision and broadened horizon we see earth's millions who are yet unconscious of the signs of the times and know not that the coming of the Lord is nigh at hand, we are overwhelmed with the desire to speed through the lands, and ring the message forth—"Jesus is coming soon—prepare to meet him!" Oh, that we might write it in flaming letters upon the sky.
—*This Is That,* p. 11

Let the giddy, laughing, thoughtless sinner, dancing on the brink of Hell, be sobered and come to Jesus in repentance, confessing his sins, or he will be eternally lost in that land where laughing and dancing are never known. The invitation is extended to all mankind, irrespective of race, creed, color, or age; all alike need Jesus, and without Him, all are undone.
—*This Is That,* p. 426

Books by Aimee Semple McPherson

Aimee: Life Story of Aimee Semple McPherson. Los Angeles: International Church of the Foursquare Gospel, 1979.

In the Service of the King: The Story of My Life. New York: Boni & Liveright, 1927.

This Is That: Personal Experiences, Sermons, and Writings of Aimee Semple McPherson. Los Angeles: Bridal Call Publishing House, 1921.

Books about Aimee Semple McPherson

Blumhofer, Edith. *Aimee Semple McPherson: Everybody's Sister.* Grand Rapids, Mich.: Wm. B. Eerdmans, 1993.

Epstein, Daniel Mark. *Sister Aimee: The Life of Aimee Semple McPherson.* New York: Harcourt Brace Jovanovich, 1993.

Organization

International Church of the Foursquare Gospel, Corporate Headquarters, 1910 W. Sunset Blvd., Ste. 200, Los Angeles, CA 90026-0176.

Other Resources

Web site: www.foursquare.org. Official web site of the International Church of the Foursquare Gospel.

"The invitation is extended to all mankind, irrespective of race, creed, color or age; all alike need Jesus, and without Him, all are undone."

ELIJAH MUHAMMAD
(1897–1975)

Although his separatist and racist views outraged many, Elijah Muhammad brought large numbers of African Americans to Islam and provided many with a sense of self-esteem and self-reliance through the Nation of Islam, a militant religious faction he helped establish as a major force within the black community.

Born Elijah Poole in Sandersville, Georgia, to sharecropper parents, he quit school at the age of nine and left home at sixteen. As a child, he said he witnessed three white men tormenting and lynching a black man. Blood from the hanged man is supposed to have dripped upon him, sealing the evil of the white men in his mind forever. In the 1920s Poole and his wife, Clara, left the South for Detroit as part of the great migration of rural blacks to urban areas in the North.

Unemployed during the Depression, Poole went to hear the preaching of Wallace D. Fard, who taught that African Americans were the "Original People," royal Muslims transplanted by evil white slavers from the holy city of Mecca. Poole believed Fard was a human incarnation of God and became his disciple. Fard created the Lost-Found Nation of Islam and opened its first temple in Detroit. Fard later renamed Poole Elijah Muhammad, establishing him as Fard's—and therefore God's—Messenger.

Muhammad held that American blacks needed to organize and fight to establish their own independent nation.

After Fard's mysterious disappearance in 1934, Muhammad declared himself his successor. He soon established a second Nation of Islam temple in Chicago, and others followed on the East Coast. Wherever he went Muhammad taught that African Americans were a noble race held down by evil whites. He held that Fard's appearance signaled the end of six thousand years of white rule and that American blacks needed to organize and fight to establish their own independent nation.

In 1942, during World War II, Muhammad was arrested and spent four years in jail for failing to register for the draft. His time in jail lent him a martyr's air and made him the undisputed leader of the Black Muslims, as his followers were known. After his release, Muhammad Ali, Malcolm X, and the Reverend Louis Farrakhan became his disciples.

Muhammad's teachings were disseminated in the periodical *Muhammad Speaks* and in several books. At the time of his death it was estimated that he had 100,000 followers in seventy temples around the United States. After his death his son Wareth Deen Mohammed dropped the Nation of Islam name and led the bulk of its members into mainstream Sunni Islam. Farrakhan continues to lead a smaller organization that still calls itself the Nation of Islam.

His Words

Why do I stress the religion of Islam for my people, the so-called American Negroes? First, and most important, Islam is actually our religion by nature. It is the religion of Allah (God), not a European organized white man's religion. . . . It dignifies the black man and gives us the desire to be clean internally and externally and for the first time to have a sense of dignity. . . . Islam will put the black man of America on top of the civilization.
—*A Message to the Blackman in America,* pp. 84–85

Let us make this clear. I am not begging. For, it please Allah, He will give us a home, and I am with Him. Today, according to Allah's word, we are living in a time of the great separation of blacks and whites. The prophecy—400 years of slavery—as to the time the so-called Negroes would serve white people ended in 1955. The so-called Negroes must return to their own. The separation would be a blessing for both sides. It was the only solution, according to the Bible, for Israel and the Egyptians. It will prove to be the only solution for America and her slaves.
—*A Message to the Blackman in America,* p. 24

Books by Elijah Muhammad

The Fall of America. 1973. Reprint, Atlanta: Secretarius Publications, 1997.

A Message to the Blackman in America. 1965. Reprint, Newport News, Va.: UB & US Communication Systems, 1992.

The Secrets of Freemasonry. Atlanta: Secretarius Publications, 1997.

The Supreme Wisdom: Solution to the So-Called Negroes' Problem. 1957. Reprint, Lawrenceville, N.J.: Red Sea Press, 1990.

Books about Elijah Muhammad

Evanzz, Karl. *The Messenger: The Rise and Fall of Elijah Muhammad.* New York: Pantheon Books, 1999.

Gardell, Mattias. *In the Name of Elijah Muhammad: Louis Farrakhan and the Nation of Islam.* Durham, N.C.: Duke University Press, 1996.

Organization

Nation of Islam, 7351 S. Stoney Island Ave., Chicago, IL 60649.

Other Resources

Web site: www.noi.org. Official web site of the Nation of Islam contains official history of the Nation and an official biographical sketch of Elijah Muhammad.

Periodical: *Final Call Online.* Official newspaper of the Nation of Islam; web site: www.finalcall.com.

"Islam will put the black man of America on top of the civilization."

BHAKTIVEDANTA PRABUPHADA
(1896–1977)

As founder of the International Society for Krishna Consciousness—ISKCON, commonly called the Hare Krishnas—Swami Bhaktivedanta Prabuphada brought to the West a unique interpretation of Hindu worship by creatively tapping into the 1960s spiritual zeitgeist. With a simple mantra oft repeated, he and his disciples made an indelible image on the culture of the period.

After earning a degree in chemistry and starting a pharmacy business, in 1922 Prabuphada met a spiritual leader, Srila Bhaktisiddhanta Sarasvati Thakur, who changed his life by urging him to spread Vaishnava Hinduism, a devotional practice centered on incarnations of the god Vishnu, especially Krishna, throughout the Western world. He was formally initiated as a disciple a decade later and threw himself into writing, lecturing, and teaching in English. In 1944 he started the still-published magazine *Back to the Godhead.* In the 1950s he renounced all family ties and by the end of the decade took vows of renunciation of the material world.

In 1965 he left for America, believing that if he could successfully preach Vaishnavism here, it would spread throughout the Western world. After six months of rootlessness he rented a storefront on New York's Lower East Side, where spiritual seekers began to gather to hear him teach the Vedic path to freedom from material want. His books became popular among college students, who increasingly sought him out, and he and his disciples began to hold outdoor chanting sessions in Tompkins Square Park.

Prabuphada's teachings rely, in part, on the powerful experience of repetitive chanting to achieve closeness with the divine.

A year after arriving in America, Prabuphada incorporated the International Society for Krishna Consciousness. He began to hold Sunday "feasts" after services as a means of distributing *prasada,* food consecrated to Krishna and distributed to devotees; these feasts would grow into a signature tradition of ISKCON. Soon the ISKCON mantra—"Hare Krishna, Hare Krishna, Krishna Krishna, Hare Hare. Hare Rama, Hare Rama, Rama Rama, Hare Hare"—was part of America's countercultural lexicon.

Prabuphada's teachings were a direct outgrowth of the bhakti yoga tradition in which he was taught, which dates to the sixteenth century and relies, in part, on the powerful experience of repetitive chanting to achieve closeness with the Divine. ISKCON also mandated strict vegetarianism and allowed sex only within marriage for procreation. Male devotees shaved their heads, except for one tuft, called a *sikha,* at the crown of the head. Initiated devotees lived in the temples and dedicated themselves to serving Krishna and proselytizing, quickly building the movement while garnering criticism and controversy over missionary tactics. After establishing temples in San Francisco, London, Berlin, and elsewhere, disciples brought the movement to India.

By the time of Prabuphada's death, there were 108 ISKCON temples worldwide, and he had published fifty-one volumes of transcendental literature. Although the movement was enmeshed in several controversies and scandals following Prabuphada's death—some involving sex abuse, drugs, and weapons—by the late 1990s there were 225 ISKCON temples worldwide.

His Words

The real disease is in the heart. If the mind is cleansed, however, if consciousness is cleansed, a person cannot be harmed by material disease. To cleanse the mind and heart from all misconceptions, one should take to this chanting of the Hare Kṛṣṇa maha-mantra. This is both easy and beneficial. By chanting the name of the Lord, one is immediately freed from the blazing fire of material existence.
—*The Nectar of Instruction,* p. 68

Books by Swami Bhaktivedanta Prabuphada

The Bhagavad-Gita as It Is. London: Bhaktivedanta Book Trust, 1985.

Easy Journey to Other Planets: By Practice of Supreme Yoga. Los Angeles: Bhaktivedanta Book Trust, 1985.

Kṛṣṇa Consciousness: The Topmost Yoga System. Boston: ISKCON Press, 1970.

Kṛṣṇa Consciousness: The Matchless Gift. New York: Bhaktivedanta Book Trust, 1995.

The Lord in the Heart. Boston: ISKCON Press, 1970.

The Nectar of Instruction. Los Angeles: Bhaktivedanta Book Trust, 1997.

Teachings of Lord Chaitanya: A Treatise on Factual Spiritual Life. New York: ISKCON Press, 1968.

Book about Swami Bhaktivedanta Prabuphada

Judah, J. Stillson. *Hare Krishna and the Counterculture.* New York: John Wiley & Sons, 1974.

For a more complete list of books by and about Bhaktivedanta Prabuphada, see Judah, *Hare Krishna,* pp. 207–210.

Organization

International Society for Krishna Consciousness, 3764 Watseka Ave., Los Angeles, CA 90034; phone: 800-927-4152.

Other Resources

Web site: www.ISKCON.com. Official web site of ISKCON.

> *"If the mind is cleansed, however, if consciousness is cleansed, a person cannot be harmed by material disease."*

BERTRAND RUSSELL
(1872–1970)

Logic, philosophy, mathematics, education, and religion were all fields that grew and changed because of the contributions of Bertrand Arthur William Russell. His committed atheism made him a spokesman for a secular age whose goal was to wrest ethics and morality from the religious world.

Born in Wales and educated in Cambridge, England, Russell received his bachelor of arts in mathematics and went on to garner prestigious prizes such as the Order of Merit and, in 1950, the Nobel Prize in literature. Although he wrestled with religious questions in his philosophical studies, Russell was an atheist and wrote extensively on his belief that faith in God is unjustifiable in the face of the depth and perpetuity of evil in the world. Deeply committed to the scientific method and logical and mathematical formulations, Russell struggled with the question of whether, and to what extent, it is possible to "know" anything. His scientific pursuit of a theory of knowledge led him to abandon the idealistic philosophy of his student days and develop a "new realism" and a "new philosophy of logic."

In addition to being a mathematician, logician, and philosopher, Russell was a long-standing social activist for progressive causes, and during the 1950s and 1960s he became a public opponent of the proliferation of nuclear weapons and the war in Vietnam. His commitment to social justice had extended to his youth, though, when he experienced two convictions and six months of jail time for antiwar protests during World War I.

Deeply committed to the scientific method and logical and mathematical formulations, Russell struggled with the question of whether, and to what extent, it is possible to "know" anything.

In 1955 Russell released, with Albert Einstein, the Einstein-Russell Manifesto, which called for an end to the development of nuclear weapons. A year earlier he had delivered a famous broadcast on the BBC titled "Man's Peril," in which he warned of the dangers of the so-called Bikini H-bomb tests. In 1961 he was imprisoned for one week for his protests of nuclear weapon development. Russell died at the age of ninety-eight in Penrhyndeudraeth, Wales.

His Words

Religion is based, I think, primarily and mainly upon fear. It is partly the terror of the unknown and partly, as I have said, the wish to feel that you have a kind of elder brother who will stand by you in all your troubles and disputes. Fear is the basis of the whole thing—fear of the mysterious, fear of defeat, fear of death. Fear is the parent of cruelty, and therefore it is no wonder if cruelty and religion have gone hand in hand.
—"Why I Am Not a Christian," in *Why I Am Not a Christian,* p. 22

1888. March 3. I shall write about some subjects, especially religious ones, which now interest me. I have, in consequence of a variety of circumstances, come to look into the very foundations of the religion in which I have been brought up. On some points my conclusions have been to confirm my former creed, where others I have been irresistibly led to such conclusions as would not only shock my people, but have given me much pain. I have arrived at certainty in few things, but my opinions, even where not convictions, are on some things nearly such. I have not the courage to tell my people that I scarcely believe in immortality.
—"First Efforts," in *My Philosophical Development,* p. 21

Books by Bertrand Russell

Atheism: Collected Essays, 1943–1949. New York: Arno Press, 1972.
The Autobiography of Bertrand Russell. New York: Routledge, 2000.
A History of Western Philosophy. New York: Simon & Schuster, 1945.
Marriage and Morals. New York: Horace Liveright, 1929.
My Philosophical Development. New York: Routledge, 1995.
On Education, Especially in Early Childhood. London: George Allen & Unwin, 1926.

The Problems of Philosophy. London: Williams & Norgate, 1912.
The Selected Letters of Bertrand Russell. Vol. 2, The Public Years, 1914–1970. Edited by Nicholas Griffin. New York: Routledge, 2001.
What I Believe. London: Kegan Paul, 1925.
Why I Am Not a Christian: And Other Essays on Religion and Related Subjects. New York: Simon & Schuster, 1957.

Books about Bertrand Russell

Blackwell, Kenneth, and Harry Ruja. *A Bibliography of Bertrand Russell.* 3 vols. New York: Routledge, 1994.
Clark, Ronald William. *The Life of Bertrand Russell.* London: Jonathan Cape, 1975.
Jager, Ronald. *The Development of Bertrand Russell's Philosophy.* London: George Allen and Unwin, 1972.
Monk, Ray. *Bertrand Russell: The Spirit of Solitude.* New York: The Free Press, 1996.

Organization

The Bertrand Russell Research Centre, TSH-619, McMaster University, Hamilton, ON L8S 4M2, Canada; phone: 905-525-9140, ext. 24896; fax: 905-577-6930; e-mail: bertruss@mcmaster.ca.

Other Resources

Web sites: www.users.drew.edu/jlenz/brs.html. Official web site of the Bertrand Russell Society. Information on meetings, publications, archives, and links to relevant web sites.

www.humanities.mcmaster.ca/~russell/brhome.htm. Web site of the Bertrand Russell Research Centre. Research on his life and work; largest collection of his papers.

Periodical: *Journal of Bertrand Russell Studies;* web site: www.humanities.mcmaster.ca/~russell/journal.htm.

"Religion is based, I think, primarily and mainly upon fear. It is partly the terror of the unknown."

ZALMAN SCHACHTER-SHALOMI
(1924–)

Best known for his ability to bring Jewish spirituality to disparate audiences, Rabbi Zalman Schachter-Shalomi is considered the father of the contemporary Jewish Renewal movement, blending the rootedness and depth of Hasidic Judaism with a zestful exploration of other forms of spirituality, meditation, and mysticism.

Schachter-Shalomi was born in Poland and raised in Vienna, Austria. The rise of Nazism led him and his family to flee Europe, landing them in New York in 1941. Ordained by the Lubavitch Hasidic movement in 1947, he later pursued graduate degrees at Boston University and Hebrew Union College.

The range of his Jewish education—from the traditional Lubavitch yeshiva to the liberal Reform seminary—led Schachter-Shalomi to think in new ways about how to make Judaism accessible and attractive to Jews who were intimidated by Orthodoxy yet uninspired by the less observant denominations. To achieve his goals, in 1962 he founded the P'nai Or (Faces of Light) Religious Fellowship, now called ALEPH: Alliance for Jewish Renewal.

The range of his Jewish education led Schachter-Shalomi to think in new ways about how to make Judaism accessible and attractive to Jews who were intimidated by Orthodoxy yet uninspired by the less observant denominations.

Jewish Renewal is based on principles of equality, feminism, and environmentalism, infused with the spiritual resources of Judaism, particularly the Kabbalah mystical tradition. However, Schachter-Shalomi's openness reaches beyond Judaism's confines. By practicing meditation with Buddhists and drawing on Sufi mystic tradition, he has forged interfaith dialogue about issues of spiritual renewal and the pursuit of social justice.

In 1978, when the Camp David peace accord was signed, Schachter added "Shalomi" (Hebrew for "my peace") to his name to demonstrate solidarity with the Middle East peace process. He has said that he will drop "Schachter" from his name when peace comes to the region.

The latest chapter in Schachter-Shalomi's career is his spiritual reflection on the experience of aging. In 1989 he founded the Spiritual Eldering Institute to help people understand the aging process in terms of expanded consciousness and spiritual growth.

His Words

I do not consider it to be dangerous for persons of Jewish background to experience and explore Eastern mysticism, provided they check it out for technique and content, rather than for ritual, dogma, and ethnic lifestyle. The process of a soul's way to God is often initiated by an excursion into the realms of the Eastern religions.
—*Fragments of a Future Scroll,* p. 7

Books by Zalman Schachter-Shalomi

The Dream Assembly: Tales of Rabbi Zalman Schachter-Shalomi. Collected and retold by Howard Schwartz. Illustrated by Yitzhak Greenfield. Nevada City, Calif.: Gateways/IDHHB, 1989.

The First Step: A Guide for the New Jewish Spirit. With Donald Gropman. New York: Bantam Books, 1983.

Fragments of a Future Scroll: Hassidism for the Aquarian Age. Edited by Philip Mandelkorn and Stephen Gerstman. Germantown, Pa.: Leaves of Grass Press, 1975.

From Age-ing to Sage-ing: A Profound New Vision of Growing Older. New York: Warner Books, 1995.

Paradigm Shift: From the Jewish Renewal Teachings of Reb. Zalman Schachter-Shalomi. Edited by Ellen Singer. Northvale, N.J.: Jason Aronson, 1993.

Organizations

ALEPH: Alliance for Jewish Renewal, 7318 Germantown Ave., Philadelphia, PA 19119.

Spiritual Eldering Institute, 970 Aurora Ave., Boulder, CO 80302; phone: 303-449-7243; fax: 303-938-1277; e-mail: info@spiritualeldering.org.

Other Resources

Web sites: www.aleph.org. Official web site of ALEPH: Alliance for Jewish Renewal.

www.spiritualeldering.org. Official web site of Spiritual Eldering Institute.

Audiotape: *Davening with Reb Zalman: An Audio Siddur.* New York: P'nai Or Religious Fellowship, 1989.

> *"The process of a soul's way to God is often initiated by an excursion into the realms of the Eastern religions."*

WILLIAM J. SEYMOUR
(1870–1922)

William J. Seymour was a minister instrumental in spreading the Holiness-Pentecostal movement, which stresses healing, prophecy, and glossolalia, or "speaking in tongues." His church in Los Angeles became the center of a great revival and helped make Pentecostalism one of the most influential religious movements of the twentieth century. Blacks and whites worshiped side by side in Seymour's church during a time of racial segregation.

Seymour was born to former slaves in Centerville, Louisiana, and raised as a Baptist. He moved to Cleveland in 1900 and was introduced to Holiness theology, which stressed John Wesley's teachings of sanctification and Christian perfection (the belief that it is possible to liberate human beings from the flaw in their moral nature that causes them to sin), divine healing, premillennialism (the belief that Jesus would return to the earth before the millennium began), and belief in the revival of the Holy Spirit before the "rapture."

In 1903 Seymour moved to Houston, Texas, where he met Charles Fox Parham, the white founder of the modern Pentecostal movement. Although local law prevented blacks and whites from studying in the same classroom, Parham encouraged Seymour to listen in on his Bible classes by standing outside the open door. Among Parham's teachings was the idea that speaking in tongues is evidence of a "true baptism in the Spirit."

In 1906 Seymour arrived in Los Angeles, where he was invited to preach at a Holiness church. The established Holiness churches rejected the notion of "tongues," however, so he began to preach in private homes. His ministry attracted larger and larger crowds as word of the services spread. Eventually he took over an

Blacks and whites worshiped side by side in Seymour's church during a time of racial segregation.

abandoned African Methodist Episcopal church on Azusa Street, which he called the Apostolic Faith Mission. The little church was soon jammed with worshipers, who engaged in traditional African-American practices such as shouting, singing, trances, and ecstatic dance. Seymour published a magazine, *Apostolic Faith,* which quickly grew from five thousand to fifty thousand subscribers.

Seymour's leadership began to decline after his mentor, Charles Parham, visited the church in 1906 and denounced what he referred to as the "fits and spasms of spiritualists." A further blow came when two white women in the movement objected to Seymour's 1908 marriage (ostensibly on the grounds that the "rapture" was approaching) and moved to Oregon, taking the magazine's subscriber list with them. That left Seymour cut off from his followers. Few of his writings survive today. Nonetheless, within just a few years he made a lasting impact, especially on African-American worship styles.

His Words

Don't go out of here talking about tongues; talk about Jesus.

Book by William J. Seymour

The Azusa Street Papers: A Reprint of the Apostolic Faith. Foley, Ala.: Together in the Harvest Publications, 1997.

Books about William J. Seymour

Bartleman, Frank. *Azusa Street.* Plainfield, N.J.: Bridge Publishing, 1980. First published in 1925 as *How Pentecost Came to Los Angeles.*

Hollenweger, Walter J. *Pentecostalism: Origins and Developments Worldwide.* Peabody, Mass.: Hendrickson Publishers, 1997.

Martin, Larry. *The Life and Ministry of William J. Seymour: And a History of the Azusa Street Revival.* Joplin, Mo.: Christian Life Books, 1999.

———. *The Words That Changed the World: Azusa Street Sermons.* Joplin, Mo.: Christian Life Books, 1999.

Martin, Larry, ed. *Holy Ghost Revival on Azusa Street: The True Believers: Eye-Witness Accounts of the Revival That Shook the World.* Joplin, Mo.: Christian Life Books, 1998.

"Don't go out of here talking about tongues; talk about Jesus."

SHIRDI SAI BABA
(c. 1835–1918)

Shirdi Sai Baba's life demonstrated that great spiritual personalities transcend traditional concepts of how saints and gurus accomplish their work. Known for his eccentric behavior, Sai Baba appeared mad to some but was widely recognized as a master of the highest caliber. His emphasis on the unity of all religions was an early model for today's ideal of religious tolerance and universalism.

His personal history is unknown, but it is thought that Sai Baba was born a Hindu of the Brahmin caste in a village of Hyderabad State, India. He appeared one day in the quiet farming village of Shirdi, Maharashtra State, as a nameless fakir (wandering ascetic) around sixteen years old. After living for some months under a tree, he took up residence in a local mosque. People began to call him Sai Baba; *Sai* meaning "Lord," and *Baba* meaning "Father." This might be translated as "Holy Father."

His magnetic presence and luminous eyes attracted devotees from both Hindu and Muslim communities. Combining traits of the two faiths, he dressed in Muslim fashion while wearing Hindu caste marks on his forehead and burned a continuous sacred fire *(dhuni)* in the mosque, a practice associated more with Hinduism (and Zoroastrianism) than with Islam.

Shirdi Sai Baba's emphasis on the unity of all religions was an early model for today's ideal of religious tolerance and universalism.

Instead of giving conventional teachings, Sai Baba bestowed his grace and help symbolically through cryptic actions, stories, and parables. He employed shock tactics, such as displaying a fiery temper or ordering a strict vegetarian to eat meat. He would demand money from visitors, then give it away or use it in mysterious rituals intended to aid the spiritual advancement of devotees. He gained renown as a wonder-worker and for his supernatural powers. On one occasion, he used his arm to stir a boiling pot without injury; on another, he deliberately burned his hand in the *dhuni* fire, explaining that he did this to save a baby who had fallen into flames in a distant village. But though his healings and miracles (such as granting progeny to childless couples) were flamboyant, he discouraged devotees from seeking powers and visions. He trained his followers to attract the grace of God through devotion and obedience to the guru, and encouraged normal family life rather than renunciation and asceticism. His other characteristics included a delight in music and dance, habitual smoking of a clay pipe, and a love for dogs.

Shirdi Sai Baba named no successor, but among his well-known disciples were Meher Baba and Upasni Maharaj, who became masters in their own right. Many accept the contemporary teacher Sathya Sai Baba as his reincarnation, while others believe that Shirdi Sai Baba himself continues to bless his devotees, who are estimated at up to 10 million people worldwide. His tomb-shrine at Shirdi is a major pilgrimage site.

His Words

He often spoke symbolically. . . . Once Deshpande, a devotee . . . , was bitten by a snake and, in his terror, rushed straight to the mosque. When he reached the steps, however, Baba shouted: "Don't come up, Brahmin! Go back! Get down!" Even in his fear of death, he did not dare disobey Sai Baba but stood there in mute supplication. A moment later Baba spoke again, this time in a gentle, kindly voice: "Come up now. The Fakir is gracious to you. You will recover."

"The Fakir" . . . was Sai Baba's way of referring to God. Deshpande now found that in the command not to come up Baba had been speaking not to him but to the poison which was entering his bloodstream.

He would sometimes speak in parables, leaving his devotees to work out the answer.

"Some robbers came and took away my money. I said nothing but quietly followed them and killed them and so recovered my money." The money is the faculties natural to man in his pure state, to Primordial Man or Adam before the Fall; the robbers are the desires; killing them and recovering the wealth is destroying desires and realizing the Self.
—Osborne, *The Incredible Sai Baba,* pp. 80–81

Books about Shirdi Sai Baba

Osborne, Arthur. *The Incredible Sai Baba.* 1958. Reprint, York Beach: Samuel Weiser, 1972.

Rigopoulos, Antonio. *The Life and Teachings of Sai Baba of Shirdi.* Albany: State University of New York Press, 1993.

Organization

Sai Baba Sanasthan, P.O. Shirdi 423109, Kopargaon, Ahmednagar, Maharashtra State, India. Established in 1922 to conduct service activities, publishing, and other work connected with Sai Baba.

Other Resources

Web site: saibaba.org/arathi.html. Archive of music and resources to promote the life and teachings of Shirdi Sai Baba.

He would sometimes speak in parables, leaving his devotees to work out the answer.

STARHAWK
(1951–)

A leading figure of the Goddess and Wicca movements, Starhawk is an activist for feminist, antimilitary, and "ecospiritual" environmental causes; a spiritual teacher who gives talks and workshops in North America and Europe; and the author of books on the Pagan religion, magick, and politics, as well as visionary fiction. Starhawk (born Miriam Simos) is a cofounder of Reclaiming, a San Francisco collective that seeks to unify earth-based spirituality and politics. The group offers classes, intensives, public rituals, and training in the Goddess and magical traditions.

Born in St. Paul, Minnesota, and of Jewish heritage, Starhawk holds an M.A. in psychology from Antioch West University and has been committed to principles of nonviolent activism since her high school days during the Vietnam war. She is involved in support work for sustainability programs and practices the system of ecological design known as permaculture.

Starhawk has been a collaborator with the director Donna Read (with whom she formed a film company, Belili Productions) on several films, including *Goddess Remembered, The Burning Times,* and a documentary on the life of the archaeologist Marija Gimbutas. Her commentaries are published widely, and she is a columnist for the journal *Reclaiming Quarterly.*

Starhawk is a cofounder of Reclaiming, a San Francisco collective that seeks to unify earth-based spirituality and politics.

Her Words

The law of the Goddess is love: passionate sexual love, the warm affection of friends, the fierce protective

love of mother for child, the deep comradeship of the coven. There is nothing amorphous or superficial about love in the Goddess religion; it is always specific, directed toward real individuals, not vague concepts of humanity. Love includes animals, plants, the earth itself—"all beings," not just human beings. It includes ourselves and all our fallible human qualities.
—*The Spiral Dance,* p. 97

Unconditional love means that regardless of the conflict we might have had with our friend, regardless of whatever still lies unfinished between us, we can honor our deep connection of spirit. Unconditional love means that we recognize the Goddess in our friend's eyes, that we allow ourselves to accept her failures, her annoying behaviors, her mistakes and weaknesses, as part of the rich brew of her personality. When my mother was dying, I remember an enormous pang of grief at the thought that she would never yell at me again.
—*The Pagan Book of Living and Dying,* p. 62

Books by Starhawk

Circle Round: Raising Children in the Goddess Tradition. With Anne Hill and Diane Baker. New York: Bantam Books, 1998.

Dreaming the Dark: Magic, Sex, and Politics. Boston: Beacon Press, 1997.

The Fifth Sacred Thing. New York: Bantam Books, 1993.

The Pagan Book of Living and Dying. With M. Macha Nightmare and the Reclaiming Collective. San Francisco: HarperSanFrancisco, 1997.

The Spiral Dance: A Rebirth of the Ancient Religion of the Great Goddess. 1979. Reprint, San Francisco: HarperSanFrancisco, 1999.

Truth or Dare: Encounters with Power, Authority, and Mystery. San Francisco: HarperSanFrancisco, 1988.

The Twelve Wild Swans: A Journey into Magic, Healing, and Action. With Hilary Valentine. San Francisco: HarperSanFrancisco, 2000.

Walking to Mercury. New York: Bantam Books, 1997.

Organization

Reclaiming, P.O. Box 14404, San Francisco, CA 94114; web site: www.reclaiming.org.

Other Resources

Web site: www.starhawk.org.

Videotapes: *Women and Spirituality: The Burning Times* (1990), *Women and Spirituality: Goddess Remembered* (1993), directed by Donna Read; available from Belili Productions.

Audiotape: *Magic, Vision, and Action: Changing Consciousness, Healing the Earth,* Sounds True, 1990.

Periodical: *Reclaiming Quarterly;* web site: www.reclaiming.org/newsletter/index.html.

Film company: Belili Productions, P.O. Box 410187, San Francisco, CA 94141-0187; web site: www.webcom.com/gimbutas/belili/about.html.

"Love includes animals, plants, the earth itself—'all beings,' not just human beings."

DESMOND TUTU
(1931–)

A leader in the ecclesiastical opposition to apartheid in South Africa, Anglican Archbishop Desmond Tutu earned worldwide recognition for his nonviolent activism for peace and racial harmony. In 1984 he was awarded the Nobel Peace Prize for his efforts to establish an international boycott of trade and investment in South Africa. He has inspired the world with his courageous moral stance, rooted in his Christian faith.

Born to Xhosa and Tswana parents in Klerksdorp, Transvaal, Desmond Mpilo Tutu grew up in a shack without plumbing or electricity. Emulating his father's career, he received a teacher's diploma at Pretoria Bantu College and went on to earn a bachelor of arts from the University of South Africa.

Tutu worked as a teacher for three years and then entered Saint Peter's Theological College in Rossettenville, Johannesburg. He was ordained a priest in 1961. For the next few years he studied in England, where he received a master of theology degree. He returned to South Africa and in 1975 became the first black person to be appointed Anglican dean of Johannesburg.

In 1979 Tutu called for sanctions against South Africa, saying they were a form of nonviolent protest that would help to end apartheid. His global popularity made him a threat to the South African government at a time when political dissenters often faced arrest, violence, or even death. For many years the South African government denied him a passport to travel abroad, but it relented in 1982 in response to international pressure.

This winner of the Nobel Peace Prize grew up in apartheid-divided South Africa in a shack without plumbing or electricity.

In 1986 Desmond Tutu was elected archbishop of Cape Town, the highest position in the South African Anglican Church. Between 1996 and 1998 he led the Truth and Reconciliation Commission, which investigated human rights abuses during apartheid. A skilled orator, he has continued to speak out against oppression and injustice even after the defeat of apartheid.

His Words

We shall be free, all of us, black and white, for it is God's intention. He enlists us to help him transfigure all the ugliness of this world into the beauty of his kingdom.
—*The Rainbow People of God,* p. 127

Be nice to whites, they need you to rediscover their humanity.
—quoted in James B. Simpson, *Simpson's Contemporary Quotations*

Revolution! They think we run away from revolution, but the people in this country do not think revolution is necessarily a bad thing. Revolution means a radical change. If it is revolution to say I work for a South Africa that is nonracial; if it is revolution to say I am working for a South Africa that is truly democratic; if it is revolution to say I am working for a South Africa where black and white and yellow and green can walk together arm in arm, then, friends, I am for that.
—*The Rainbow People of God,* p. 142

Books by Desmond Tutu

The African Prayer Book. New York: Doubleday, 1995.
No Future without Forgiveness. New York: Doubleday, 2000.
The Rainbow People of God: The Making of a Beautiful Revolution. New York: Doubleday, 1984.
The Words of Desmond Tutu. New York: Newmarket Press, 1996.

Books about Desmond Tutu

Battle, Michael. *Reconciliation: The Ubuntu Theology of Desmond Tutu.* Cleveland, Ohio: Pilgrim Press, 1997.

______, comp. *The Wisdom of Desmond Tutu.* Louisville, Ky.: Westminster John Knox Press, 2000.

Hulley, L. D., ed., et al. *Archbishop Tutu: Prophetic Witness to South Africa.* n.p.: BHB International, 1997.

Pieterse, H. J. C., ed. *Desmond Tutu's Message: A Qualitative Analysis.* Empirical Studies in Theology, vol. 5. Boston: Brill Academic Publishers, 2001.

Other Resources

Videotapes: *Bishop Desmond Tutu,* Vision Video, 2001; *The Church of God Goes On,* Episcopal Radio-TV Foundation, 1982; *Tutu and Franklin: A Journey toward Peace,* dialogue between Bishop Desmond Tutu and John Hope Franklin, PBS, 2001.

"[God] enlists us to help him transfigure all the ugliness of this world into the beauty of his kingdom."

2

THEY BORE **WITNESS** WITH THEIR LIVES

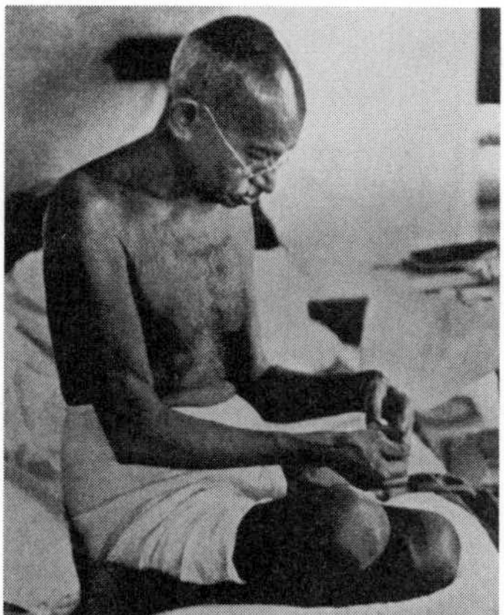

There is a price to be paid for understanding in the depth of one's soul that there is a right course and a wrong course, and that the right one must be followed regardless of danger. Sometimes the consequences are accepted willingly. More often they are imposed through force and violence. The twentieth century was wracked by extraordinary brutality, and imposed martyrdom was, sadly, all too common. Whole communities paid the price; individuals were subjected to insufferable horrors. Yet the light of hope, though sometimes dimmed, was ever present because of the courage of those few willing to risk all. This is, perhaps, the toughest of spiritual tests.

Religious intolerance certainly predated the century. Nor did it end with the dawn of a new millennium. The Middle East, a wellspring of spiritual visions that became global, remains in the forefront of world hot-spots where firm belief both uplifts and divides. Such was the experience of 'Abdu'l Bahá, son of the founder of the Bahá'í faith. Bahá spent much of his life in prison, kept there by the Islamic Ottoman Empire, which sought to repress his father's teachings as heretical. Yet Bahá did not waver in his inner vision. "Love is the light that guideth in darkness," he wrote.

Bahá survived his trials. But the century's best-known witnesses to their faith did not. They were murdered in public view—as were Mahatma Gandhi, Malcolm X, Martin Luther King, Jr., and Oscar Romero—and in the secretive hell of concentration camps, as was Dietrich Bonhoeffer.

Bonhoeffer, a German Protestant theologian, was the first of this group to die. He sealed his fate with his passionate condemnation of

Hitler's "final solution." For Bonhoeffer, the burden of Christian discipleship took precedence over life itself. Gandhi was next, felled by a fanatical assassin because he saw Hindu and Muslim as equal before God in an India made independent by his simple spirituality yoked to an indomitable political will.

Of all those profiled in this chapter, Malcolm X perhaps most dramatically represents the depth of transformation that spiritual insight can spur. Narcotics, prostitution, and gambling composed his early career; racial hatred informed his creed. Yet he died because he came to espouse humanity's essential oneness after experiencing it in Mecca, the Islamic holy city.

King, unlike Malcolm, spent the entirety of his public life speaking of his belief in a divinely ordained human oneness. His words inspired national self-reflection and healing, and made him the personification, with Gandhi, of nonviolent revolutionary struggle rooted in the power of faith. He, too, was murdered by an enemy blinded to the essential truth of the one human destiny. The same may be said for Oscar Romero, the Roman Catholic archbishop of El Salvador, whose epiphany was forged in the caldron of Latin America's historic class distinctions compounded by cold war politics.

A truth of martyrdom is its ability to inspire from beyond the grave, or funeral pyre, and such is the case with the five men noted here. Each has become an icon in his community. Yet the power of their actions was such that they have also transcended cultural, racial, and religious boundaries to live on as global examples of all that is most elevated, and universally exalted, in the human species.

Bearing witness, fortunately, does not always lead to death, as was true for Bahá. So too for Daniel Berrigan and Gustavo Gutiérrez. Of the two, Berrigan has paid the heftier price for his witness. Bringing the Roman Catholic tradition to bear on current issues, this Jesuit priest has repeatedly been arrested for his antimilitary activism. Gutiérrez, by contrast, would seem to have triumphed in his commitment. The acknowledged founder of Liberation theology, which interprets the Christian Gospel as demanding solidarity with the poor and oppressed, he has been honored internationally for his work while escaping direct condemnation by his church and violence from his opponents.

It could be said, though, that the true triumph of bearing witness is the very act itself.

'ABDU'L BAHÁ
(1844–1921)

The son of the founder of the Bahá'í faith, this missionary and teacher was responsible for the propagation of this modern religion in the Western world, drawing people to its teachings of unity and equality through his own humble and radiant personality.

Born Abbas Effendi in Persia but later called 'Abdu'l Bahá (Servant of the Glory), he lived the greater part of his life in persecution and prison. When he was a child, his father, Bahá'u'lláh, proclaimed himself the founder of a new religion, the Bahá'í faith, which stresses the unity and equality of humankind and the truth and harmony found in all religions. The new prophet suffered a harsh fate at the hands of the Islamic Ottoman Empire that ruled Persia at the time, being forced after his great proclamation to spend the rest of his life in prison and in exile—dying in prison in the city of Akko, now in Israel, in 1892. 'Abdu'l Bahá was imprisoned and exiled along with his father and became his devoted student and designated successor during those years.

After he was freed in 1908, 'Abdu'l Bahá governed the Bahá'í community, and he wasted no time in traveling throughout the Western world to spread the Bahá'í message of peace and universal brotherhood—his quiet, charismatic presence drawing attention wherever he went. Because of his work, the Bahá'í faith went from being a small and persecuted Persian sect to an influential religious movement with adherents around the world.

The son of the founder of the Bahá'í faith, 'Abdu'l Bahá lived the greater part of his life in persecution and in prison.

His Words

Know thou of a certainty that Love is the secret of God's holy Dispensation, the manifestation of the All-Merciful, the fountain of spiritual outpourings. Love is heaven's kindly light, the Holy Spirit's eternal breath that vivifieth the human soul. Love is the cause of God's revelation unto man, the vital bond inherent, in accordance with the divine creation, in the realities of things. Love is the one means that ensureth true felicity both in this world and the next. Love is the light that guideth in darkness, the living link that uniteth God with man, that assureth the progress of every illumined soul.
—*Selections from the Writings of 'Abdu'l Bahá,* p. 27

Books by 'Abdu'l Bahá

The Promulgation of Universal World Peace. Wilmette, Ill.: Bahá'í Publishing Trust, 1974.

Selections from the Writings of 'Abdu'l Bahá. Haifa, Israel: Bahá'í World Centre, 1982.

Wisdom of the Master: The Spiritual Teaching of 'Abdu'l Bahá. Edited by Steven Sholl. Ashland, Ore.: White Cloud Press, 1997.

Book about 'Abdu'l Bahá

Balyuzi, H. M. *'Abdu'l Bahá: The Centre of the Covenant of Baha'u'llah.* London: George Ronald, 1971.

Organization

Bahá'í House of Worship, 112 Linden Ave., Wilmette, IL 60091-2839. Bahá'í's U.S. headquarters.

Other Resources

Web site: www.bahai.org. Official web site of the Bahá'í faith.

"Love is the light that guideth in darkness, the living link that uniteth God with man, that assureth the progress of every illumined soul."

DANIEL BERRIGAN
(1921–)

Often jailed for his protests against the Vietnam war, weapons manufacturers, and militarism, the Jesuit priest, poet, and activist Daniel Berrigan has brought the Roman Catholic social tradition to bear on current events for a half century.

Raised in Syracuse, New York, Berrigan entered the Order of the Society of Jesus in 1939 and taught at Catholic preparatory schools. He was ordained a priest in 1952. Berrigan then traveled to France, where he studied further and was influenced by the worker-priest movement. A sense of the responsibility that comes with Christian faith pervaded his work. He returned to the United States and in 1957 assumed a teaching post at Le Moyne College in Syracuse. His teaching vocation continued throughout his career, as he held positions at Cornell and Yale Universities, among other schools.

Berrigan pursued his passion for justice by becoming associate director of United Religious Work from 1966 to 1969. He also used poetry as a vehicle for social protest; he actively opposed the Vietnam war and wrote a collection of poems, *Night Flight to Hanoi,* after a moving 1968 trip to Vietnam to obtain the release of three American pilots.

Berrigan is perhaps most famous for destroying draft registration files in Catonsville, Maryland—an incident for which he was sentenced to three years in prison in 1970. After fleeing underground for several months, he was captured by the authorities and served eighteen months before his release on parole. Berrigan continued to challenge the political and military establishment

Berrigan's work is infused with the sense of the responsibility that comes with Christian faith.

with his brother (and onetime priest) Philip, with whom he had orchestrated the Catonsville incident. In 1980 the brothers led the first Plowshares Action, a protest at a General Electric weapons plant in King of Prussia, Pennsylvania. For the next twelve years Berrigan was repeatedly arrested for his protest demonstrations at weapons manufacturing plants and other sites.

Berrigan lives in a Jesuit community in New York and remains active in social justice causes. Just a month before his eightieth birthday, he was arrested on Good Friday 2001 for blocking the entrance to a Navy aircraft carrier turned into a floating military museum in New York. Later he said that, despite his age, he would continue to speak out on the issues that have defined his life's work: "The day after I'm embalmed, that's when I'll give it up," he said. Berrigan also continues to conduct retreats and to write. He has authored more than fifty books of prose and poetry.

His Words

In 1980 and frequently since, groups of us have labored to break the clutch on our souls of wars and rumors of wars, of "inevitable" wars, of "just" wars, of "necessary" wars, of "victorious" wars. For us, repeated arrests, and the discipline of nonviolence in a religious tradition, have been summed up in the ethic of the resurrection surpassing all ideologies and justifications. Simply put, and daring to speak for others, some of whom are in jail tonight, we have longed to taste the resurrection. We have longed to welcome its thunders and quakes, and to echo its great gifts. We want to test the resurrection in our bones. We want to see if we might live in hope instead of in the . . . twilight thicket of cultural despair in which standing implies many are lost. May I add that in all this, we have not been disappointed.
—1999 Unitarian Universalist Peace Fellowship Lecture

DEFENSE: Could you state to the court what your intent was in burning the draft files?

DANIEL BERRIGAN: I did not want the children or the grandchildren of the jury or of the judge to be burned with napalm.

—*The Trial of the Catonsville Nine*

Books by Daniel Berrigan

And the Risen Bread: Selected Poems, 1957–1997. Edited by John Dear. New York: Fordham University Press, 1998.

Daniel Berrigan: Poetry, Drama, Prose. Edited by Michael True. Maryknoll, N.Y.: Orbis Books, 1988.

The Geography of Faith: Underground Conversations on Religious, Political, and Social Change. Woodstock, Vt.: SkyLight Paths, 2001.

Job: And Death No Dominion. Ashland, Ohio: Sheed & Ward, 2000.

Night Flight to Hanoi: War Diary with Eleven Poems. New York: Macmillan, 1968.

Prison Poems. Greensboro, N.C.: Unicorn Press, 1973.

The Trial of the Catonsville Nine. Boston: Beacon Press, 1970.

Steadfastness of the Saints: A Journal of Peace and War in Central and North America. Maryknoll, N.Y.: Orbis Books, 1985.

To Dwell in Peace: An Autobiography. San Francisco: Harper & Row, 1987.

Books about Daniel Berrigan

Curtis, Richard. *The Berrigan Brothers: The Story of Daniel and Philip Berrigan.* New York: Hawthorn Books, 1974.

Klejment, Anne. *The Berrigans: Bibliography of Published Works by Daniel, Philip, and Elizabeth McAlister Berrigan.* New York: Garland Publishers, 1979.

Lockwood, Lee. *Daniel Berrigan: Absurd Convictions, Modest Hopes.* New York: Random House, 1972.

Polner, Murray, and Jim O'Grady. *Disarmed and Dangerous: The Radical Lives and Times of Daniel and Philip Berrigan.* New York City: HarperCollins, 1997.

"I never wanted only to be a fugitive—to stay out of jail only for the sake of staying out. That was never, never the idea. I wanted to stay out in order to take risks. If not, then I might as well go to jail and remain there."

DIETRICH BONHOEFFER
(1906–1945)

The most prominent Protestant martyr of World War II, Dietrich Bonhoeffer was a leading theological voice in opposition to the Nazi regime and a key proponent of the ecumenical movement. Although his opposition to Nazism began mostly as a protest against churches' loss of autonomy, it grew into a passionate condemnation of the Nazis' treatment of the Jews and a powerful example of the meaning of discipleship.

Educated at Tübingen, Berlin, and Union Theological Seminary in New York, the Reverend Dietrich Bonhoeffer served as vicar at a German church in Barcelona after his ordination in the German Evangelical Church. While abroad he began to make contacts that would prove vital in both his ecumenical efforts and his resistance to Hitler. In 1931 he joined the faculty of the University of Berlin. When Hitler rose to power two years later, many in the Evangelical Church—Germany's main denomination, long allied with the state—welcomed the new leader.

Bonhoeffer's disillusionment began with a controversy over the so-called Aryan paragraph, which barred non-Aryans from the ministry and was championed by the *Deutsche Christen* (German Christians), the Evangelical Church's pro-Nazi element. Opponents of the rule favored the evangelization and conversion of Jews and opposed barring Jewish converts from church positions. Bonhoeffer said the rule surrendered the church's religious values

In a 1933 essay, "The Church and the Jewish Question," Bonhoeffer argued for aiding the victims of Nazism and strove to inform the world of what was happening in Germany.

to political ideology, and he urged ministers to resign from the Evangelical Church in protest. In 1934 the Confessing Church, an alternative and independent denomination, was born.

In a 1933 essay, "The Church and the Jewish Question," Bonhoeffer argued for aiding the victims of Nazism, although his argument was predicated on Christian supersessionism, the belief that Christianity has replaced Judaism as God's true covenant. He also strove to inform the world of what was happening in Germany. Later that year he took a pulpit in London and worked successfully to have the Confessing Church recognized by international ecumenical bodies. He returned to Germany in 1935 to help train clergy for the Confessing Church. His best-known books, *The Cost of Discipleship* and *Life Together,* emerged from this experience.

As Gestapo pressure on the church increased, Bonhoeffer was banned from Berlin and began to work in secret. He also began to speak increasingly of Judaism as equal in God's eyes to Christianity. After a brief stint in New York, he became a key player in resistance to Nazism. Bonhoeffer was arrested after helping a handful of Jews escape from Germany. While he was in jail, the Nazis became aware of the extent of his participation in the resistance, including his role in an ill-conceived attempt to assassinate Hitler. On April 9, 1945, he was hanged at the Flössenburg concentration camp.

His Words

I believe that God can and will bring good out of evil, even out of the greatest evil. For that purpose, he needs men who make the best use of everything. I believe that God will give us all the strength we need to help us to resist in all times of distress. But he never gives it in advance, lest we should rely on ourselves and not on him alone. A faith such as this should allay all our fears for the future. I believe that even our mistakes and shortcomings are turned to good account, and that it is no harder for God to deal with them than with our supposedly good deeds. I believe that God is no timeless fate, but that he waits for and answers sincere prayers and responsible actions.

—"After Ten Years," in *Letters and Papers from Prison,* p. 11

Books by Dietrich Bonhoeffer

The Cost of Discipleship. Minneapolis: Fortress Press, 2001.
Ethics. London: SCM, 1955.
Letters and Papers from Prison. New York: Touchstone, 1971.
Life Together. New York: Harper & Row, 1954.

Books about Dietrich Bonhoeffer

Bethge, Eberhard. *Dietrich Bonhoeffer: A Biography.* Translated by Eric Mosbacher et al. Minneapolis: Fortress Press, 2000.
Morris, Kenneth Earl. *Bonhoeffer's Ethic of Discipleship: A Study in Social Psychology, Political Thought, and Religion.* University Park: Pennsylvania State University Press, 1986.

For a more complete list of books by and about Dietrich Bonhoeffer, see *The Cost of Discipleship,* pp. 319–340.

Organization

Dietrich Bonhoeffer Society; U.S. contact: Reverend Nancy J. Farrell, 1282 Greenview Dr., Woodburn, OR 97071.

Other Resources

Web site: www.dbonhoeffer.org. Official web site of the Dietrich Bonhoeffer Society.
Statue: Westminster Abbey, along with other twentieth-century martyrs, dedicated in 1998.
Opera: *Bonhoeffer,* by Robert S. Hatten; premiered by Houston Baptist University, May 2000.

"I believe that God can and will bring good out of evil, even out of the greatest evil."

MAHATMA GANDHI
(1869–1948)

Architect of the nonviolent protest movement that ousted the British from India, Mahatma Gandhi is among the most beloved personalities of the twentieth century. Political and social change movements around the world have looked to him as an example while seeking to adapt his philosophy and tactics to their own situations. He was instrumental in three major twentieth-century struggles: against racism, violence, and colonialism.

Mohandas Karamchand Gandhi (*Mahatma* is an honorific meaning "great soul") was raised steeped in Hinduism and Jainism, giving him an appreciation for ahimsa (non-injury for all living beings), vegetarianism, and fasting. He was married at thirteen, and his family decided he should study law in England, for which he set sail in 1888. There he met many social reformers and rebellious souls who would greatly influence his later work. Ironically, it was in England that Gandhi was introduced to the Hindu classic the Bhagavad Gita, the most influential book in his life.

After a brief return stay in India, Gandhi accepted a one-year contract from a South African firm; he would stay in South Africa for twenty years. There he experienced the discrimination all Indians faced, and he dedicated himself to winning justice for South Africa's Indians. He organized the Indian community, exposed the injustices to the outside world, and won press attention in and out of the country.

Gandhi was instrumental in three major twentieth-century struggles: those against racism, violence, and colonialism.

Gandhi delved into a spiritual quest, studying Leo Tolstoy's writings on Christianity, as well as Hindu philosophy and Quaker beliefs. He developed a fascination for Jesus, whose message and example loom large in the development of Gandhi's nonviolence, and he was attracted to simple living and manual labor. Gandhi called on Indians to defy discriminatory laws and suffer the consequences. This call marked the birth of satyagraha ("devotion to truth"), a method of resistance without violence. The government, under British pressure, eventually accepted a compromise, and Gandhi then returned to India.

After initially keeping a low profile, he returned to the public eye in India to push for satyagraha against British rule. By 1920 Gandhi was the dominant figure in the struggle as head of the Indian National Congress. He taught that it was Indians' own imperfections that maintained their servitude, and his strategy of nonviolent non-cooperation with the British led to boycotts, fasts, and imprisonment for many followers. Gandhi himself was imprisoned for two years, and upon his 1924 release he found the congress—and Hindu-Muslim relations—badly fractured.

In 1930 Gandhi led a massive march against the salt tax, among the most successful actions of the struggle. Four years later he quit the congress and devoted himself to building the nation "from the bottom up"—educating the poor and removing the caste stigma of the untouchables.

When India and Pakistan gained independence, Gandhi bitterly opposed the sectarian division of the two nations. He threw himself into healing the wounds between Muslims and Hindus. Although his fasts and entreaties won some major victories, in 1948 a Hindu nationalist assassinated him while Gandhi was on his way to evening prayers.

His Words

Man and his deed are two distinct things. Whereas a good deed should call forth approbation and a wicked deed disapprobation, the doer of the deed, whether good or wicked always deserves respect or pity as the case may be. "Hate the sin and not the sinner" is a precept which, though easy enough to understand, is rarely practiced, and that is why the poison of hatred spreads in the world.
—*An Autobiography,* p. 274

The first step in non-violence is that we cultivate in our daily life, as between ourselves, truthfulness, humility, tolerance, and loving kindness.
—quoted in *Mahatma,* p. 267

If my non-violence is to be contagious and infectious, I must acquire greater control over my thoughts.
—quoted in *The Mind of Mahatma Gandhi,* p. 277

Books by Mahatma Gandhi

An Autobiography: The Story of My Experiments with Truth. With Sissela Bok. Translated by Mahadev Desai. Boston: Beacon Press, 1993.

The Essential Writings of Mahatma Gandhi. Edited by Raghavan Iyer. New York: Oxford University Press, 2000.

Gandhi on Non-Violence. Edited by Thomas Merton. New York: W. W. Norton, 1965.

Books about Mahatma Gandhi

Chatterjee, Margaret. *Gandhi's Religious Thought.* Notre Dame: University of Notre Dame Press, 1983.

Easwaran, Eknath. *Gandhi the Man: The Story of His Transformation.* Tomales, Calif.: Nilgiri Press, 1997.

Jordens, G. T. F. *Gandhi's Religion: A Homespun Shawl.* New York: St. Martin's Press, 1998.

Prabhu, R. K., and U. R. Rao, eds. *The Mind of Mahatma Gandhi.* London: Oxford University Press, 1946.

Tendulkar, D. G. *Mahatma: Life of Mohandas Karamchand Gandhi.* Vol. 4. 2d ed. Delhi: Publications Division, Ministry of Information and Broadcasting, 1960.

Wolpert, Stanley. *Gandhi's Passion: The Life and Legacy of Mahatma Gandhi.* New York: Oxford University Press, 2001.

For a more complete list of books by and about Mahatma Gandhi, see *Essential Writings of Mahatma Gandhi.*

Organization

M. K. Gandhi Institute for Nonviolence, 650 East Parkway S., Memphis, TN 38104; phone: 901-452-2824; web site: www.gandhiinstitute.org. Founded by Gandhi's grandson Arun Gandhi.

Other Resources

Web site: www.mkgandhi.org. India-based web site that includes the complete text of Gandhi's autobiography, research information, photographs, and more.

Film/Videotape/DVD: *Gandhi,* directed by Richard Attenborough, Columbia Pictures, 1982.

Museum: Gandhi Museum, Ring Rd., Delhi, India. In addition to exhibits, includes a library and information center.

Memorial: Raj Ghat, the site of Gandhi's last rites in Delhi, features a much-visited memorial stone.

"The first step in non-violence is that we cultivate in our daily life, as between ourselves, truthfulness, humility, tolerance, and loving kindness."

GUSTAVO GUTIÉRREZ
(1928–)

A Roman Catholic priest and theologian, Gustavo Gutiérrez is viewed as the founder of the influential theology of liberation in Latin America (later called liberation theology). His work has been an inspiration for liberation movements in Third World countries, and for African Americans, women, and other groups.

Part Quechua Indian, Gutiérrez was born in Lima, Peru, where he grew up among the poor. After studying in Rome and France, he taught at the Pontificia Universidad Católica del Perú in Lima while continuing to live among the city's impoverished masses and serving as a parish priest. A prolific writer, he published his best-known book, *A Theology of Liberation,* in Spanish in 1971. In it he challenged the church to work for social justice and help change the economic and political systems that create and perpetuate poverty. His thought is deeply rooted in the Gospel, read as a revolutionary story of liberation that demands solidarity with the oppressed as a logical consequence of a fully lived Christian spirituality. Although the church has issued general cautions against Liberation theology, Gutiérrez's work has not been directly criticized by the Vatican.

Gutiérrez's thought is deeply rooted in the Gospel, read as a revolutionary story of liberation that demands solidarity with the oppressed as a logical consequence of a fully lived Christian spirituality.

Gutiérrez has been a visiting professor at Union Theological Seminary in New York and Cambridge University in Great Britain, as well as elsewhere, and has received more than a dozen honorary degrees. He is a member of the Peruvian Academy of Language and in 1993 was named a member of the French Legion of Honor for his "tireless work for human dignity and life, and against oppression, in Latin America and the Third World."

In 2000 Gutiérrez relocated to France and joined the Dominican Order's French Province, a move seen as an attempt to distance himself from Lima's conservative church hierarchy. He also began teaching philosophy and theology at the University of Notre Dame in Indiana.

His Words

Poverty is an act of love and liberation. It has a redemptive value. If the ultimate cause of human exploitation and alienation is selfishness, the deepest reason for voluntary poverty is love of neighbor. Christian poverty has meaning only as a commitment of solidarity with the poor, with those who suffer misery and injustice. The commitment is to witness to the evil which has resulted from sin and is a breach of communion. It is not a question of idealizing poverty, but rather of taking it on as it is—an evil—to protest against it and to struggle to abolish it. . . . Christian poverty, and expression of love, is solidarity *with the poor* and is a protest *against poverty.*
—*A Theology of Liberation,* p. 172

We often see poverty as an economic and social issue, but we must have a deeper understanding. In the ultimate analysis, poverty is death. It is unjust and early death. It is the destruction of persons, of people and nations.
—Address at the Brown University graduation ceremony, 2000

Books by Gustavo Gutiérrez

The Density of the Present: Selected Writings by Gustavo Gutiérrez. Maryknoll, N.Y.: Orbis Books, 1999.

The God of Life. Translated by Matthew J. O'Connel. Maryknoll, N.Y.: Orbis Books, 1991.

Gustavo Gutiérrez: Essential Writings. Edited by James B. Nickoloff. Maryknoll, N.Y.: Orbis Books, 1996.

Las Casas: In Search of the Poor of Jesus Christ. Translated by Robert R. Barr. Maryknoll, N.Y.: Orbis Books, 1993.

On Job: God-Talk and the Suffering of the Innocent. Translated by Matthew J. O'Connel. Maryknoll, N.Y.: Orbis Books, 1987.

Sharing the Word through the Liturgical Year. Translated by Colette Joly Dees. Maryknoll, N.Y.: Orbis Books, 1997.

A Theology of Liberation: History, Politics, and Salvation. Rev. ed. Translated by Caridad Inda and John Eagleson. Maryknoll, N.Y.: Orbis Books, 1988. First published in Spanish in 1971.

The Truth Shall Make You Free: Confrontations. Maryknoll, N.Y.: Orbis Books, 1990.

We Drink from Our Own Wells. Translated by Matthew J. O'Connel. Maryknoll, N.Y.: Orbis Books, 1984.

Books about Gustavo Gutiérrez

Duncan, William B. *The Political Philosophy of Peruvian Theologian Gustavo Gutiérrez.* Toronto Studies in Theology, vol. 85. Lewiston, N.Y.: Edwin Mellen Press, 2001.

Nava, Alexander. *The Mystical and Prophetic Thought of Simone Weil and Gustavo Gutiérrez: Reflections on the Mystery and Hiddenness of God.* Albany: State University of New York Press, 2001.

Ramsey, William M. *Four Modern Prophets: Walter Rauschenbusch, Martin Luther King, Jr., Gustavo Gutiérrez, Rosemary Radford Ruether.* Louisville, Ky.: Westminster John Knox Press, 1986.

"Christian poverty, and expression of love, is solidarity with the poor *and is a protest* against poverty."

MARTIN LUTHER KING, JR.
(1929–1968)

Among the best-known personalities in American history, the Reverend Martin Luther King, Jr., was a civil rights leader motivated by his deeply held religious beliefs. Often comparing the plight of African Americans with that of the Israelites in Egypt, King movingly wove together biblical imagery, prophetic language, and motifs from African-American religion and its spirituals. He was called a modern-day Moses who told twentieth-century pharaohs to "let my people go."

The son and grandson of Baptist ministers, King entered Crozer Theological Seminary in Chester, Pennsylvania, in 1948; there he was first exposed to Mahatma Gandhi's nonviolent thought. Pursuing a Ph.D. at Boston University after seminary, he focused on God's relationship with humanity. While in Boston, he met Coretta Scott, whom he married in 1953 and with whom he had four children.

King became pastor of Dexter Avenue Baptist Church in Montgomery, Alabama. About a year later a local black woman named Rosa Parks refused to surrender her seat on a public bus to a white person, and the Montgomery Bus Boycott began. The city's transit system was integrated a little more than a year after the boycott started.

On the heels of that struggle, King founded the Southern Christian Leadership Conference, giving his efforts a national platform. A month in India studying Gandhi's philosophy convinced him of the need for nonviolence, and in 1960 he returned to his native Atlanta to become co-pastor, with his father, of Ebenezer Baptist Church.

King was called a modern-day Moses who told twentieth-century pharaohs to "let my people go."

In 1963 King was jailed in Birmingham, Alabama, after leading a protest that had been opposed by many clergy, black and white. From his cell King issued his influential "Letter from a Birmingham Jail," in which he spelled out in explicit form his nonviolent philosophy.

In April 1963 King led the March on Washington, an interracial gathering of 200,000 people. On the steps of the Lincoln Memorial, he delivered his "I Have a Dream" speech, invoking biblical images to imagine a world in which justice reigns and from which racism is absent. The following year the Civil Rights Act of 1964 was passed, and King received the Nobel Peace Prize.

Opposition from radical blacks to King's nonviolence began to appear in 1965. In his later years King increasingly focused on fighting poverty and opposing the Vietnam war. In Memphis, Tennessee, on April 3, 1968, he preached his most apocalyptic sermon, in which he likened himself to Moses, who saw the Promised Land from a mountaintop but died before leading his people there. King's own mission was cut short the next day by an assassin's bullet.

His Words

And when we allow freedom to ring, when we let it ring from every village and hamlet, from every state and city, we will be able to speed up that day when all of God's children—black men and white men, Jews and Gentiles, Catholics and Protestants—will be able to join hands and sing in the words of the old Negro spiritual, "Free at last, free at last; thank God Almighty, we are free at last."
—"I Have a Dream," in *A Testament of Hope,* p. 220

Oppressed people cannot remain oppressed forever. The urge for freedom will eventually come. This is what happened to the American Negro. Something within him has reminded him of his birthright of freedom; something without has reminded him that he can gain it.
—"Letter from a Birmingham Jail," in *A Testament of Hope,* p. 297

Books by Martin Luther King, Jr.

Strength to Love. 1963. Reprint, Philadelphia: Fortress Press, 1981.
A Testament of Hope: The Essential Writings and Speeches of Martin Luther King, Jr. Edited by James Melvin Washington. San Francisco: HarperSanFrancisco, 1986.

Why We Can't Wait. 1963. Reprint, New York: New American Library, 2000.

Books about Martin Luther King, Jr.

Branch, Taylor. *Parting the Waters: America in the King Years, 1954–63.* New York: Simon & Schuster, 1988.

Farris, Christine King. *Martin Luther King, Jr.: His Life and Dream.* Lexington, Mass.: Silver Burdette Ginn, 1986.

Frady, Marshall. *Martin Luther King, Jr. (Penguin Lives).* New York: Viking, 2002.

Witherspoon, William Roger. *Martin Luther King, Jr.: To the Mountaintop.* Garden City, N.Y.: Doubleday, 1985.

For a more complete list of books by and about Martin Luther King, Jr., see *Testament of Hope,* pp. 681–688.

Other Resources

Museum and Research Center: Martin Luther King, Jr., Center for Nonviolent Social Change, 449 Auburn Ave. NE, Atlanta, GA 30312; phone: 404-526-8900.

Historic Site: Martin Luther King, Jr. National Historic Site, 450 Auburn Ave. NE, Atlanta, GA 30312; phone: 404-331-5190.

Videotape: *Eyes on the Prize,* directed by Ken Burns, documentary on the civil rights movement, 1986.

"Oppressed people cannot remain oppressed forever. The urge for freedom will eventually come."

OSCAR ROMERO
(1917–1980)

Oscar Romero was thought to be a conservative who would moderate between the Salvadoran Roman Catholic Church's two factions—those wanting the church to remain neutral in the country's economic struggle, and those wanting the church to take a stand with the poor against the rich. However, events persuaded him to act otherwise as archbishop, and he became an outspoken advocate for the poor of El Salvador and the world. He paid for it with his life.

Born in the hills of Ciudad Barrios, El Salvador, Oscar Arnulfo Romero y Goldamez became a carpenter when he left school at age twelve. The call to the priesthood led him to study at seminaries in San Miguel and San Salvador and later in Rome, where he was ordained in 1942. He returned home to become a rural priest. In 1970 he became a bishop and in 1977 archbishop.

Three weeks after his installation, Father Rutilio Grande, an ardent preacher against the oppression of the poor, was shot. The killing of his friend catapulted Romero into action. Even though he did not see himself as a revolutionary, his words and caring for his people caused a revolution of ideas. Instead of sitting in an office, he visited the poorest villages throughout his country, participating in confirmations, first communions, or local celebrations. In his preaching and writing, he condemned the economic and social systems that beleaguered the poor, and he denounced the violence that kept these systems in place.

Even though Romero did not see himself as a revolutionary, his words and caring for his people caused a revolution of ideas.

Thousands attended Mass every Sunday to hear Romero's homilies, and the church's radio station carried his messages to the far reaches of the country and beyond. People in the remotest villages gathered in small groups to listen to and discuss the archbishop's sermons and his reflections on the prior week's political happenings. He said, "When I focus on the week gone by, I attend to a work that is proper for the Church. . . . We turn the Gospel's light onto the political scene, but the main thing for us is to light the lamp of the Gospel in our communities."

Romero was celebrating Mass on March 24, 1980, when he was felled by an assassin's bullet. A few days before his death, he said, "The only thing that matters is to radically follow the Gospel, which not all can understand. One can yield in certain nonessential aspects, but there can be no yielding on radically following the Gospel." A United Nations commission determined that right-wing opponents murdered Romero. At the Vatican, the process of naming him a saint is under way.

His Words

We ought to be clear from the start that the Christian faith and the activity of the church have always had socio-political repercussions. By commission or omission, by associating themselves with one or another social group, Christians have always had an influence upon the socio-political makeup of the world in which they lived.
—"The Political Dimension of the Faith from the Perspective of the Option for the Poor," in *Voice of the Voiceless,* p. 178

The peace in which we believe is, however, the fruit of justice: *opus iustitiae pax*. . . . We therefore regard as a most urgent task the establishment of social justice.
—"The Church and Popular Political Organizations," in *Voice of the Voiceless,* p. 109

Book by Oscar Romero

Voice of the Voiceless: The Four Pastoral Letters and Other Statements. Maryknoll, N.Y.: Orbis Books, 1985.

Books about Oscar Romero

Brockman, James R. *Romero: A Life.* Maryknoll, N.Y.: Orbis Books, 1989.

______. *The Word Remains: A Life of Oscar Romero.* Maryknoll, N.Y.: Orbis Books, 1982.

Sobrino, Jon. *Archbishop Romero: Memories and Reflections.* Maryknoll, N.Y.: Orbis Books, 1990.

Other Resources

Web site: www.napf.org/hero/oscar_romero.html. Nuclear Age Peace Foundation, Oscar Romero page.

Videotape: *Romero,* directed by John Duigan, dramatized biography of Romero starring Raul Julia, 1989.

Image: Painted icon by Robert Lentz, Bridge Building Images, Inc.; web site: www.bridgebuilding.com.

> *"We ought to be clear from the start that the Christian faith and the activity of the church have always had socio-political repercussions."*

MALCOLM X
(1925–1965)

Born Malcolm Little in Omaha, Nebraska, Malcolm X was a pioneering American Muslim who popularized ideas of black separatism and nationalism in the 1950s and 1960s but later tempered his ideas to envision peaceful cooperation of the races.

He spent his early life as a petty criminal, landing in repeated trouble with the law. While serving time for robbery, he read the works of Elijah Muhammad, leader of the Nation of Islam, the radical black nationalist group. He converted in 1946, taking the name Malcolm X. After his release from prison in 1952, he became a speaker and organizer for the group and, two years later, minister of one of its main mosques in New York's Harlem neighborhood. His compelling sermons and charismatic personality brought many new adherents to the Nation of Islam, but his racist statements alienated many others, white and black.

As a minister of the Nation of Islam, Malcolm X taught that the civil rights movement, integration, and racial equality were shams, the pabulum offered by a ruling class directed by evil whites. He promoted the ideas of African-American self-reliance, a separate independent nation for blacks, and the use of violence as a means of self-protection. His views made him distinctly unpopular with the country's establishment, as well as with civil rights leaders, and in 1963 Elijah Muhammad censured him for his comments implying that the assassination of President John F. Kennedy had been deserved.

Malcolm X's compelling sermons and charismatic personality brought many new adherents to the Nation of Islam.

In 1964 Malcolm X broke with the Nation of Islam, because of a shift in his religious beliefs but also because of disillusionment with Elijah Muhammad and the movement. In March of that year, he announced that he was founding his own Islamic religious movement. In April, after a trip to Mecca, Islam's holiest site, he revised his ideas about racial separatism and said he no longer thought whites an evil race. Later he announced his conversion to Islam's mainstream Sunni branch and took the name El-Hajj Malik El-Shabazz. That move only increased the tensions between his followers and those he left behind in the Nation of Islam. On February 21, 1965, Malcolm was shot to death in Harlem's Audubon Ballroom. Three members of the Nation of Islam were later convicted of his murder.

His Words

Bending my knees to pray—that act—well, that took me a week. You know what my life had been. Picking a lock to rob someone's house was the only way my knees had ever been bent before. I had to force myself to bend my knees. And waves of shame and embarrassment would force me back up. For evil to bend its knees, admitting its guilt, to implore the forgiveness of God, is the hardest thing in the world. It's easy for me to see and say that now. But then, when I was the personification of evil, I was going through it. Again, again I would force myself back down into the praying-to-Allah position. When finally I was able to make myself stay down—I didn't know what to say to Allah.
—*The Autobiography of Malcolm X*, p. 196

When I am dead . . . the white man, in his press, is going to identify me with "hate." He will make use of me dead, as he has made use of me alive, as a convenient symbol of "hatred"—and that will help him to escape facing the truth that all I have been doing is holding up a mirror to reflect, to show, the history of unspeakable crimes that his race has committed against my race. . . . I know that societies have often killed the people who have helped to change those societies. And if I can die, having brought any light, having exposed any meaningful truth that will help to destroy the racist cancer that is malignant in the body of America—then all the credit is due to Allah. Only the mistakes have been mine.
—*The Autobiography of Malcolm X*, pp. 439–440

Books by Malcolm X

The Autobiography of Malcolm X. With Alex Haley. 1965. Reprint, New York: Ballantine Books, 1999.

The End of White World Supremacy: Four Speeches. Edited and with an introduction by Benjamin Karim. New York: Seaver Books, 1971.

Malcolm X: The Last Speeches. Edited by Bruce Perry. New York: Pathfinder Press, 1989.

Books about Malcolm X

Cone, James H. *Martin and Malcolm and America: A Dream or a Nightmare.* Maryknoll, N.Y.: Orbis Books, 1991.

Dyson, Michael Eric. *Making Malcolm: The Myth and Meaning of Malcolm X.* New York: Oxford University Press, 1994.

Evanzz, Karl. *The Judas Factor: The Plot to Kill Malcolm X.* New York: Thunder's Mouth Press, 1993.

Other Resources

Film/Videotape/DVD: *Malcolm X,* directed by Spike Lee, dramatic presentation starring Denzel Washington, 1992.

"I know that societies have often killed the people who have helped to change those societies."

3

THEIR **PRESENCE** CHANGED THE WORLD

Global communications, global travel, global impact. The twentieth century was a time of great change, with no innovations more representative of the period than these three. As they did for commerce and politics, they affected the inner lives of people in unforeseen and profound ways that have yet to be fully understood.

The advances began slowly—at least that is how it appears in hindsight, given the dizzying pace of change that marked the century's waning decades. Swami Vivekananda, for example, died soon after the century began, and the extent of his impact seems, at first glance, limited. In fact, the appearance of this exponent of Hinduism's Vedantic path at the Parliament of the World's Religions in Chicago in 1893 set the stage for the West's broad acceptance of Eastern spirituality, which followed decades later.

Vivekananda's work, it can be argued, also opened the way for the critical and popular acceptance afforded Rabindranath Tagore, the first Asian writer to be awarded the Nobel Prize in literature. Through Tagore the core values of Indian culture—peace, tolerance, unity, and divine love reflected in human love—gained appreciation in the West and were incorporated into the century's utopian vision of a global village steadily progressing toward an idealized human society, which, it was assumed, would follow.

Abraham Joshua Heschel's long-lasting impact was of another sort. As a theologian, teacher, and social activist, he helped restore a lost mysticism to mainstream American Judaism while leading his community into the modern era of interfaith dialogue and interracial social action.

In five short years Pope John XXIII set in motion changes within the Roman Catholic world that transformed the church beyond anything it has experienced in modern history. There has been no turning back from the Second Vatican Council convened by John, whose papacy was among the shortest of the twentieth century. Reform became the watchword, and the changes he initiated continue to convulse the Catholic world as it seeks to balance modernity and tradition.

John, then, was an unlikely spiritual revolutionary. The same might be said for Ram Dass, the middle-class son of acculturated American Judaism who was once a tenured professor at Harvard University named Richard Alpert. But just about all that John and Ram Dass have in common is the willingness to follow the spirit of experimentation, wherever it might lead, that so characterized the 1960s. For Ram Dass that spirit led to psychedelic drugs—and then to the path blazed by Vivekananda and Tagore, Eastern mysticism. And as John became an icon to a generation of liberal Catholics, Ram Dass became an icon to a generation turned on by recovery of a spirit it found lacking in contemporary Western society.

But when it comes to impact, none in the century approach Billy Graham, Tenzin Gyatso, better known as the fourteenth Dalai Lama, and Pope John Paul II. Each in his own way is an example of that unique late twentieth century's creation: the spiritual leader as pop celebrity and commodity. Not since the rise of Islam, the newest of the world's great religions, has a spiritual leader affected the global stage to such a degree.

Graham, confidant of presidents and kings, transformed the Protestant tent revival into a worldwide multimedia stadium extravaganza. The Dalai Lama employed a lighthearted touch to make Buddhism, the ornate Tibetan branch in particular, fashionable to non-Buddhists everywhere, including Hollywood celebrities. John Paul turned the papal Mass into the religious equivalent of a traveling rock tour, and the Vatican into a political powerhouse on issues of morality.

Of the three, the Dalai Lama is the youngest. But even he is no youngster. When these three pass from the scene, their legacies will endure for decades, if not longer. Take nothing away from their forceful personalities and indomitable spiritual strengths. But give a fair share of the credit for their international impact to the ease with which global communications and travel were made possible at the close of the twentieth century.

DALAI LAMA (TENZIN GYATSO)
(1935–)

For the past half century, since he was forced to flee his Tibetan homeland, Tenzin Gyatso, better known as H. H. (His Holiness) the Dalai Lama, has inspired the world with his wisdom, compassion, and courage.

He was born to a peasant family, but when he was two, Buddhist lamas from Tibet's capital city, Lhasa, were led to his remote house by special indicators, including images in their dreams. There they tested whether he could identify certain significant items left behind by the thirteenth Dalai Lama (literally, "Ocean [or Great] Teacher"), the spiritual leader of Tibet who had recently died. The infant Gyatso passed the tests and was declared the fourteenth Dalai Lama, a reincarnation of his predecessor. Three years later he was enthroned in his palace in Lhasa. His new role also made him de facto political head of the country.

In 1951 Communist troops from China invaded Tibet and reclaimed it as a Chinese territory for the first time in centuries. As part of subsequent truce negotiations, the Dalai Lama was formally made the head of the now regional Tibetan government. In 1959, after years of small, sporadic rebellions by native Tibetans, the Chinese launched a massive repression. Thousands of Tibetans were killed, hundreds of Buddhist temples and monasteries were destroyed, and the Dalai Lama felt compelled to go into exile. He settled just beyond Tibet's southern, Himalayan border in the Indian city of Dharamsala, where he gradually attracted a community of displaced

Forced into exile by the Chinese occupation of Tibet, the Dalai Lama has traveled extensively, acting as an advocate for conflict resolution by peaceful means.

Tibetans and disciples that currently numbers more than one hundred thousand.

During his years of exile, the Dalai Lama has traveled extensively, keeping the Tibetan cause alive on the international stage while spreading the Buddhist *dharma* (teachings) and acting as an advocate for conflict resolution by peaceful means. His engaging personality shines through in his books, several of which have been *New York Times* bestsellers. In 1989 he received the Nobel Peace Prize in recognition of his efforts.

His Words

The more altruism we develop in a day, the more peaceful we find ourselves. Similarly, the more self-centered we remain, the more frustrations and trouble we encounter. All these reflections lead us to conclude that a good heart and an altruistic motivation are indeed true sources of happiness and are therefore genuine wish-granting jewels.
—*Path to Bliss,* p. 18

A sad human being cannot influence reality. If you are sad or depressed, you cannot influence reality. When you face a so-called enemy, that enemy only exists on a relative level. Then, if you harbor hatred or ill feelings toward that person, the feeling itself does not hurt the enemy. It only harms your own peace of mind and eventually your own health.
—*The Buddha Nature,* p. 78

Books by the Dalai Lama

The Art of Happiness: A Handbook for Living. New York: Riverhead, 1998.

The Buddha Nature. Woodside, Calif.: Bluestone Communications, 1996.

The Buddhism of Tibet. Ithaca, N.Y.: Snow Lion Publications, 1975.

Ethics for a New Millennium. New York: Penguin Putnam, 1999.

The Good Heart. Somerville, Mass.: Wisdom Publications, 1996.

Kindness, Clarity, and Insight. Ithaca, N.Y.: Snow Lion Publications, 1984.

My Land and My People. New York: McGraw-Hill, 1977.

An Open Heart: Practicing Compassion in Everyday Life. Edited by Nicholas Vreeland. Boston: Little, Brown, 2001.

Path to Bliss. Ithaca, N.Y.: Snow Lion Publications, 1991.
A Policy of Kindness. Ithaca, N.Y.: Snow Lion Publications, 1990.

Books about the Dalai Lama

Avedon, John F. *In Exile from the Land of Snows.* New York: Alfred A. Knopf, 1984.
Farrar-Halls, Gill. *The World of the Dalai Lama: An Inside Look at His Life, His People, and His Vision.* Wheaton, Ill.: Theosophical Publishing, 1998.
Morgan, Tom, ed. *A Simple Monk: Writings on His Holiness the Dalai Lama.* Introduction by Robert Thurman. Photographs by Alison Wright. Novatoa, Calif.: New World Library, 2001.

Organization

Tibet Center, 359 Broadway, New York, NY 10013; phone and fax: 212-966-8504.

Other Resources

Web sites: www.tibet.com. Web site of the Government of Tibet in Exile.
www.savetibet.org. Web site of the International Campaign for Tibet.
Videotape: *Compassion in Exile,* documentary, Lemle Pictures, 1992; available from Direct Cinema Limited, P.O. Box 10003, Santa Monica, CA 90410; phone 310-396-4774.
Film/Videotape/DVD: *Kundun,* dramatization, Touchstone Pictures, directed by Martin Scorsese, 1997.

"The more altruism we develop in a day, the more peaceful we find ourselves."

BILLY GRAHAM
(1918–)

The foremost Protestant evangelist of the twentieth century, the Reverend Billy Graham has employed the latest in technology and marketing techniques to modernize the format and style of traditional revival meetings, attracting large audiences worldwide. Many of his contemporaries became associated solely with political conservatives, but Graham befriended and advised U.S. presidents of both major parties, while consistently preaching the need to make a personal decision to live for Jesus Christ. And at a time when many prominent religious figures were tainted by sexual or financial misdeeds, he remained free from scandal.

Born near Charlotte, North Carolina, Graham committed his life to Christ at a revival in 1934. He was ordained five years later by a Southern Baptist church, studied at the Florida Bible Institute (now Trinity College), and graduated from Wheaton College in Illinois in 1943. He joined Youth for Christ, which spread the Gospel to servicemen, and became a rising star in the world of evangelism. In 1949 his stardom was sealed by a Los Angeles crusade that extended more than five weeks past its original three-week target. Around the same time the media mogul William Randolph Hearst boosted Graham's career by ordering that positive stories be written in his newspapers about the evangelist.

In tent meetings and revivals for over fifty years, Graham's message has been consistent and simple: Surrender to Jesus and you will be saved.

Graham's first overseas crusade was held in 1954 in London. Three years later more than two million people attended a sixteen-week crusade at New York's Madison Square Garden. Graham established the Hour of Decision radio show in 1950 and staged his first televised crusade in 1957. He has written a newspaper column and penned eighteen books, and his ministerial organization has produced numerous evangelistic films. His message has been consistent and simple: Surrender to Jesus and you will be saved. He talks little of hell, social or political concerns, intellectualized theology, or denominational concerns.

Throughout his career Graham has consulted with and advised U.S. presidents. Although Harry Truman dubbed him a counterfeit, Dwight Eisenhower, John F. Kennedy, Lyndon Johnson, Richard Nixon, Gerald Ford, Jimmy Carter, Ronald Reagan, George Bush, and Bill Clinton all met with him. He offered the prayer at Nixon's 1968 inaugural and in 1991 appeared on television alongside President George H. W. Bush—who called him America's pastor—at the start of the Persian Gulf War.

In his mid-eighties, Graham, slowed by age and illness, turned much of his ministry over to his son Franklin while still preaching. Franklin Graham continues the family tradition of advising American presidents; he is a confidant of President George W. Bush. Billy Graham has preached to more than 210 million people in over 185 countries and territories.

His Words

At the loneliest moments in your life you have looked at other men and women and wondered if they too were seeking—something they couldn't describe but knew they wanted and needed. Some of them seemed to have found fulfillment in marriage and family living. Others went off to achieve fame and fortune in other parts of the world. Still others stayed at home and prospered, and looking at them you may have thought: "These people are not on the Great Quest. These people have found their way. They knew what they wanted and have been able to grasp it. It is only I who travel this path that leads to nowhere. It is only I who goes asking, seeking, stumbling along this dark and despairing road that has no guideposts." But you are not alone. All mankind is traveling with you, for all mankind is on this same quest. All humanity is seeking the answer to the confusion, the moral sickness, the spiritual emptiness that oppresses the world. All mankind is crying out for guidance, for comfort, for peace.
—*Peace with God,* pp. 1–2

Books by Billy Graham

Billy Graham: The Inspirational Writings: Peace with God, The Secret of Happiness, Answers to Life's Problems. n.p.: Budget Book Service, 2000.

How to Be Born Again. Dallas: Word Publishing, 1989.

Just as I Am: The Autobiography of Billy Graham. San Francisco: HarperSanFrancisco, 1997.

For a more complete list of books by Billy Graham, see *Just as I Am,* pp. 741–742.

Books about Billy Graham

Drummond, Lewis, and John R. W. Stott. *The Evangelist.* Nashville: W Publishing, 2001.

McLoughlin, William G., Jr. *Billy Graham: Revivalist in a Secular Age.* New York: Ronald Press, 1960.

Paul, Ronald C. *Billy Graham: Prophet of Hope.* New York: Ballantine Books, 1978.

Walker, Jay. *Billy Graham: A Life in Word and Deed.* New York: Avon Books, 1998.

Wooten, Sara McIntosh. *Billy Graham: World-Famous Evangelist (People to Know).* Berkeley Heights, N.J.: Enslow Publishers, 2001.

Organization

Billy Graham Evangelistic Association, P.O. Box 779, Minneapolis, MN 55440; phone: 877-2GRAHAM. (In November 2001, Graham announced that the ministry's headquarters would relocate to his native Charlotte, North Carolina, to a building on a street named for him.)

Other Resources

Web site: www.billygraham.org. Official web site of the Billy Graham Evangelistic Association.

Periodical: *Decision,* magazine founded in 1960, published by the BGEA, which features Graham's messages.

"All humanity is seeking the answer to the confusion, the moral sickness, the spiritual emptiness that oppresses the world. All mankind is crying out for guidance, for comfort, for peace."

ABRAHAM JOSHUA HESCHEL
(1907–1972)

Theologian, teacher, and social activist, Rabbi Abraham Joshua Heschel profoundly influenced Jewish thinking in the late twentieth century. His writing expounded on Jewish mysticism and prophecy, and his fusion of Jewish scholarship with involvement in the civil rights movement made him a patron saint to legions of Jews who drew their spiritual inspiration from his example. He was also influential in improving Catholic-Jewish ties in the Vatican II era.

Born into a Hasidic dynasty in Warsaw, Poland, Heschel earned a doctorate in philosophy at the University of Berlin, an unusual foray into secular culture for someone with his background. He taught in Berlin and Frankfurt before leaving Nazi Germany for the United States, where in 1940 he joined the faculty of Hebrew Union College, a Reform Jewish seminary in Cincinnati, Ohio. But he never fit in religiously at the liberal school and five years later moved to the Jewish Theological Seminary, a Conservative Jewish school in New York, where he remained a professor of Jewish ethics and mysticism until his death.

Heschel's belief that scholarship must be twinned with action led him to march with the civil rights leader Martin Luther King, Jr., and photographs of the two walking arm in arm remain an indelible image from the era.

Heschel's writings span an array of languages—German, Hebrew, Yiddish, and a lyrically beautiful English he acquired only late in life. In his books, both academic and spiritual, he formulated a philosophy of Judaism uniquely suited to his time while drawing on and encouraging the piety, spontaneity, and emotion of the Hasidism of his youth. He posited a God who yearns for human companionship as much as humans yearn for God, an "ineffable" divinity who suffers whenever his creations suffer and is deeply saddened when they sin. Heschel's short work on the Jewish Sabbath, in which he called the seventh day a "palace in time," remains a classic and much-read volume.

Heschel retained traditional Jewish observance throughout his life as he broke new ground in interfaith relations and social activism. A meeting with Pope Paul VI helped pave the way for Vatican II's positive statements on Jews and Judaism, and in 1965 Heschel became the first Jew appointed to the faculty of Union Theological Seminary, the liberal Protestant seminary in New York. His belief that scholarship must be twinned with action led him to march with the civil rights leader Martin Luther King, Jr., and photographs of the two walking arm in arm remain an indelible image from the era. Of his participation in the civil rights movement, Heschel said, "When I march in Selma, my feet are praying."

Since his death in 1972, Heschel has grown in popularity among Jews and others seeking greater connectedness between spirituality and social action.

His Words

Time is like a wasteland. It has grandeur but no beauty. Its strange, frightful power is always feared but rarely cheered. Then we arrive at the seventh day, and the Sabbath is endowed with a felicity which enraptures the soul, which glides into our thoughts with a healing sympathy. It is a day on which hours do not oust one another. It is a day that can soothe all sadness away.
—*The Sabbath,* p. 20

Resorting to the divine invested in us, we do not have to bewail the fact of His shore being so far away. In our sincere compliance with His commands, the distance disappears. It is not in our power to force the beyond to become here; but we can transport the here into the beyond.
—*Man Is Not Alone,* p. 131

Books by Abraham Joshua Heschel

Between God and Man: An Interpretation of Judaism. New York: Free Press, 1997.

The Earth Is the Lord's: The Inner World of the Jew in Eastern Europe. Woodstock, Vt.: Jewish Lights, 1995.
Israel: An Echo of Eternity. Woodstock, Vt.: Jewish Lights, 1995.
Man Is Not Alone: A Philosophy of Religion. New York: Noonday Press, 1997.
A Passion for Truth. Woodstock, Vt.: Jewish Lights, 1995.
The Sabbath. New York: Noonday Press, 1996.

Books about Abraham Joshua Heschel

Kaplan, Edward K., and Samuel H. Dresner. *Abraham Joshua Heschel: Prophetic Witness.* New Haven: Yale University Press, 1998.
Moore, Donald J. *The Human and the Holy: The Spirituality of Abraham Joshua Heschel.* New York: Fordham University Press, 1989.

For a more complete list of books by and about Abraham Heschel, see *Between God and Man,* pp. 275–298.

Organization

Shalom Center, 6711 Lincoln Dr., Philadelphia, PA 19119; phone: 215-844-8494. Founded by Rabbi Arthur Waskow, the center reflects Heschel's values and propagates his message. Articles on its web site (www.shalomctr.org) reflect on his legacy, and the center has set up a council to commemorate the annual anniversary of his death.

"It is not in our power to force the beyond to become here; but we can transport the here into the beyond."

POPE JOHN XXIII
(1881–1963)

Although his papacy was among the shortest of the twentieth century, the impact of Pope John XXIII is still felt throughout the Roman Catholic world and beyond. The first pope in centuries to admit that the church was in need of reform, he convened the Second Vatican Council, setting in motion and supporting a major overhaul of Catholic life and worship. Vatican II substituted the vernacular for Latin in the Catholic Mass, improved interfaith and ecumenical relations, and generally revolutionized the church.

Born Angelo Giuseppe Roncalli on November 25, 1881, he grew up the son of sharecroppers in Sotto il Monte, Italy, and entered a seminary at twelve. After a hiatus to serve in the Italian army, he was ordained in 1904 and was appointed secretary to the bishop of Bergamo. Following service as a military chaplain in World War I, he was appointed spiritual director of the seminary he had attended and was called to the Vatican in 1921 to reorganize the Society for the Propagation of the Faith. He then served the Vatican in a variety of roles around Europe before being named cardinal-patriarch of Venice in 1953.

His 1958 election as pope was a surprise. He was a compromise choice, winning on the twelfth ballot, his age, seventy-six, having made him attractive as a transitional leader whose papacy would be relatively short. He was expected to be a caretaker who would continue the policies of the long-serving Pius XII, but such was not the case.

Three months into Pope John XXIII's papacy, he called for an ecumenical council—the first in over a century—to meet in Rome in 1962 and "bring the church up to date."

Although it lasted only five years, the papacy of John XXIII was a busy and monumental one. Three months into his papacy he called for an ecumenical council—the first in over a century—to meet in Rome in 1962 and "bring the church up to date." Vatican II radically changed the face of the church, internally and externally, and John imagined it a "New Pentecost," or outpouring of the Holy Spirit.

Pope John XXIII was a strong voice for world peace and ecumenical relations. His encyclical *Pacem in terris,* "Peace on Earth," was addressed to all of humankind. It reflected the fears of living in the nuclear age and called human freedom the basis of world peace. He created the Secretariat for Promoting Christian Unity and appointed the Vatican's first representative to the Assembly of the World Council of Churches held in New Delhi. He traveled more than his predecessors and worked to depoliticize—and demystify—the papacy. He removed from the liturgy words offensive to Jews and on at least one occasion greeted Jewish visitors with the biblical quote "I am Joseph, your brother."

He died on June 3, 1963, and was remembered fondly in the world media for his jovial nature and rotund figure, as well as for his accomplishments, even though the work of Vatican II was far from completed. In September 2000, Pope John XXIII was beatified, the second of three steps toward being declared a saint in the Roman Catholic Church.

His Words

The Council now beginning rises in the Church like daybreak, a forerunner of most splendid light. It is now only dawn. And already at this first announcement of the rising day, how much sweetness fills our heart. Everything here breathes sanctity and arouses great joy. Let us contemplate the stars, which with their brightness augment the majesty of this temple.
—Opening speech to Vatican II, in *Documents of Vatican II*

All must realize that there is no hope of putting an end to the building up of armaments, nor of reducing the present stocks, nor, still less—and this is the main point—of abolishing them altogether, unless the process is complete and thorough and unless it proceeds from inner conviction.
—*Pacem in terris*

Books by Pope John XXIII

Encyclicals and Other Messages of John XXIII. Washington: TPS Press, 1964. Includes *Pacem in terris* and *Mater et magistra,* his two most influential encyclicals.

Journal of a Soul. 1980. Reprint, Garden City, N.Y.: Image Books, 1999.

Books about Pope John XXIII

Feldman, Christian. *Pope John XXIII: A Spiritual Biography.* New York: Crossroad, 2000.

Johnson, Paul. *Pope John XXIII.* Boston: Little, Brown, 1974.

O'Brien, David, and Thomas Shannon. *Catholic Social Thought: The Documentary Heritage.* Maryknoll, N.Y.: Orbis Books, 1998.

For a more complete list of books by and about John XXIII, see Johnson, *Pope John XXIII,* p. 245.

Other Resources

Web sites: www.vatican.va/archive/hist_councils/ii_vatican_council/index.htm. The Vatican web site's section on Vatican II. www.vatican.va/holy_father/john_xxiii/index.htm. The Vatican web site's section on Pope John XXIII.

Grave: Basilica of St. Peter, in the Vatican. Has become a major pilgrimage site.

"The Council now beginning rises in the Church like daybreak, a forerunner of most splendid light."

POPE JOHN PAUL II
(1920–)

The first non-Italian pontiff in 456 years, Pope John Paul II has built bridges between the Roman Catholic Church and other religions even as he has reinforced his church's traditional positions on controversial sexuality and gender issues, and the authority of the papacy.

Born Karol Józef Wojtyła in Wadowice, Poland, he was an actor before being ordained a priest in 1946. By the time he became archbishop of Kraków in 1963, he was widely known for speaking out against Poland's Communist government. In 1978 he was elected pontiff after the death of Pope John Paul I. He is the most widely traveled pope in history, having made multiple visits to the Americas, Australia and the Pacific islands, Europe, Africa, and Asia. In March 2000 he made a historic trip to the Holy Land, visiting both Israelis and Palestinians within borders the two groups dispute.

More than any other pope, John Paul II has fostered dialogue with non-Christians, including Jews, Muslims, Buddhists, Hindus, and members of various tribal religions. In his first year as pope he visited Auschwitz, the notorious Nazi concentration camp in his native Poland, in a gesture of outreach to Jews. In 1986 he became the first pope to pray in a synagogue, during a meeting with Roman Jews, and he later issued a pastoral letter condemning anti-Semitism as a sin. He has also reached out to non-Catholic Christian groups, notably meeting with Ecumenical Patriarch Bartholomew I, titular leader of the Eastern Orthodox Church, which split with

> *More than any other pope, John Paul II fostered dialogue with non-Christians, including Jews, Muslims, Buddhists, Hindus, and members of various tribal religions.*

the Roman Catholic Church in 1054. The most overtly political modern pope, John Paul II has met with over five hundred heads of state and frequently comments on international issues, always urging justice and reconciliation. His staunch anti-Communism is credited with aiding Lech Wałesa's Solidarity movement in Poland and helping to cause the Soviet Union's collapse.

Under his leadership the church has also staunchly opposed abortion, the ordination of women, sexual promiscuity, birth control, and divorce while insisting upon priestly celibacy and the primacy of Rome's authority in acceptable Catholic teaching. Yet John Paul II has steadfastly spoken for the poor and oppressed, and against capital punishment, moral ambiguity, and the excesses of capitalism and consumerism. He survived an assassination attempt in 1981 and continues to travel, offering himself as a sort of chaplain to the world despite his age and steadily deteriorating health.

His Words

The first and fundamental structure for a "human ecology" is the family, founded on marriage, in which the mutual gift of self as husband and wife creates an environment in which children can be born and grow up. Too often life is considered to be a series of sensations rather than as something to be accomplished. The result is a lack of freedom to commit oneself to another person and bring children into this world. The family is sacred; it is the sanctuary of life. It is life's heart and culture. It is the opposite of the culture of death, the destruction of life by abortion.
—*Centesimus annus,* in *John Paul II: The Encyclicals in Everyday Language,* p. 190

The Church of Christ discovers her "bond" with Judaism by "searching into her own mystery." The Jewish religion is not "extrinsic" to us, but in a certain way is "intrinsic" to our own religion. With Judaism, therefore, we have a relationship which we do not have with any other religion. You are our dearly beloved brothers, and, in a certain way, it could be said that you are our elder brothers.
—Speech to representatives of the Jewish community in Rome, April 13, 1986, in *John Paul II and Interreligious Dialogue,* p. 72

The religiosity of the Muslims deserves respect. It is impossible not to admire, for example, their fidelity to prayer. The image of believers in Allah who, without caring about time or place, fall to their knees and immerse themselves in prayer remains a model for all those who invoke the true God, in particular for those Christians who, having deserted their magnificent cathedrals, pray only a little or not at all. —*Crossing the Threshold of Hope*

Books by John Paul II

Crossing the Threshold of Hope. New York: Alfred A. Knopf, 1995.

The Encyclicals of John Paul II. Edited by J. Michael Miller. Huntington, Ind.: Our Sunday Visitor, 1996.

The Place Within: The Poetry of Pope John Paul II. New York: Random House, 1994.

The Wisdom of John Paul II: The Pope on Life's Most Vital Questions. New York: Vintage Books, 2001.

Books about John Paul II

Cornwell, John. *Breaking the Faith: The Pope, the People, and the Fate of Catholicism.* New York: Viking Press, 2001.

Sherwin, Byron L., and Harold Kasimow, eds. *John Paul II and Interreligious Dialogue.* Maryknoll, N.Y.: Orbis Books, 1999.

Shivanandan, Mary. *Crossing the Threshold of Love: A New Vision of Marriage in the Light of John Paul II's Anthropology.* Washington, D.C.: Catholic University Press of America, 1999.

Willey, David. *God's Politician: Pope John Paul II, the Catholic Church, and the New World Order.* New York: St. Martin's Press, 1993.

Other Resources

Web site: www.vatican.va/holy_father/john_paul_ii/index.htm. Official Vatican web site on John Paul II.

"The first and fundamental structure for a 'human ecology' is the family."

RAM DASS
(1931–)

Born Richard Alpert to middle-class Jewish parents, Ram Dass is an iconic teacher of Eastern religious traditions, especially as they are practiced in the West. He is widely credited with imparting Eastern religious philosophy and the practice of yoga to the generation of spiritually hungry young Americans that came of age in the 1960s and 1970s.

Born in Boston, Alpert earned a Ph.D. in psychology from Stanford University and by the late 1950s was one of the youngest tenured professors at Harvard University. But the direction of his life changed forever when Timothy Leary, a Harvard colleague, introduced Alpert to psilocybin and other hallucinogens. They saw drugs as a means of mind expansion and publicized their views widely. Alpert, in particular, equated his drug-induced trips with a kind of religious experience. He later wrote that while high on psilocybin he came to recognize the difference between his ego and what he called "that which was I beyond Life and Death." Still later he dubbed this the "soul nature" and taught others to find it through meditation and study.

Ram Dass came to recognize the difference between his ego and what he called "that which was I beyond Life and Death." He dubbed this the "soul nature" and taught others to find it through meditation and study.

In 1963, as an experiment, Leary and Alpert administered psychedelic drugs to some students and were subsequently fired by Harvard. This censure set Alpert on a spiritual quest. He was increasingly frustrated with "coming down" from the semi-religious highs he felt with psychedelics and wanted something more permanent. In 1967 he went to India and met Neem Karoli Baba, a Hindu holy man who became his guru. Baba, known as Maharajji to his followers, renamed Alpert "Ram Dass," which means "servant of God."

Ram Dass returned to the United States and, in 1971, wrote his classic, *Be Here Now.* Part memoir, part meditation, the book describes his religious philosophy, combining Hinduism, Buddhism, Taoism, and even some Christianity. It sold over 2 million copies and is often credited with launching the New Age movement. In subsequent years Ram Dass founded or helped found the Hanuman Foundation, which fosters spiritually directed social action in the West; the Prison Ashram Project, which teaches inmates spiritual values through service projects; the Seva Foundation, which promotes health care in developing nations, and the Dying Project, which attempts to instill spiritual meaning in end-of-life experiences.

In 1997 Ram Dass suffered a massive stroke that he said gave him a new understanding of suffering, patience, and acceptance of death. He called the stroke, which slurred his speech and put him in a wheelchair, a "gift" from Maharajji, who died in 1973. Three years after his stroke, he wrote *Still Here: Embracing Aging, Changing, and Dying,* in which he tried to guide readers to a spiritually rich maturity. Ram Dass continues to write, lecture, and teach around the world.

His Words

This is the place of pure being. That inner place where you dwell, you just be. There is nothing to be done in that place. From that place, then, it all happens, it manifests in perfect harmony with the universe. Because you are the laws of the universe. You are the laws of the universe! This is what man's journey into consciousness is all about. This is Om (home). It's going Om, this is the place! Becoming one with God, returning. It's the return to the roots that the Tao talks about. . . . It's Buddha consciousness, it's Christ consciousness. Jesus says: I and my Father are One. When Buddha says: You give up attachment and you finish with the illusion. This is the place!"

—*Be Here Now,* pp. 85–87

Books by Ram Dass

Be Here Now. San Cristobol, N.M.: Lama Foundation, 1971, distributed by Crown Publishing, New York, 1971.

Grist for the Mill. With Stephen Levine. Santa Cruz, Calif.: Unity Press, 1977.

How Can I Help? Stories and Reflections on Service. With Paul Gorman. New York: Alfred A. Knopf, 1985.

Journey of Awakening: A Meditator's Guidebook. New York: Bantam Books, 1990.

The Meditative Mind: Varieties of Meditative Experience. With Daniel P. Goleman. New York: Jeremy P. Tarcher, 1996.

Miracle of Love: Stories about Neem Karoli Baba. New York: Button Books, 1979.

The Only Dance There Is: Talks Given at the Menninger Foundation. Garden City, N.Y.: Anchor Press, 1974.

The Psychedelic Experience: A Manual Based on the Tibetan Book of the Dead. As Richard Alpert, with Timothy Leary and Ralph Metzner. New Hyde Park, N.Y.: University Books, 1964.

Still Here: Embracing Aging, Changing, and Dying. New York: Riverhead Books, 2000.

Organizations

Human Kindness Foundation (Prison Ashram Project), P.O. Box 61619, Durham, NC 27715; phone: 919-304-2220; web site: www.humankindness.org.

Seva Foundation, 1786 Fifth St., Berkeley, CA 94710; phone: 800-223-7382; web site: www.seva.org.

Other Resources

Web site: www.ramdasstapes.org. The Ram Dass Tape Library Foundation's nonprofit web site offering tapes of Ram Dass's lectures with updates about his health and speaking schedule.

Videotapes: *Evolution of a Yogi.* Hartley Film Foundation, 1970; *Fierce Grace,* Lemle Pictures, 2001; available at lemlepix@worldnet.att.net.

Audiotape: *Promises and Pitfalls of the Spiritual Path,* Hanuman Foundation Tape Library, 1988.

"This is Om (home). It's going Om, this is the place! Becoming one with God, returning."

RABINDRANATH TAGORE
(1861–1941)

The great Hindu poet and philosopher Rabindranath Tagore was the first Asian writer to be awarded the Nobel Prize in literature. Through the popular medium of verse, Tagore conveyed to the world the beauty of India's mystical ideal of divine love, with its poignant echoes in the realm of human love. He became the voice of India's sacred and artistic heritage, and through him the fundamental values of Indian culture became more widely known outside of his homeland—despite the fact that only a fraction of his vast output has been translated from his native Bengali into other languages. The spread of these values—peace, tolerance, and unity—contributed to the century's movement toward a new world culture founded on diversity and universality.

Tagore was born in Calcutta to a celebrated Brahmin family; his father, Debendranath Tagore, was a mystic and a leader of the Brahmo Samaj, a religious reform movement. Although Rabindranath was also a playwright, novelist, and author of short stories and essays, he is chiefly known for his lyrical poetry, influenced by the love poems of the Bengali Vaishnavas (worshipers of Lord Vishnu), the mystical songs of the tantric Baul sect of Bengal, and the medieval North Indian poet-saint Kabir. Tagore's *Gitanjali* (Song Offerings), published in 1912 in England and the United States, was his first English translation of his own work. Championed by famous poets of the day, including W. B. Yeats and Ezra Pound, it won

Tagore's reputation in Bengal to this day is akin to that of Shakespeare in the English-speaking world. He is the only person ever to author the national anthems of two different nations: Bangladesh and India.

him the 1913 Nobel Prize. Yeats wrote in his introduction to the published work that *Gitanjali* "stirred my blood as nothing has for years." Tagore was knighted in 1915 but gave up the title in 1919 in protest against the infamous Amritsar massacre of four hundred Indian demonstrators by British troops. His poetry in English enjoyed great popularity in the West, and in 1930 he went on a world tour that included meetings with Albert Einstein, Thomas Mann, George Bernard Shaw, Robert Frost, and other eminent people of the day.

Tagore's verse reflects his belief in the oneness of God, nature, and humanity—a concept he wrote about directly in books such as *Sadhana, Creative Unity,* and *The Religion of Man.* Among his best-known works are *The Gardener, The Crescent Moon,* his translation *Songs of Kabir, Cycle of Spring, Fireflies, Sheaves,* and the plays *The Post Office* and *Chitra.* He was also a much-admired painter and a composer of songs as well as a reformer and critic of colonialism, nationalism, and the Indian caste system. Shantiniketan (Abode of Peace), a school he founded in Bolpur in 1901, was inspired by traditional Hindu ideals of education; in 1921 it became the internationally attended Visva-Bharati University. In the 1960s some of Tagore's hauntingly beautiful fiction was brought to the screen by the internationally known Bengali filmmaker Satyajit Ray.

His Words

That I want thee, only thee—let my heart repeat without end. All desires that distract me, day and night, are false and empty to the core.

As the night keeps hidden in its gloom the petition for light, even thus in the depth of my unconsciousness rings the cry—I want thee, only thee.

As the storm still seeks its end in peace when it strikes against peace with all its might, even thus my rebellion strikes against thy love and still its cry is—I want thee, only thee.
—*Gitanjali,* vol. 38

The same stream of life that runs through my veins night and day runs through the world and dances in rhythmic measures.

It is the same life that shoots in joy through the dust of the earth in numberless blades of grass and breaks into tumultuous waves of leaves and flowers.

It is the same life that is rocked in the ocean-cradle of birth and death, in ebb and in flow.

I feel my limbs are made glorious by the touch of this world of life. And my pride is from the life-throb of ages dancing in my blood this moment.
—*Gitanjali,* vol. 69

Books by Rabindranath Tagore

Gitanjali: A Collection of Indian Songs. Introduction by W. B. Yeats. 1912. Reprint, New York: Dover, 2000. Prose versions translated by the author from the original Bengali.

Reminiscences. 1917. Reprint, Madras: Macmillan India, 1987.

Selected Poems. Translated by William Radice. New York: Penguin Books, 1994.

Selected Short Stories. Translated by William Radice. New York: Penguin Books, 1994.

Songs of Kabir. Translated by Rabindranath Tagore. 1915. Reprint, York Beach, Maine: Samuel Weiser, 1995.

A Tagore Reader. Edited by Amiya Chakravarty. Boston: Beacon Press, 1971.

Books about Rabindranath Tagore

Dutta, Krishna, and Andrew Robinson. *Rabindranath Tagore: The Myriad-Minded Man.* London: Bloomsbury, 1997.

Hudson, Yeager. *Emerson and Tagore: The Poet as Philosopher (Asia and the Wider World Series, vol. 1).* South Bend, Ind.: Cross Cultural Publications, 1988.

Other Resources

Films/Videotape: *Two Daughters,* directed by Satyajit Ray, 1961, available on videotape; *The Home and the World,* directed by Satyajit Ray, 1984.

Audiotape: *The Crescent Moon: Prose Poems,* narrated by Deepak Chopra, Amber-Allen, 1996.

"The same stream of life that runs through my veins night and day runs through the world and dances in rhythmic measures."

VIVEKANANDA
(1863–1902)

Swami Vivekananda became the first teacher from the Hindu tradition to bring to a large Western audience the teachings of Vedanta, a philosophy of the divine nature of all things, based on the Vedas, the Bhagavad Gita, and other Indian scriptures.

As a child named Narendranath Datta, Vivekananda was fascinated by the wandering monks who were a regular feature of the Indian countryside, and he would sometimes try to imitate their meditation. He was a bright student in school and university, specializing in Western philosophy and logic, and he came to be very skeptical about the Hindu beliefs in which he had been raised, placing his faith solely in reason and logic. Then he met the God-intoxicated sage Ramakrishna, and everything changed for him. Ramakrishna was no intellectual, yet he radiated an atmosphere Vivekananda had never experienced before, and the young skeptic's faith was restored. Vivekananda was convinced beyond any doubt that God-realization is the most important thing in life, and he became one of Ramakrishna's disciples.

After Ramakrishna's death in 1886, Vivekananda decided it was necessary to take Vedanta to the West—a revolutionary idea at the time. In 1893 he traveled to the United States to be present at the first Parliament of the World's Religions in Chicago, where his teaching generated great interest—and some commotion among conservative Christians. The *New York Herald* called him "undoubtedly the greatest figure in

Vivekananda's teaching formed the foundation for the much larger Western interest in Hindu philosophy that arose in the second half of the twentieth century.

the Parliament of Religions. After hearing him, we feel foolish to send missionaries to this learned nation." Following the parliament, Vivekananda traveled throughout the United States and England for four years, lecturing and teaching. A number of his talks were recorded and collected into books.

Vivekananda spent the rest of his relatively brief life in India, where he founded the Ramakrishna Mission and Order and began a series of educational, philanthropic, and health-care concerns aimed at improving material and spiritual conditions among his countrymen. He was able to make one further teaching trip to the United States in 1899 and died at the age of thirty-nine. His Ramakrishna Order continues to flourish both inside and outside India, and his teaching formed the foundation for the much larger Western interest in Hindu philosophy that arose in the second half of the twentieth century.

His Words

This is the gist of all worship—to be pure and to do good to others. He who sees Śiva in the poor, in the weak, and in the diseased, really worships Śiva, and if he sees Śiva only in the image, his worship is but preliminary. He who has served and helped one poor man seeing Śiva in him, without thinking of his caste, creed, or race, or anything, with him Śiva is more pleased than with the man who sees Him only in temples.
—*The Complete Works of Swami Vivekananda, vol. 3,* p. 141

It is impossible to find God outside of ourselves. Our own souls contribute all of the divinity that is outside of us. We are the greatest temple. The objectification is only a faint imitation of what we see within ourselves.
—*The Complete Works of Swami Vivekananda, vol. 7,* p. 59

Books by Swami Vivekananda

The Complete Works of Swami Vivekananda. Calcutta: Advaita Ashrama, 1985.

Jnana-Yoga. New York: Ramakrishna-Vivekananda Center, 1980.

Karma-Yoga and Bhakti-Yoga. New York: Ramakrishna-Vivekananda Center, 1980.

Living at the Source: Yoga Teachings of Vivekananda. Edited by Ann Myren and Dorothy Madison. Boston: Shambhala Publications, 1996.

Raja-Yoga. New York: Ramakrishna-Vivekananda Center, 1980.

Books about Swami Vivekananda

Chetanananda, Swami. *Vivekananda: East Meets West: A Pictorial Biography.* St. Louis: Vedanta Society, 1995.

Nikhilananda, Swami. *Vivekananda: A Biography.* New York: Ramakrishna-Vivekananda Center, 1989.

Organization

Ramakrishna-Vivekananda Center of New York, 17 East Ninety-fourth St., New York, NY 10128-0611; phone: 212-534-9445; fax: 212-828-1618; e-mail: rvcnewyork@worldnet.att.net; web site: www.ramakrishna.org.

"We are responsible for what we are, and whatever we wish ourselves to be, we have the power to make ourselves."

4

THEY MADE **INTELLECT** A SPIRITUAL FORCE

Intellect has been called the cognitive power of the soul, the means by which humans conduct inquiry into the nature of ultimate truth, Socrates' "divine voice." A Buddhist might call it right thinking: enlightenment meets the Enlightenment. As with all centuries, the twentieth had its share of extraordinary thinkers.

Evelyn Underhill was one of them. Poet, novelist, scholar of religious mysticism, Underhill moved from British naval intelligence during World War I to Anglican pacifism by World War II. *Mysticism: A Study in the Nature and Development of Man's Spiritual Consciousness,* her classic work, was written while she was still in her early thirties. She believed modern science and ageless contemplative practice to be complementary and, in the grand tradition of the fully engaged, divided her days between her prolific literary career and working with the poor and giving spiritual guidance.

For liberal Protestants, New York's Union Theological Seminary is a bastion of progressive Christian thought, and it was there, during the century's violent midpoint, that Reinhold Niebuhr and Paul Tillich wrestled with the moral and intellectual question of evil, exemplified for them by Nazi ideology. Tillich, a Lutheran pastor, experienced the Hitler regime firsthand in his native Germany until his outspoken opposition to the Third Reich forced him to leave for the United States. Niebuhr, born in Missouri, came to his social ethic through liberalism and socialism, which he abandoned because of American socialist pacifism over entering World War II. "Christian Realism," he concluded, forced the recognition of great evil, even as it embraced the great good expressed by individuals.

Orthodox religiosity often rejects intellectual inquiry as a threat to tradition, hierarchy, and belief—all the more reason for including Alexander Schmemann and Joseph Soloveitchik among the century's spiritual giants. Their orthodoxies were very different, of course. Schmemann was a Russian Orthodox Christian priest, Soloveitchik an Orthodox Jewish rabbi. Yet both men helped their coreligionists steer a course between unquestioned acceptance of Old World dogmas, unworkable for many in twentieth-century America, and wholesale abandonment of the wisdom embedded in the tenets that had sustained so many of the faithful over centuries. Changing times, they insisted, required changed religious patterns, arrived at through intellectual engagement with modernity.

Hans Küng sought a similar reformist path within the Roman Catholic world. The tightly structured Roman Church, however, proved more resistant to Küng's unorthodoxy. Despite his having been an official theological consultant to the Second Vatican Council, Küng's intellectual forthrightness in opposition to papal infallibility and other key dogma eventually prompted Rome to revoke his credentials to teach Catholic theology at Catholic universities. Despite that, he remained a Catholic educator while pursuing interfaith dialogue and peacemaking.

The twentieth century inherited scores of religious and philosophical schools for deconstructing reality. One of the century's unique contributions in this realm was the extraordinary faith (at least in the West) placed in psychology as a balm for the human condition. Carl Gustav Jung and Abraham Maslow helped restore spirit to Sigmund Freud's spiritless creation. Jung, who had worked with Freud, plumbed the dream world and religious imagery to link human archetypes and illuminate our "collective unconscious." Maslow injected into modern psychology the idea of spiritual development as a key component of mental health.

The end of the twentieth century saw great emphasis on the development of artificial intelligence. However, it will be some time before computers make superfluous the likes of Ken Wilber. Wilber, born as the century reached the halfway mark, is a modern rarity, an independent scholar whose goal is nothing less than a "theory of everything." For Wilber, *everything* means science as well as spirituality, East and West, the perennial philosophy and the latest thinking on human psychology, sociology, the arts, and even alternative medicine. He is at once premodern, modern, and postmodern, denying none their partial truth. “Everybody is right, to a certain degree,” says Wilber. Only in his fifties, he may well be the late twentieth century’s intellectual gift to the twenty-first.

CARL GUSTAV JUNG
(1875–1961)

• • • • • • •

Responsible for the juxtaposition of spiritual and psychological growth, Carl Gustav Jung spent his life exploring "inner space" through dreams, symbols, mythology, and art. Born in Kesswil, Switzerland, the son of a clergyman, Jung studied medicine at the University of Basel and later worked with Sigmund Freud in Vienna. Their relationship was intense and ended, after just a few years, with the publication in 1912 of Jung's groundbreaking *Symbols of Transformation.*

Among Jung's greatest contributions, both to analytical psychology and to spiritual growth, is his work on dream interpretation and his understanding of archetypes. Archetypes are part of the "collective unconscious," a concept he developed by studying world religions and myths. He determined that some symbols cross religious and cultural boundaries throughout history, and that all humans connect to this set of symbols primarily through dreams. Examples of archetypes are the "mother," the "father," the "hero," and the "trickster."

Personality theorists generally believed that the psychological process was either mechanistic—one thing leads to another—or teleologic—future ideas lead us on. Jung believed in a synthesis of the two and added a third component, synchronicity, two events happening at the same time, which is not logical but from which an individual gains understanding about the self. For Jung, these synchronistic events were not coincidence but evidence of the collective unconscious and the connectedness of all humans, animals, and nature.

Jung's development of the concepts of archetypes and collective unconscious have transformed how we discuss both psychological and spiritual growth.

Jung's primary goal for humans was to become whole, both psychologically and spiritually. In his personality typology—consisting of four functions: sensing, acquiring information through the senses; feeling, evaluating information through one's emotional response; intuiting, integrating information from sources outside conscious ones; and thinking, evaluating information rationally and logically—he stated that for each person one function is most developed (superior) and one is least developed (inferior). Humans process their world primarily through their superior function, but consciously developing one's inferior function leads to wholeness and brings about balance in one's psyche and life. Katharine Briggs and Isabel Briggs Myers used Jung's typology as the basis for the Myers-Briggs Type Indicator of personality type.

Because he combined evidence about the human psyche from his clinical work; his own dreams, fantasies, and visions; as well as an in-depth study of alchemy, Eastern religions, astrology, mythology, and fairy tales, Jung's work has greatly influenced the spiritual growth movement in mainline as well as New Age religious communities.

His Words

The fact that religious statements frequently conflict with the observed physical phenomena proves that in contrast to physical perception the spirit is autonomous, and that psychic experience is to a certain extent independent of physical data. The psyche is an autonomous factor, and religious statements are psychic confessions, which in the last resort are based on unconscious, i.e., on transcendental processes. These processes are not accessible to physical perception but demonstrate their existence through the confessions of the psyche. . . . That is why whenever we speak of religious contents we move in a world of images that point to something ineffable.
—*Answer to Job,* p. 7

The hypothesis of a collective unconscious belongs to the class of ideas that people at first find strange but soon come to possess and use as familiar conceptions. . . . A more or less superficial layer of the unconscious is undoubtedly personal. I call it *the personal unconscious.* But this personal unconscious rests upon a deeper layer, which does not derive from personal experience and is not a personal acquisition but is inborn. This deeper layer I call the *collective unconscious.*
—*Four Archetypes,* p. 3

The general function of dreams is to try to restore our psychological balance by producing dream material that re-establishes, in a subtle way, the total psychic equilibrium.
—*Man and His Symbols,* p. 34

Books by Carl G. Jung

Analytical Psychology: Its Theory and Practice. New York: Vintage Books, 1968.

Answer to Job. Princeton: Princeton University Press, 1973.

The Archetypes and the Collective Unconscious. Translated by R. F. C. Hull. New York: Pantheon Books, 1959.

The Collected Works of Carl G. Jung. Bollingen Series 20. Translated by R. F. C. Hull. Edited by H. Read, M. Fordham, and G. Adler. Princeton: Princeton University Press, 1953–1979.

Four Archetypes: Mother/Rebirth/Spirit/Trickster. Translated by R. F. C. Hull. Princeton: Princeton University Press, 1959.

Man and His Symbols. Garden City, N.Y.: Doubleday, 1964.

Memories, Dreams, Reflections. Translated by Richard and Clara Winston; edited by Aniela Jaffe. 1963. Reprint, New York: Vintage Books, 1989.

Books about Carl G. Jung

Dunne, Claire. *Carl Jung: Wounded Healer of the Soul.* New York: Parabola Books, 2000.

Hayman, Ronald. *A Life of Jung.* New York: W. W. Norton, 2001.

Stevens, Anthony. *On Jung.* Princeton: Princeton University Press, 1999.

Storr, Anthony. *C. G. Jung.* New York: Viking Press, 1973.

Organization

C. G. Jung Institute–Boston, chartered by the New England Society of Jungian Analysts (NESJA) and dedicated to the healing discipline of analytical psychology; web site: www.cgjungboston.com, lists other Jung affiliates.

"The statements of the conscious mind may easily be snares and delusions, lies, or arbitrary opinions, but this is certainly not true of the statements of the soul."

HANS KÜNG
(1928–)

A leading Roman Catholic theologian, Hans Küng is known for his work on behalf of interfaith dialogue and his call to religious leaders to help bring about world peace by unifying around a common ethic: "Treat others as you would have them treat you." Although appointed by Pope John XXIII as the official theological consultant to the Second Vatican Council in 1962, Küng subsequently challenged the Holy See on papal infallibility and other key Catholic teachings. Despite church censure, he has remained a loyal Christian and continued his life's mission as a Catholic educator.

The 1995 founding of the Global Ethic Foundation, of which Küng is president, was inspired by his draft of the "Declaration Towards a Global Ethic," adopted by the 1993 Parliament of the World's Religions in Chicago. This document proposed a set of universal ethical values for both believers and nonbelievers and declared a commitment to a culture of nonviolence and respect for life, a just economic order, tolerance and truthfulness, and equal rights and partnership between men and women.

Hans Küng was born in the canton of Lucerne, Switzerland, and studied at the Papal Gregorian University in Rome and at the Sorbonne and the Institut Catholique in Paris, receiving his ordination in 1954 and his doctorate in theology in 1957. A dedicated ecumenist for the past forty-five years, Küng focused his first book on the doctrine of justification by faith, showing the often overlooked similarities between the Protestant

Küng urged a "global ethic"—a commitment to a culture of nonviolence and respect for life, a just economic order, tolerance and truthfulness, and equal rights and partnership between men and women.

and Roman Catholic positions. He has held many teaching posts, but because of his dissident stance the Vatican revoked his right to teach as a Catholic theologian at the University of Tübingen in 1979. He thereafter became a popular lecturer at the university's Institute for Ecumenical Research until his retirement in 1996. A prolific author, Küng has tackled a wide range of subject matter, including Judaism, Freud, art, and euthanasia. Many of his later books have been collaborative efforts with key figures from other religious traditions. Küng's seven-part German-language television special about religions around the world, titled *Spurensuche: Die Weltreligionen auf dem Weg* (Exploring the Tracks of the World Religions), was issued on videotape in 1999.

His Words

Men and women with a religious commitment all over the world have not lost hope: wherever they can be activated—whether in Poland or in South Africa, in the Philippines or in South America—the religions are still a spiritual force which could change the face of the earth for the better

—*Yes to a Global Ethic*, p. 2

Books by Hans Küng

The Catholic Church: A Short History. New York: Modern Library, 2001.

Christianity and World Religions: Paths of Dialogue with Islam, Hinduism, and Buddhism. Maryknoll, N.Y.: Orbis Books, 1993.

Does God Exist? Garden City, N.Y.: Doubleday, 1980.

Freud and the Problem of God. Translated by Edward Quinn. New Haven: Yale University Press, 1990.

Global Responsibility: In Search of a New World Ethic. Translated by John Bowden. New York: Crossroad, 1991.

Infallible? An Unresolved Enquiry. New York: Continuum, 1994.

Judaism: Between Yesterday and Tomorrow. Translated by John Bowden. New York: Continuum, 1995.

On Being a Christian. Translated by Edward Quinn. Garden City, N.Y.: Image Books, 1984.

Theology for the Third Millennium: An Ecumenical View. Translated by Peter Heinegg. New York: Doubleday, 1988.

Why I Am Still a Christian. Translated by David Smith, et al. Nashville: Abingdon Press, 1987.

Yes to a Global Ethic. Edited by Hans Küng. Translated by John Bowden. New York: Continuum, 1996.

Books about Hans Küng

Häring, Hermann. *Hans Küng: Breaking Through.* New York: Continuum, 1998.

Kuschel, Karl-Josef, and Hermann Häring, ed. *Hans Küng: New Horizons for Faith and Thought.* New York: Continuum, 1993.

Pitchers, Alrah. *The Christology of Hans Küng: A Critical Examination.* New York: Peter Lang, 1997.

Organizations

Council for a Parliament of the World's Religions, P.O. Box 1630, Chicago, IL 60690; phone: 312-629-2990; e-mail: info@cpwr.org.

Global Ethic Foundation for Inter-cultural and Inter-religious Research, Education, and Encounter; web site: www.uni-tuebingen.de/stiftung-weltethos/dat_eng/index_e.htm.

Institute for Ecumenical Research (Institut für Ökumenische Forschung), at the University of Tübingen, Wilhelmstr. 7, 72074 Tübingen, Germany; web site (in German): www.uni-tuebingen.de/uni/uoi/Institut/index.html.

"The religions are still a spiritual force which could change the face of the earth for the better."

ABRAHAM MASLOW
(1908–1970)

A pioneer of humanistic psychology, Abraham Maslow taught that human beings are motivated by a range of needs that are organized like a ladder, from the most basic to the highest. This "hierarchy of needs" starts with physiological, survival, and security needs; proceeds through emotional needs for love, belonging, and self-esteem; and culminates in "self-actualization," the need to fulfill one's human potential. He said that only when basic needs are fulfilled do people pursue the higher needs.

Abraham Harold Maslow was born in Brooklyn, New York, to Jewish immigrants from Russia. By 1934 he had earned bachelor's, master's, and doctoral degrees in psychology from the University of Wisconsin. After a period of teaching at Brooklyn College, in 1951 he joined Brandeis University and remained there until his retirement in 1969. At Brandeis he met Dr. Kurt Goldstein (a specialist in psychiatric and neurological disorders), who introduced him to the idea of self-actualization, and began to produce his own theoretical work. In 1965 Maslow published a study of human behavior in the workplace, *Eupsychian Management,* which is now available under the title *Maslow on Management.*

Maslow's theory of self-actualization influenced the subsequent establishment of transpersonal psychology, which recognizes spiritual development as a component of mental health.

Maslow was especially interested in studying the traits of self-actualized people (such as Abraham Lincoln, Frederick Douglass, Albert Einstein, and Eleanor Roosevelt), which include benevolence, justice, self-sufficiency, and humor. He also studied life-transforming moments of profound understanding, love, or ecstasy, which he called peak experiences. In these experiences, he said, one perceives reality with clarity, effortlessness, and a profound sense of meaning. Self-actualizing development and peak experiences, he believed, are within the reach of all and enable people to live fully rounded, engaged, happy lives.

The field of humanistic psychotherapy that grew out of Maslow's work in the 1960s is aimed at helping individuals to become self-actualized. His focus on study of the positive, healthy potential of individuals was a radical departure from the emphasis on pathology that characterized the Freudian and behavioral schools of psychology dominant at the time. Maslow's theory of self-actualization influenced the subsequent establishment of transpersonal psychology, which recognizes spiritual development as a component of mental health.

His Words

I have used the words *therapy, psychotherapy,* and *patient.* Actually, I hate all these words, and I hate the medical model that they imply because the medical model suggests that the person who comes to the counselor is a sick person, beset by disease and illness, seeking a cure. Actually, of course, we hope that the counselor will be the one who helps to foster the self-actualization of people, rather than the one who helps to cure a disease.
—*The Farther Reaches of Human Nature,* p. 51

If the variant religions may be taken as expressions of human aspiration, i.e., what people would like to become if only they could, then we can see here too a validation of the affirmation that all people yearn toward self-actualization or tend toward it.
—*Toward a Psychology of Being,* p. 173

The human being needs a framework of values, a philosophy of life, a religion or a religion-surrogate to live by and understand by, in about the same sense that he needs sunlight, calcium or love.
—*Toward a Psychology of Being,* p. 226

Books by Abraham Maslow

The Farther Reaches of Human Nature. New York: Penguin Arkana, 1993.

Future Visions: The Unpublished Papers of Abraham Maslow. Edited by Edward Hoffman. Thousand Oaks, Calif.: Sage Publications, 1996.

Motivation and Personality. 3d ed. Reading, Mass.: Addison-Wesley, 1987.

The Psychology of Science: A Reconnaissance. New York: Harper & Row, 1966.

Religions, Values, and Peak Experiences. New York: Penguin Books, 1976.

Toward a Psychology of Being. 3d ed. New York: John Wiley & Sons, 1998.

Books about Abraham Maslow

Decarvalho, Roy José. *The Growth Hypothesis in Psychology: The Humanistic Psychology of Abraham Maslow and Carl Rogers.* Lewiston, N.Y.: Edwin Mellen Press, 1991.

Hoffman, Edward. *The Right to Be Human: A Biography of Abraham Maslow.* Los Angeles: Jeremy P. Tarcher, 1988. Reprint, Four Worlds Press, 1998.

Organization

Association for Humanistic Psychology, 1516 Oak St., No. 320A, Alameda, CA 94501; phone: 510-769-6495; web site: ahpweb.org.

Other Resources

Films: *Being Abraham Maslow,* interview with Warren Bennis; New York: Filmmaker's Library, 1972. *Maslow and Self-Actualization,* Santa Ana, Calif.: Psychological Films, 1968.

Audiotapes: *Self-Actualization, Psychology of Religious Awareness,* and others; available from Big Sur Tapes, Tiburon, Calif.; web site: www.bigsurtapes.com.

"If you deliberately plan to be less than you are capable of being, then I warn you that you'll be deeply unhappy the rest of your life."

REINHOLD NIEBUHR
(1892–1971)

The son of a minister, the Reverend Reinhold Niebuhr became one of the most popular and influential pastor-theologians in America, affecting political thought, ecumenical dialogue, and the Christian social ethic.

Niebuhr was born in Wright City, Missouri, and the pastoral influence of his father led to his early interest in theology. In 1910, at the age of eighteen, he graduated from Elmhurst College, the seminary of the Evangelical Synod of North America, a denomination now part of the United Church of Christ. After this early education, Niebuhr went to Eden Theological Seminary in St. Louis, from which he graduated in 1913, and then received bachelor of divinity and master of arts degrees from Yale University. He was ordained in 1915.

Niebuhr went to Detroit to serve as pastor at Bethel Evangelical Church, where he remained until 1928. During his tenure at Bethel, he observed the hardships of autoworkers before they were protected by labor unions or social legislation. Accordingly, his philosophy shifted from the prevailing liberalism of the day to a socialist critique of capitalism. Later he abandoned socialism because of socialist support of pacifism on the eve of World War II. He left Detroit to assume a professorship at Union Theological Seminary in New York, where he would remain a formidable intellectual force until his retirement in 1960.

Despite his belief in the pervasiveness of sin and evil, Niebuhr considered himself a hopeful man, and his political activism reflected his belief that there are "indeterminate possibilities" for human beings to do good.

At Union, Niebuhr developed the theological concept for which he is best known, Christian Realism. This idea and *Moral Man and Immoral Society,* the book in which it is developed, stress the persistence of evil in society and in the human experience, even as individual human beings are capable of great moral good.

Despite his belief in the pervasiveness of sin and evil, Niebuhr considered himself a hopeful man, and his political activism reflected his belief that there are "indeterminate possibilities" for human beings to do good so long as they accept that not everything is within their control. He sought to convince Christian pacifists to rethink their position as Hitler rose to power.

Niebuhr also accomplished much in the area of ecumenical dialogue. He was perhaps the first influential Christian theologian to advocate against Christians' seeking to convert Jews. After he suffered a stroke in 1952, Niebuhr's public activities were severely curtailed, but he continued teaching and writing until his death at age seventy-nine in Stockbridge, Massachusetts.

His Words

THE SERENITY PRAYER

God grant me the serenity to accept the things I cannot change,
The courage to change the things I can,
And the wisdom to know the difference.
—1934 monthly bulletin of the Federal Council of Churches

American Christianity tends to be irrelevant to the problems of justice because it persists in presenting the law of love as a simple solution for every communal problem.
—"The Spirit of Justice," in *Love and Justice,* p. 25

The world's most urgent problem is the establishment of a tolerable system of mutual security for the avoidance of international anarchy. Such a system will not meet all the requirements of perfect justice for decades to come. There is a sense in which it will probably never meet them. Yet it is possible to avoid both a tyrannical unification of the world, and the alternative anarchy, if each nation is ready to make commitments commensurate with its power.
—"American Power and World Responsibility," in *Love and Justice,* p. 205

Books by Reinhold Niebuhr

Leaves from the Notebook of a Tamed Cynic. Louisville, Ky.: Westminster John Knox Press, 1991.

Love and Justice: Selections from the Shorter Writings of Reinhold Niebuhr. Edited by D. B. Robertson. Louisville, Ky.: Westminster John Knox Press, 1992.

Moral Man and Immoral Society: A Study in Ethics and Politics. 1932. Reprint, Louisville, Ky.: Westminster John Knox Press, 2002.

The Nature and Destiny of Man. Louisville, Ky.: Westminster John Knox Press, 1996.

The Self and the Dramas of History. Lanham, Md.: University Press of America, 1988.

Books about Reinhold Niebuhr

Bingham, June. *Courage to Change: An Introduction to the Life and Thought of Reinhold Niebuhr.* Lanham, Md.: University Press of America, 1992.

Fox, Richard Wrightman. *Reinhold Niebuhr: A Biography.* New York: Pantheon Books, 1985.

Gilkey, Langdon. *On Niebuhr: A Theological Study.* Chicago: University of Chicago Press, 2001.

"American Christianity tends to be irrelevant to the problems of justice because it persists in presenting the law of love as a simple solution for every communal problem."

ALEXANDER SCHMEMANN
(1921–1983)

A priest and brilliant theologian of the postrevolutionary Russian emigration, Father Alexander Schmemann was instrumental in opening up the spiritual riches of Eastern Orthodox Christianity to the Western world and in establishing a vibrant Orthodox Christianity in America.

Schmemann was born in Estonia and brought up in France among the community of intellectual Russian émigrés. He studied at Saint Sergius Theological Institute in Paris, which, because of the suppression of religion in the Soviet Union, had become a center for the study of Russian Orthodox theology. His specialty became liturgical theology. He was ordained a priest in 1947 and taught at Saint Sergius until 1951, when he emigrated to the United States to teach at the recently formed Saint Vladimir's Seminary in Crestwood, New York, where he became dean in 1961 and remained for the rest of his life.

Schmemann's charismatic personality, his deep love of the church, and his particular emphasis on liturgical renewal made him perhaps the most influential figure in the Orthodox Church in the United States in the twentieth century. Before the 1950s the Orthodox churches in America with roots in Russia and Eastern Europe were on the decline and in danger of dying out. In the 1950s and 1960s, a revival of sorts that reversed this trend began: attendance at services increased as did education in the Orthodox faith, founding of new parishes, and openness to sharing the faith. Schmemann's influence on this phenomenon was foundational.

Schmemann's charismatic personality, his deep love of the church, and his particular emphasis on liturgical renewal made him perhaps the most influential figure in the Orthodox Church in the United States in the twentieth century.

He was active in the ecumenical movement and believed that churches have a responsibility to express their faith through social action. "Christ came to save the whole man and not part of him," Schmemann said. The contemporary world in all its complexities requires answers as well as good theories, he said, adding that true ecumenism depends not only on the unity of the church but also on the unity of all people. The churches, he continued, must constantly review and revalue their relations with a changing world order; only in so doing can they function as creative organisms.

His Words

Many people often find religion's most important aspect to be the rituals and customs, the beauty of services, the possibility of encountering the sacred, heavenly, and divine. But Christ's parable of the last judgment (Matt. 25:31–46) reveals that all of this, if it is not based on love and directed toward love, makes religion fruitless, needless, empty, and dead.
—*Celebration of Faith,* p. 121

Again and again we come to recognize that the most essential, joyful mystery of Christianity is the mystery of the person, of what makes each human being valuable to God, of what we can and must love in him or her. It is precisely this mystery which the world and its ruling ideologies have repudiated.
—*Celebration of Faith,* p. 97

Books by Alexander Schmemann

The Eucharist: Sacrament of the Kingdom. Crestwood, N.Y.: St. Vladimir's Seminary Press, 1987.
For the Life of the World: Sacraments and Orthodoxy. Crestwood, N.Y.: St. Vladimir's Seminary Press, 1997.
Introduction to Liturgical Theology. Crestwood, N.Y.: St. Vladimir's Seminary Press, 1997.

Other Resources

Web sites:
www.concentric.net/~Kyinsman/Schmemann.html. Father Alexander Schmemann home page.
www.schmemann.org. Protopresbyter Alexander Schmemann web site.

"The most essential, joyful mystery of Christianity is the mystery of the person, of what makes each human being valuable to God, of what we can and must love in him or her."

JOSEPH SOLOVEITCHIK
(1903–1993)

As the foremost expositor of modern—or centrist—Orthodox Judaism, Rabbi Joseph Soloveitchik offered observant American Jews a path between liberal denominations and secularism on the one hand and insular ultra-Orthodoxy and Hasidism on the other. He exemplified unwavering fidelity to Jewish tradition alongside an almost unprecedented comfort with secular, Western intellectual traditions, carving a niche for observant Jews to remain true to their religious ideals and lifestyle while participating in the secular culture. So influential is his contribution that few major opinions or decisions are issued in the modern Orthodox world today without claiming the mantle of "the Rav"—the rabbi—as he is widely known.

Born into a dynasty of distinguished Lithuanian Talmudic scholars, Soloveitchik focused on Maimonides' philosophical presentation of Jewish law. He received a Ph.D. in philosophy from the University of Berlin. In 1932 he moved to Boston and soon after established the Maimonides School, the first Jewish "day school" that emphasized secular and Judaic studies equally. (Previously Jewish educational options included after-school programs or *yeshivot* limited to Judaic studies only.)

Soloveitchik exemplified unwavering fidelity to Jewish tradition alongside an almost unprecedented comfort with secular, Western intellectual traditions.

Soloveitchik began teaching Jewish philosophy in 1941 at New York's Yeshiva University and became head of the school's Rabbi Isaac Elchanan Seminary, in effect the only rabbinical seminary in America for centrist Orthodox Jews. The position gave him profound influence on the Orthodox rabbinate, and he was responsible for ordaining more than two thousand rabbis. He was active in the religious Zionist movement before and during the establishment of modern Israel.

Although he published little in his lifetime, hundreds of hours of Soloveitchik's lectures and classes were taped, and scholars have only begun mining this vast collection. In his two most important published works, *Halakhic Man* and *The Lonely Man of Faith*, he applied academic philosophical methods to Jewish thought. The first explores the system of Jewish law as a method of applying divinely inspired order on the world. The second explores the tension between faith and reason.

Soloveitchik often took progressive stances on issues, and much debate about his legacy centers on how far in that direction he would have gone were he still alive. In a then-novel move the Maimonides School taught Talmud to girls. Soloveitchik also gave the first lecture on Talmud at Yeshiva's Stern College for Women.

His Words

The contemporary man of faith looks upon himself as a stranger in modern society, which is technically minded, self-centered, and self-loving, almost in a sickly narcissistic fashion, scoring honor upon honor, piling up victory upon victory, reaching for the distant galaxies, and seeing in the here-and-now sensible world the only manifestation of being. What can a man of faith like myself, living by a doctrine which has no technical potential, by a law which cannot be tested in the laboratory, steadfast in his loyalty to an eschatological vision whose fulfillment cannot be predicted with any degree of probability, let alone certainty, even by the most complex, advanced mathematical calculations—what can such a man say to a functional, utilitarian society which is *saeculum*-oriented and whose practical reasons of the mind have long ago supplanted the sensitive reasons of the heart?
—*The Lonely Man of Faith*, p. 6

Books by Joseph Soloveitchik

Fate and Destiny: From Holocaust to the State of Israel. Hoboken: KTAV, 2000.
Halakhic Man. Philadelphia: Jewish Publication Society, 1983.

The Lonely Man of Faith. New York: Doubleday, 1992.
Reflections of the Rav: Lessons in Jewish Thought. Adapted by Abraham R. Besdin. Hoboken: KTAV, 1993.

Books about Joseph Soloveitchik

Confrontation: The Existential Thought of Rabbi J. B. Soloveitchik. Hoboken: KTAV, 1993.
Genack, Menachem. *Rabbi Joseph B. Soloveitchik: Man of Halacha, Man of Faith.* Hoboken: KTAV, 1998.
Hartman, David. *Love and Terror in the God Encounter: The Theological Legacy of Rabbi Joesph B. Soloveitchik.* Woodstock, Vt.: Jewish Lights, 2001.
Rakeffet-Rothkoff, Aaron. *The Rav: The World of Rabbi Joseph B. Soloveitchik.* Hoboken: KTAV, 1999.

For a more complete list of books by and about Joseph Soloveitchik, see *Confrontation,* pp. 175–176.

Organization

Rabbi Joseph B. Soloveitchik Institute, 2 Clark Rd., Brookline, MA 02445. Dedicated to disseminating Soloveitchik's teachings.

"The contemporary man of faith looks upon himself as a stranger in modern society, which is technically minded, self-centered, and self-loving."

PAUL TILLICH
(1886–1965)

Best known for his public criticisms of Nazism and his unorthodox liberal theology, Professor Paul Tillich had a gift for harmonizing secular philosophy with relevant theology.

The son of a Lutheran pastor, Tillich was born in Starzeddel, Germany, and spent his childhood there. In 1904 he completed his high school education at the prestigious Friedrich Wilhelm Gymnasium, a Berlin school for advanced students. Tillich went on to study the theology of Kant, Schleiermacher, and Hegel at universities in Tübingen, Berlin, and Halle. In 1911 he was awarded a doctorate in philosophy from the University of Breslau, and he received his licentiate in theology the next year from the university in Halle. In 1912 he was ordained in the Evangelical Lutheran Church.

Two years after his ordination, with World War I raging, Tillich was called to serve as a military chaplain. Four years of witnessing the cruelty and brutality of war deeply affected his theology. Before his war experience Tillich's theological foundation was the Romantic movement, which saw a distinct relation between man, nature, and history. But witnessing the violence of war led him to reject his earlier thought as immature and incomplete. He expanded his theological horizons and began to develop his own systematic theology.

After the war Tillich went to the University of Berlin to become a lecturer on the philosophy of religion. He then went to the University of Marburg, where Karl Barth's "neo-orthodox" theology was popular. At Marburg, Tillich met and was deeply

Tillich articulated a popular theology to answer the eternal philosophical and theological question on the nature of humanity, "What am I?"

influenced by Martin Heidegger, a theologian who brought existentialist thought—the search for an intellectual way to describe the human condition—to bear on the problems of the twentieth century.

In 1925 Tillich moved on to Dresden, where his view of culture was greatly shaped by his exposure to the arts, and later to Leipzig, where he continued to teach and lecture. In Frankfurt, in 1929, Tillich found himself teaching at the most liberal educational institution in Germany. His public criticisms of the growing Nazi movement cost him his professorship, though, and with an invitation from his fellow theologian Reinhold Niebuhr to teach at New York's Union Theological Seminary, Tillich and his family moved to the United States.

Tillich taught at Union until 1955. While there he developed a theology to answer the eternal philosophical and theological question on the nature of humanity, "What am I?" He concluded that life is meaningful and unified. In his classic book, *The Courage to Be*, he wrote: "Courage is the self-affirmation of being in spite of the fact of nonbeing. It is the act of the individual self in taking the anxiety of nonbeing upon itself by affirming itself either as part of an embracing whole or in its individual selfhood." After his retirement from Union, he became a professor at Harvard; then, from 1962 until his death three years later, he taught at the University of Chicago as the Nuveen Professor of Theology.

His Words

Being religious means asking passionately the question of the meaning of our existence and being willing to receive answers, even if the answers hurt.
—*Saturday Evening Post*, June 14, 1958

The total movement with which we are concerned is the slowly developing defeat of the spiritual temper of the nineteenth century. The self-sufficient this-worldliness of capitalist culture and religion is being disturbed. Questions and doubts are arising on all sides; they point toward something beyond time and threaten the security of a present which has cut itself loose from the eternal.
—*The Religious Situation*, p. 24

The first duty of love is to listen.

Books by Paul Tillich

The Courage to Be. 2d ed. New Haven: Yale University Press, 2000.

The Essential Tillich: An Anthology of the Writings of Paul Tillich. Edited by F. Forrester Church. Chicago: University of Chicago Press, 1999.

The Protestant Era. Translated by James Luther Adams. Chicago: University of Chicago Press, 1948.

The Religious Situation. Translated by H. Richard Niebuhr. New York: Henry Holt, 1932.

The Socialist Decision. Translated by Franklin Sherman. New York: Harper & Row, 1977.

Systematic Theology. 3 vols. Chicago: University of Chicago Press, 1951–1963.

Books about Paul Tillich

Parrella, Frederick J., ed. *Paul Tillich's Theological Legacy: Spirit and Community.* Berlin, N.Y.: Walter de Gruyter, 1995.

Pauck, Wilhelm, and Marion Pauck. *Paul Tillich: His Life and Thought.* New York: Harper & Row, 1976.

Other Resources

Memorial Park: Paul Tillich Park, New Harmony, Ind. Tillich's ashes were interred here in 1965. Web site: www.newharmony.evansville.net.

"Being religious means asking passionately the question of the meaning of our existence and being willing to receive answers, even if the answers hurt."

EVELYN UNDERHILL
(1875–1941)

A poet and novelist, Evelyn Underhill wrote elegantly on mysticism and devotional life and advocated the integration of personal spirituality and worldly action. The only child of a British barrister and his wife, Underhill was educated primarily at home in Wolverhampton, England, and later at London's King's College for Women, where she studied history and botany. At the age of sixteen, she published her first book, a volume of light verse about the legal profession titled *A Bar-Lamb's Ballad Book*—hardly a harbinger of the sweeping and incisive studies of religious mysticism that would bring her eminence throughout the West as an author and lecturer.

Although she converted to Christianity in 1907, the year of her marriage to Hubert Stuart Moore, Underhill did not immediately affiliate with a denomination. She was drawn to Roman Catholicism but felt some of its tenets conflicted with her growing attraction to the burgeoning modernist intellectual movement. While researching *Mysticism: A Study in the Nature and Development of Man's Spiritual Consciousness*, her 1911 classic, she met Baron Friedrich von Hügel, the expert on mysticism who greatly influenced her thinking and became her spiritual director. In 1921, the year she became a practicing member of the Anglican Church, Underhill delivered the Upton Lecture on the Philosophy of Religion at Manchester College, Oxford, becoming the first woman to do so. During this time, she also traveled throughout Western Europe, studying its art and culture. *Mysticism,* which explores the works of the great mystics, including Meister Eckhart, St. John of the Cross,

Evelyn Underhill recognized that contemplative prayer is not just for monks and nuns but for anyone willing to undertake it.

St. Teresa of Ávila, and Rumi, is still considered the consummate investigation of human spiritual awareness.

Underhill believed that contemplative prayer is not just for monks and nuns but for anyone willing to undertake it. She considered the study of modern science not a threat to contemplation but rather an enhancement of it. She was an advocate of an integrated life, balanced between active and passive spirituality. As a routine she spent mornings writing and afternoons working with the poor and giving spiritual direction. A prolific writer, she published novels, books of verse, philosophical and religious works, accounts of retreats and conferences she conducted, and critical essays and reviews in various publications, including the *Spectator,* where she served for a time as theological editor. She frequently lectured on matters of religion and spirituality. Her Upton Lecture was later published as *The Life of the Spirit and the Life of Today.* Another of her books, *Worship,* published in 1936, led her to a profound interest and involvement in the Greek Orthodox Church.

Underhill worked in naval intelligence during World War I, but by 1939 she had joined the Anglican Pacifist Fellowship. The following year she authored a forceful pamphlet on Christian pacifism entitled *The Church and War.* Although she studied the personalities of mystics and ascetics, she was widely known as a passionate individual interested in all aspects of life.

Her Words

It is the "inclusive" mystic, whose freedom and originality are fed but not hampered by the spiritual tradition within which he appears, who accepts the incarnational status of the human spirit, and can find the "inward in the outward as well as the outward in the inward," who shows us in their fullness and beauty the life-giving possibilities of the soul transfigured in God.
—*Mysticism,* p. xvi

Visions and voices, then, may stand in the same relation to the mystic as pictures, poems, and musical compositions stand to the great painter, poet, musician. They are the artist's expressions and creative results (a) of thought, (b) of intuition, (c) of direct perception. All would be ready to acknowledge how conventional and imperfect of necessity are those transcripts of perceived Goodness, Truth, and Beauty which we owe to artistic genius: how unequal is their relation to reality. But this is not to say that they are valueless or absurd. So too with the mystic, whose proceedings in this respect are closer to those of the artist than is generally acknowledged. In both types there is a constant and involuntary work of translation going on, by which Reality is interpreted in the terms of appearance. In both, a peculiar mental make-up conduces to this result. —*Mysticism,* p. 272

Books by Evelyn Underhill

Fragments from an Inner Life: The Notebooks of Evelyn Underhill. Edited and with an introduction by Dana Greene. Harrisburg, Pa.: Morehouse, 1993.

The Letters of Evelyn Underhill. Edited and with an introduction by Charles Williams. Westminister, Md.: Christian Classics, 1989.

The Life of the Spirit and the Life of Today. New York: E. P. Dutton, 1922.

Mysticism: A Study in the Nature and Development of Man's Spiritual Consciousness. 1911. Reprint, Mineola, N.Y.: Dover Publications, 2002.

Practical Mysticism: A Little Book for Normal People. New York: E. P. Dutton, 1915.

Worship. 1936. Reprint, Westport, Conn.: Hyperion Press, 1979.

Books about Evelyn Underhill

Cropper, Margaret. *The Life of Evelyn Underhill.* 1958. With a new foreword by Dana Greene. Woodstock, Vt.: SkyLight Paths, 2002.

Greene, Dana. *Evelyn Underhill: Artist of the Infinite Life.* Notre Dame: University of Notre Dame Press, 1998.

Organization

Evelyn Underhill Association, 7315 Brookville Rd., Chevy Chase, MD 20815; web site: www.evelynunderhill.org.

"It is the 'inclusive mystic' . . . who shows us in their fullness and beauty the life-giving possibilities of the soul transfigured in God."

Other Resources

Virginia Theological Seminary Archives, Bishop Payne Library, 3737 Seminary Road, Alexandria, VA, 22304-5201; phone: 703-461-1850; email: jrandle@vts.edu.

KEN WILBER
(1949–)

Ken Wilber is one of the few intellectual visionaries to offer a unifying view that seeks to reconcile all the discordant elements of our postmodern world—to embrace equally science and spirituality, and to include all the disciplines in one grand "theory of everything." With his model of human growth and development, synthesizing Eastern contemplative traditions and Western science into a comprehensive "spectrum of consciousness," Wilber laid the philosophical foundations for the transpersonal psychology movement. His writings have renewed appreciation of the perennial philosophy, the worldview common to the great wisdom traditions, in which reality is seen as a multilayered phenomenon, ranging from matter to body to mind to soul to the Divine Spirit. Wilber criticizes contemporary materialist culture as a "flatland" that denies the existence of higher levels of consciousness. To counter this perspective, he argues for an integration of science and religion through the development of a science that embraces all the various stages, structures, and states of human consciousness.

Born in 1949 in Oklahoma City, Wilber was educated at Duke University and the University of Nebraska, acquiring two bachelor of science degrees and a master's degree in biochemistry. However, his explorations of psychology and philosophy led him to abandon his pursuit of a Ph.D. to concentrate on his own studies and writing. His reputation was established with his first book, *The Spectrum of Consciousness,* written

> *Wilber argues for an integration of science and religion through the development of a science that embraces all the stages, structures, and states of human consciousness.*

when he was twenty-three years old. As an independent scholar he has found a respectful audience all over the world, in addition to attracting controversy for his critique of New Age thought.

From 1983 on Wilber has distanced himself from the transpersonal movement in favor of an approach that both "transcends and includes" the essentials of all the major schools of psychology. Applying this integral vision to the social sciences, he has brought new insights to developmental psychology; anthropology; psychotherapy; the sociology of religion; the philosophy of science, health, and alternative medicine; and art and literary theory. Seeing these diverse fields from an integral perspective, he brings together the best of the premodern, modern, and postmodern periods, denying no school of thought its partial truth but asserting that "everybody is right, to a certain degree." To give integral philosophy a firmer grounding in the academic world, he founded the Integral Institute, which aims to document the scientific evidence for spiritual development and transformation. The first eight volumes of his *Collected Works* were published in 2000.

His Words

At this point in history, the most radical, pervasive, and earth-shaking transformation would occur simply if everybody evolved to a mature, rational, and responsible ego.
—*Up from Eden,* p. 328

So the call of the nondual traditions is: Abide as Emptiness, embrace all Form. The liberation is in the Emptiness, never in the Form, but Emptiness embraces all forms as a mirror all its objects. So the Forms continue to arise, and, as the sound of one hand clapping, you are all those Forms. You are the display. You and the universe are One Taste. Your original Face is the purest Emptiness, and therefore every time you look in the mirror, you see only the entire Kosmos.
—*A Brief History of Everything,* p. 240

Books by Ken Wilber

The Atman Project. Wheaton, Ill.: Quest Books, 1980.
Boomeritis: A Novel That Will Set You Free. Boston: Shambhala Publications, 2002.

A Brief History of Everything. Boston: Shambhala Publications, 1996.
The Collected Works of Ken Wilber. Vols. 1–8. Boston: Shambhala Publications, 2000.
Integral Psychology. Boston: Shambhala Publications, 2000.
The Marriage of Sense and Soul: Integrating Science and Religion. New York: Random House, 1998.
One Taste: Daily Reflections on Integral Spirituality. Boston: Shambhala Publications, 2000.
Sex, Ecology, Spirituality. 2d ed. Boston: Shambhala Publications, 2000.
The Spectrum of Consciousness. Wheaton, Ill.: Quest Books, 1977.
A Theory of Everything. Boston: Shambhala Publications, 2000.
Up from Eden: A Transpersonal View of Human Evolution. New York: Anchor Books, 1981.

Organization

Integral Institute, 4450 Arapahoe, Ste. 100, Boulder, CO 80303. A nonprofit organization dedicated to the integration of body, mind, soul, and spirit in self, culture, and nature.

Other Resources

Web site: wilber.shambhala.com. Original writing by and about Wilbur, frequently updated, with archive and link to newsletter.

"At this point in history, the most radical, pervasive, and earth-shaking transformation would occur simply if everybody evolved to a mature, rational, and responsible ego."

5

THEY CHANGED THE WORLD BY **WRITING**

“In the beginning was the Word, and the Word was with God, and the Word was God.”

For Christians, that opening passage from the Gospel of John is foundational to their faith. For others, it reflects humankind’s reliance on language to comprehend, as best we can, that which is beyond language.

In the twentieth century the power of language to influence acquired extraordinary reach, spurred by previously unimaginable advances in literacy, leisure time, and technology. Suddenly ordinary men and women had access to information and inspiration previously restricted to the elite or the nearby. The impact was nothing short of a revolution in the dissemination of ideas that undoubtedly would leave Johannes Gutenberg flabbergasted. For communicators, the changes presented vast opportunities, larger and broader potential audiences, and problems, the Babel of competing and contradictory voices. The individuals profiled here managed to remain rooted in ageless spiritual soil while navigating these unprecedented challenges.

Thomas Berry’s concerns reflect the downside of the century’s “advances”—the degradation of God’s natural world and faith in material progress above all else. A Roman Catholic priest, Berry has pushed his tradition, and other traditions, to redefine the human penchant for creating environmental havoc as a sign of spiritual blindness toward our place in the cosmos. Martin Buber also wrote of the need for a spiritual link between humankind and God as he strove for a reversal of the widespread alienation endemic to the century. Buber lived and worked within a Jewish context, often using traditional Hasidic tales to make his points. Yet the influence of his writing went far beyond the parameters of his religious community. His philosophical signature, what he termed the I-Thou relationship, entered the universal spiritual lexicon.

After Joseph Campbell's death, a six-part television series in 1988 propelled his ideas into the popular consciousness with a swiftness impossible in any previous century. Through television's visual text, Campbell's pioneering exploration of how the building blocks of mythology transcend cultural differences was introduced to vast audiences. Mythology's psychological insights and their relevance to modern society were made clear by the new literary form. Huston Smith, a thoroughly modern spiritual explorer who embraced firsthand the extraordinary range of religious experience he studied, also mastered the age's distinct mode of communication to the benefit of his audiences.

Mircea Eliade was another of the century's seminal scholars in the history of religion. But unlike that of Campbell and Smith, Eliade's writing remained largely confined to academic circles and students of the development of mystical traditions. Together, the three underscore how important personality and showmanship became to the dissemination of ideas in the latter half of the twentieth century.

C. S. Lewis and D. T. Suzuki represent spiritual writing of an earlier yet modern time. The contemplative reality—not reality programming—was their sphere. Yet both men, from very different backgrounds and perspectives, also benefited from the century's emphasis on mass marketing and popular culture. Lewis, among the best-selling authors of all time, was the subject of an acclaimed movie about—how twentieth-century!—his love life. His *Chronicles of Narnia* gave him posthumous celebrity status among children beguiled by his wistful imagination, just as adults are won by his deeply Christian sensibilities. Suzuki, meanwhile, was embraced by leading Beat Generation Buddhists—the century's literary equivalent of the Transcendentalists—making him a popular public figure in his own right.

Abraham Isaac Kook and Simone Weil were as much participants in the history of the century as they were chroniclers of the period's inner life. Both sprang from Jewish roots, but they traveled very different paths. Kook cast his lot with Jewish nationalism, seeing in it a manifestation of biblical prophecy. Though intensely involved with worldly pursuits, he wrote widely on spiritual and philosophical themes in a variety of literary forms. Weil, in contrast, published little during her lifetime, which was defined, tragically, by the century's two world wars. Moreover, she embraced Christian faith even as she stayed apart from the official church.

In that, she represented much of the century's spiritual zeitgeist—a soul buffeted by horrendous human pain, searching wherever the path might take her for a spiritual language that approximated her inner longing and realizations.

THOMAS BERRY
(1914–)

Considered one of the elders of the environmental movement, Thomas Berry was initially a cultural historian of Europe and Asia, who became a historian of the earth. He considers himself a "geologian," a term that encompasses his role as a cosmological historian and his attention to the new planetary civilization. One of his primary concerns is that society and educational institutions foster an appreciation of the world rather than continue a human-centered cultural consciousness that exploits the earth for its own purposes.

Berry was born in the hill country of North Carolina and ordained a Roman Catholic priest. He received his Ph.D. from the Catholic University of America in European intellectual history and directed the Riverdale Center for Religious Research in New York City while teaching at Fordham University.

Berry has observed that each age has its "great work." The classical period produced reason and democracy; the medieval period gave us glorious cathedrals; and the age of discovery opened lines of transportation and communication. Berry argues that modern society's "great work" is to connect technological advances to environmental concerns. He proposes that we are entering the "Ecozoic Age," an era when humanity must work to reconnect to the earth and create a way of life that reverses the destruction it has inflicted on the planet. He believes that we should extend legal rights to "other than human" interests and that corporations should be limited by law to morally accountable activities.

Through his books and lectures, Berry has urged us to change nothing less than our cosmology—for the sake of the future of the earth.

In *The Universe Story,* Berry and his coauthor, Brian Swimme, developed the idea that science is now telling us a "new story," which began with the "Great Unfolding," their term for the big bang. Humans, says Berry, need to rediscover their place in an evolving cosmos and their creative role in the changing world.

His Words

We need to move from our human-centered to an earth-centered norm of reality and value. Only in this way can we fulfill our human role within the functioning of the planet we live on. Earth, within the solar system, is the immediate context of our existence. Beyond the sun is our own galaxy and beyond that the universe of galactic systems that emerged into being some fifteen billion years ago through some originating source beyond human comprehension.

Establishing this comprehensive context of our thinking is important in any consideration of human affairs, for only in this way can we identify any satisfying referent in our quest for a viable presence of the human within the larger dynamics of the universe. The universe itself is *the* enduring reality and *the* enduring value even while it finds expression in a continuing sequence of transformations.

—*The Great Work,* pp. 56–57

Books by Thomas Berry

The Dream of the Earth. San Francisco, Calif.: Sierra Club Books, 1990.

The Great Work: Our Way into the Future. New York: Bell Tower, 2000.

The Universe Story: From the Primordial Flaring Forth to the Ecozoic Era—A Celebration of the Unfolding of the Cosmos. With Brian Swimme. San Francisco: HarperSanFrancisco, 1994.

Book about Thomas Berry

Lonergan, Anne, and Caroline Richards, eds. *Thomas Berry and the New Cosmology.* Mystic, Conn.: Twenty-third Publications, 1987.

Other Resources

Web site: www.ecoethics.net. Harvard Divinity School's Environmental Ethics and Public Policy Center.

Event: Annual Colloquium with Thomas Berry. Each year Berry and a speaker from another discipline discuss a particular aspect of the human-earth relationship. Web site: www.web.net/~eaite/programm.htm.

Videotapes: *Thomas Berry: Dreamer of the Universe,* First Run Features, 1994; *A Tribute to Fr. Thomas Berry,* Passionist Community of Canada; *The Universe Story,* Centre for Ecology and Theology.

Audiotape: *The Collected Thoughts of Thomas Berry,* Center for the Story of the Universe.

"*The universe itself is* the *enduring reality and* the *enduring value even while it finds expression in a continuing sequence of transformations.*"

MARTIN BUBER
(1878–1965)

Among the foremost twentieth-century philosophers of human relations and Jewish thought, Martin Buber is best known for expounding on the need to be in dialogue with other humans and with God on the basis of an "I-Thou," as opposed to an "I-It," relationship. His work on Hasidic thought *(Tales of the Hasidim),* Zionism, and religious philosophy continues to influence both the academic study of Judaism and religious thinking more broadly. He also inspired the trend toward neo-Hasidism among modern Jews.

Buber was born to assimilated Jews; his mother left the family when he was three, and he was raised in what is today Ukraine by his maternal grandparents, who were immersed in Jewish culture and Jewish enlightenment movements. At university he studied art and philosophy, and his doctoral dissertation at the University of Vienna dealt with mysticism. At that time he also became influenced by Friedrich Nietzsche's attack on modern culture, which led Buber to advocate for Zionism as a means of returning to a people's roots and a more wholesome culture.

Buber served as editor of the Zionist magazine *Die Welt* (The World) at the invitation of Theodor Herzl, the founder of modern Zionism. But the two soon broke over disagreements about priorities and beliefs: Buber saw Zionism primarily as a means of Jewish cultural and social renewal, and disagreed with Herzl's single-minded emphasis on the goal

I-Thou relationships between humans are those that treat the other as an equal and autonomous being, Buber wrote, and represent the pinnacle of human relationships.

of attaining land in Palestine for Jews. In 1916 Buber created a monthly called *Der Jude* (The Jew), which rose to prominence in the German-speaking Jewish world, and he used the forum to advocate for Jewish-Arab cooperation and a binational state in Palestine.

In the early part of the twentieth century, Buber also took up the study of Hasidism, in which he saw answers for Judaism's spiritual decline and the alienation endemic to the times. In Hasidism he saw the achievement of three vital relationships: between human and God, human and human, and human and nature. His retelling of Hasidic tales remains popular, along with his scholarly works on the topic.

His seminal work, *I and Thou,* was published in 1923. Although I-Thou relationships—those that treat the other as an equal and autonomous being—are rare and difficult, he wrote, they represent the pinnacle of human relationships. More often, humans interact with each other in an I-It relation, treating the other as an object, a means to an end. When it comes to God, I-Thou relations are essential. God, he wrote, can be known through the revelation of everyday existence, and the Bible itself is a record of this human experience of and dialogue with God.

From 1924 to 1933 Buber lectured at the University of Frankfurt, where he was influenced by the great Jewish philosopher Franz Rosenzweig, with whom he collaborated on a German translation of the Hebrew Bible. At age sixty, after the Nazis forbade him from public lecturing, Buber immigrated to Palestine. He taught at Hebrew University in Jerusalem and worked tirelessly until his death in 1965 for Arab-Jewish understanding.

His Words

A time of genuine religious conversations is beginning—not those so-called but fictitious conversations where none regarded and addressed his partner in reality, but genuine dialogues, speech from certainty to certainty, but also from one open-hearted person to another open-hearted person. Only then will genuine common life appear, not that of an identical content of faith which is alleged to be found in all religions, but that of the situation, of anguish and expectations.
—*Between Man and Man,* pp. 7–8

To Hasidism, the true meaning of life is revealed in the deed. Here, even more distinctly and profoundly than in early Christianity, what matters is not what is being done, but the fact that every act carried out in sanctity—that is, with God-oriented intent—is a road to the heart of the world. There is nothing that is evil in itself; every passion can become a virtue, every inclination a "vehicle of God."
—*On Judaism*, p. 48

Books by Martin Buber

Between Man and Man. New York: Collier Books, 1965.

I and Thou. Translated by Ronald Gregor Smith. 1923. Reprint, New York: Charles Scribner's Sons, 2000.

The Letters of Martin Buber: A Life of Dialogue. Edited by Nahum N. Glatzer. Translated by Paul Mendes-Flohr. Syracuse, N.Y.: Syracuse University Press, 1996.

On Judaism. New York, Schocken Books, 1967.

The Tales of Rabbi Nachman. Introductions by Paul R. Mendes-Flohr and Ze'ev Gries. Amherst, N.Y.: Prometheus Books, 1999.

Tales of the Hasidim. New York: Schocken Books, 1991.

Books about Martin Buber

Herman, Jonathan R. *I and Tao: Martin Buber's Encounter with Chuang Tzu.* Albany: State University of New York Press, 1996.

Hodes, Aubrey. *Martin Buber: An Intimate Portrait.* New York: Viking Press, 1971.

Moore, Donald J. *Martin Buber: Prophet of Religious Secularism.* New York: Fordham University Press, 1996.

For a more complete list of books by and about Martin Buber, see Hodes, *Martin Buber,* pp. 235–237.

Other Resources

Web site: www.buber.de. Martin Buber home page.

Artwork: William Kallfelz, 1992 painting, *Martin Buber—"I And Thou."*

Andy Warhol, 1980 screenprint, part of the *Ten Portraits of Jews of the Twentieth Century Suite.*

"The close association of the relation to God with the relation to one's fellow-men . . . is my most essential concern."

JOSEPH CAMPBELL
(1904–1987)

• • • • • • •

Joseph Campbell was an American scholar and author who became internationally known for his work in comparative mythology. With his masterful storytelling ability, he made the study of myths enjoyable and meaningful to a broad audience. His books explored connections between the myths of different cultures, psychological insights into mythology, and the relevance of ancient myths to modern life.

Campbell was born in New York City, where as a youth he became interested in myths, especially those of American Indians. He acquired a master's degree in medieval literature from Columbia University in 1926 and continued his studies at universities in Paris and Munich over the next few years. During this period he became acquainted with the works of Sigmund Freud and Carl Jung, whose psychological theories influenced the development of his thoughts on mythology.

In 1934 Campbell joined the literature department at Sarah Lawrence College, where he taught for thirty-eight years. He secured his place as the leading mythologist of his time with the publication of his first book, *The Hero with a Thousand Faces,* in 1949. In it he described an archetypal hero that occurred in the myths of many of the world's cultures.

Campbell's expression "Follow your bliss" became a popular reminder that happiness results when we listen to our deepest intuitions and pursue our most passionate interests.

Over the years, in addition to his writing, Campbell did important work as an editor, assisting Swami Nikhilananda in translating *The Gospel of Sri Ramakrishna* and the Upanishads; editing works on the art, myths, and philosophy of India by the German Indologist Heinrich Zimmerman; compiling the anthology *The Portable Jung;* and editing papers from the *Eranos Yearbooks,* which published important writings on symbology and other subjects related to Jungian psychology.

In 1988, a year after his death, *Joseph Campbell and the Power of Myth,* a six-part television series of interviews with Bill Moyers, introduced Campbell's ideas and work to millions of viewers. His expression "Follow your bliss" became a popular reminder that happiness results when we listen to our deepest intuitions and pursue our most passionate interests.

His Words

It would not be too much to say that myth is the secret opening through which the inexhaustible energies of the cosmos pour into human cultural manifestation. Religions, philosophies, arts, the social forms of primitive and historic man, prime discoveries in science and technology, the very dreams that blister sleep, boil up from the basic, magic ring of myth.
—*The Hero with a Thousand Faces,* p. 3

In France, they name streets after their poets; we have them named after generals. When you think of Melville, Mark Twain, and Emerson, and you go to the places where those men lived, there's no recognition of their having been there; names of former mayors are on five or six different street corners, but not the poets and the artists.
—*An Open Life,* p. 102

Books by Joseph Campbell

The Hero with a Thousand Faces. 1949. Reprint, New York: Fine Creative Media, 1996.

A Joseph Campbell Companion: Reflections on the Art of Living. Edited by Diane K. Osborn. New York: HarperCollins, 1995.

The Masks of God. 4 vols. Vol. 1: *Primitive Mythology* (1991). Vol. 2: *Oriental Mythology* (1995). Vol. 3: *Occidental Mythology* (1995). Vol. 4: *Creative Mythology* (1995). New York: Arkana.

Myths to Live By. New York: Arkana, 1993.

An Open Life: Joseph Campbell in Conversation with Michael Toms. New York: Harper & Row, 1990.

The Power of Myth. New York: Anchor Books, 1991.
Thou Art That: Transforming Religious Metaphor. Edited by Eugene C. Kennedy. San Rafael, Calif.: New World Library, 2001.

Books about Joseph Campbell

Ellwood, Robert S. *The Politics of Myth: A Study of C. G. Jung, Mircea Eliade, and Joseph Campbell.* Albany, N.Y.: State University of New York Press, 1999.
Larson, Stephen. *A Fire in the Mind: The Life of Joseph Campbell.* New York: Anchor Books, 1993.
Noel, Daniel C., ed. *Paths to the Power of Myth: Joseph Campbell and the Study of Religion.* New York: Crossroad, Herder & Herder, 1994.

Organization

Joseph Campbell Foundation, P.O. Box 36, San Anselmo, CA 94979-0413; phone: 800-330-6984; e-mail: info@jcf.org; web site: www.jcf.org.

Other Resources

Videotapes/DVDs: *Joseph Campbell and the Power of Myth,* PBS-TV; *Joseph Campbell: The Hero's Journey; Mythos I* and *Mythos II;* all available from Mystic Fire Video.

Audiotapes: *Joseph Campbell Audio Collection:* vol. 1, *Mythology and the Individual,* HighBridge Audio; *Myth and Metaphor in Society,* Joseph Campbell talks with Jamake Highwater, Mystic Fire Audio.

"Myth is the secret opening through which the inexhaustible energies of the cosmos pour into human cultural manifestation."

MIRCEA ELIADE
(1907–1986)

One of the twentieth century's preeminent religious scholars, Mircea Eliade was a pioneer in the systematic study of the history of religion and a seminal influence on a generation of scholars in the field. His work in comparative religion influenced an entire generation of scholars, including Wendy Doniger and Lawrence E. Sullivan.

Born in Romania, Eliade received his M.A. in philosophy from the University of Bucharest in 1928. He then studied Sanskrit and Indian philosophy at the University of Calcutta and lived for six months in an Indian ashram. During his time in India he began to develop his views on the meaning of language, symbolism, and systems employed by the various religious traditions. It was his aim to resolve and incorporate this view of meaning and symbolism within underlying primordial myths that provide the basis for mystical phenomena. He coined the word *hierophanies* to mean manifestations of the sacred world, applying the term to all religious experience in traditional and contemporary societies.

In 1931 Eliade returned to Romania and completed his Ph.D. with a dissertation on yoga and its relationship to Indian mysticism, after which he taught the history of religions and Indian philosophy at the University of Bucharest. He spent World War II in England and Portugal, moving to Paris and the Sorbonne after the war, when the political situation made it impossible for him to return to Romania. In 1956 he became professor of the history of religions at the University of Chicago, where he remained for the rest of his career.

Eliade coined the word hierophanies *to mean manifestations of the sacred world, applying the term to all religious experience in traditional and contemporary societies.*

Eliade's interpretation of traditional religious cultures and his analysis of the forms of mystical experience found in them was the primary subject of his major works. He was editor in chief of the University of Chicago's monumental sixteen-volume *Encyclopedia of Religion.*

His Words

All of the culture of the traditional person, translated into everyday rites and daily symbols, is but a continuous memorial, in gesture and mind, of the invisible plane, of the sacrality of the world, and a constant offering of thanks and reverence to the deity, to the *numina* (spirit, or creative energy) that are perpetually generating us.
—*The Sacred and the Profane,* chapter 4

I wanted to engineer a confrontation between two mythologies: the mythology of folklore, of the people, which is still alive, still welling up in the old man, and the mythology of the modern world, of technocracy. . . . These two mythologies meet head on.
—*Ordeal by Labyrinth,* p. 182

Books by Mircea Eliade

The Myth of the Eternal Return. Translated by Willard Trask. Princeton: Princeton University Press, 1971.

Ordeal by Labyrinth: Conversations with Claude-Henri Rocquet. Translated by Derek Coltman. Chicago: University of Chicago Press, 1982. (Bibliography of works by and about Eliade, pp. 213–225.)

The Sacred and the Profane: The Nature of Religion. Translated by Willard Trask. Orlando, Fla.: Harcourt, 1972.

Shamanism. Translated by Willard Trask. Princeton: Princeton University Press, 1972.

Yoga: Immortality and Freedom. Translated by Willard Trask. Princeton: Princeton University Press, 1972.

"All of the culture of the traditional person, translated into everyday rites and daily symbols, is but a continuous memorial, in gesture and mind, . . . of the sacrality of the world."

Books about Mircea Eliade

Olson, Carl. *The Theology and Philosophy of Eliade.* New York: St. Martin's Press, 1992.

Rennie, Bryan. *Reconstructing Eliade: Making Sense of Religion.* Albany: State University of New York Press, 1996.

ABRAHAM ISAAC KOOK
(1865–1935)

Both a mystic and a master of Talmudic law, a visionary and a realist, Abraham Isaac Kook played an influential role in the rebirth of Jewish life in Israel and was influential in gaining Orthodox backing for the new state through his support of the movement known as religious Zionism. He served as the first Ashkenazi chief rabbi of Palestine, before modern Israel was founded. (Ashkenazi Jews are those with roots in northern and eastern Europe.)

Avraham Yitzhak ha-Cohen Kook (his full Hebrew name, affectionately shortened to Rav Kook) was born in Greiva, Latvia, and received his rabbinical training at the renowned Talmudic Academy in Volozhin, Lithuania. In 1904 he immigrated to Palestine, where he was named chief rabbi of Jaffa. At the outbreak of World War I, Kook was stranded in Europe, where he had gone to attend a religious convention. Upon his return to Palestine in 1919, he became chief rabbi of Jerusalem and, in 1921, chief rabbi of the entire Jewish community of Palestine.

Kook produced numerous works on a wide variety of subjects, including philosophical essays, spiritual meditations, and poetry. His most important work is the *Orot ha-Kodesh* (Lights of Holiness), written in the form of a spiritual diary. Among his interests were social issues, the place of religion in the modern world, and the quest for unity and harmony among all peoples. He loved the land of Israel and the Jewish people, believing that nationalism was a necessary step toward achieving the ideal of universalism in

Kook taught that Jews were obligated to play an active role in their destiny rather than rely on God alone.

the world. Although his universal views attracted criticism and controversy, he was loved and revered by secular kibbutz farmers and deeply religious Talmudic scholars alike.

As a traditional Orthodox Jew, Kook was unusual in his openness to new ideas. He supported Zionism despite the antireligious stance of the early pioneers, because he saw Jewish settlement of the Holy Land as the beginning of the divine redemption foretold by the prophets. He taught that Jews were obligated to play an active role in their destiny rather than rely on God alone. Unlike most Orthodox rabbis of his time, he accepted Jews who did not obey Judaism's religious laws while seeking to guide them back to traditional observance. Kook did not see a sharp division between the sacred and the "profane"; he therefore advocated the study of secular subjects, such as the sciences and literature, in the *yeshivot* (Jewish academies). The yeshiva he founded in Jerusalem, Yeshivat Merkaz ha-Rav, remains a major center of Talmudic study today.

His Words

All the deficiencies in the world, both the physical and the spiritual, derive from the fact that every individual comprehends only one aspect of existence which appeals to him, and all other aspects which are outside his comprehension, as far as he is concerned, might as well disappear. . . . To cope with these deficiencies, of which the whole world suffers, and we especially, is the mission of the *zaddikim* [the righteous] who, by reason and will, strive for unification. It is their vocation to mend, to integrate, and to extend peace in the world by effecting peace in the inner realm of their own soul, by exemplifying an outlook which is comprehensive and universal, which always releases life and light in all directions.

—*Orot ha-Kodesh* I, in *The Essential Writings of Abraham Isaac Kook,* p. 152

Books by Abraham Isaac Kook

Abraham Isaac Kook: The Lights of Penitence, the Moral Principles, Lights of Holiness, Essays, Letters, and Poems. Translated and edited by Ben Zion Bokser. New York: Paulist Press, 1978.

The Art of T'Shuva: Orot HaT'Shuva. Edited by David Samson and Tzvi Fishman. Jerusalem: Beit Orot, 1999.

The Essential Writings of Abraham Isaac Kook. Edited by Ben Zion Bokser. Warwick, N.Y.: Amity House, 1988.

In the Desert—a Vision: Midbar Shur on the Torah Portion of the Week. Translated by Bezalel Naor. Spring Valley, N.Y.: Orot, 2001.

Of Societies Perfect and Imperfect: Selected Readings from Eyn Ayah, Rav Kook's Commentary to Eyn Yaakov Legends of the Talmud. Translated and annotated with an introduction by Bezalel Naor. Brooklyn: Sepher-Hermon Press, 1995.

Orot: The Annotated Translation of Rabbi Abraham Isaac Kook's Seminal Work. Translated by Bezalel Naor. Northvale, N.J.: Jason Aronson, 1993.

The Teachings of HaRav Avraham Yitzhak Kook. Edited by David Samson and Tzvi Fishman. Jerusalem: Torat Eretz Yisrael Publications, 1996.

Books about Abraham Isaac Kook

Bokser, Ben Zion. *Abraham Isaac Kook.* Boston: Element Books, 1991.

Cohen, Jack J. *Guides for an Age of Confusion: Studies in the Thinking of Avraham Y. Kook and Mordecai M. Kaplan.* Bronx, N.Y.: Fordham University Press, 1999.

Elkins, Dov Peretz. *Shepherd of Jerusalem: A Biography of Rabbi Abraham Isaac Kook.* Northvale, N.J.: Jason Aronson, 1995.

Organization

Rabbi Kook Foundation (Mosad ha-Rav Kook), Rehov Maimon 1, Kiryat Moshe, Jerusalem; phone: 02-652-6231. A research center and publishing house.

"[The vocation of the righteous is] . . . to extend peace in the world by effecting peace in the inner realm of their own soul, by exemplifying an outlook which is comprehensive and universal, which always releases life and light in all directions."

C. S. LEWIS
(1898–1963)

• • • • • • •

Writing prolifically in four different genres—literary criticism, science fiction, children's literature, and Christian apologetics—C. S. Lewis was among the twentieth century's most popular Christian writers and one of the best-selling authors of all time.

Born and raised in Belfast, Northern Ireland, Clive Staples Lewis spent his childhood surrounded by books, ideas, and conversation. Jack, as he preferred to be called, reveled in a fantasy life, drawing pictures of animals imitating human behavior; with his brother, Warren, he invented Animal Land, an imaginary world complete with personified animals, a geography, a history, and a political system. Lewis attended University College, Oxford, and served in the British army during World War I. For twenty-nine years he served as a tutor and popular lecturer in English language and literature at Magdalen College, Oxford. In 1954 he accepted a chair in Medieval and Renaissance English at Cambridge University.

Lewis's first published works, other than articles in school papers and magazines, are books of poetry, *Spirits in Bondage* (1919) and *Dymer* (1926). Receiving little acclaim for his poetry, he began to write prose. In 1933 he wrote his first book on theology, *The Pilgrim's Regress,* a story of his reaffirmation of his Christian roots. Although baptized into the Church of England as a child, he had resisted religion in any form until one night in 1929, about which he said in his 1955 autobiography, *Surprised by Joy,* "In the Trinity Term of 1929 I gave in, and admitted

Decades after his death, Lewis's works of literary criticism, science fiction, children's literature, and Christian apologetics continue to appeal to children and theologians alike.

that God was God, and knelt and prayed: perhaps, that night, the most dejected and reluctant convert in all England; I did not then see what is now the most shining and obvious thing; the Divine humility which will accept a convert even on such terms."

Lewis's influence on the Christian community began in earnest when *The Screwtape Letters* appeared in a serial in the *Guardian* newspaper. World fame followed with the publication of the letters as a book in 1941. His contribution to Christian theology and thought grew with a three-year series of broadcasts for the British Broadcasting Company, compiled as *Broadcast Talks* (1942), *The Christian Idea of God* (1944), and *Mere Christianity* (1952). These talks were so popular that *Time* magazine labeled Lewis an "apostle to the skeptics." He also wrote the highly acclaimed and vastly popular children's series *The Chronicles of Narnia* (1950–1956). Decades after his death Lewis's works continue to appeal to children and theologians alike.

His Words

Morality, then, seems to be concerned with three things. Firstly, with fair play and harmony between individuals. Secondly, with what might be called tidying up or harmonizing the things inside each individual. Thirdly, with the general purpose of human life as a whole: what man was made for: what course the whole fleet ought to be on: what tune the conductor of the band wants it to play.
—*Mere Christianity,* p. 5

There are no *ordinary* people. You have never talked to a mere mortal. . . . It is immortals whom we joke with, work with, marry, snub, and exploit—immortal horrors or everlasting splendours. This does not mean that we are to be perpetually solemn. We must play. But our merriment must be of that kind (and it is, in fact, the merriest kind) which exists between people who have, from the outset, taken each other seriously—no flippancy, no superiority, no presumption. And our charity must be a real and costly love, with deep feeling for the sins in spite of which we love the sinner. . . . Next to the Blessed Sacrament itself your neighbour is the holiest object presented to your senses.
—"The Weight of Glory," in *The Essential C. S. Lewis,* p. 369

Books by C. S. Lewis

The Complete Chronicles of Narnia. 1950–1956. Reprint, New York: HarperCollins, 1998.

The Essential C. S. Lewis. Edited by Lyle Dorsett. New York: Collier Books, 1988.

A Grief Observed. 1961. Reprint, New York: Bantam Books, 1976.

Mere Christianity. New York: Macmillan, 1943.

Surprised by Joy: The Shape of My Early Life. New York: Harcourt, Brace, 1955.

Till We Have Faces. New York: Harcourt, Brace, 1956.

Books about C. S. Lewis

Carpenter, Humphrey. *The Inklings: C. S. Lewis, J. R. R. Tolkien, Charles Williams, and Their Friends.* London: Allen & Unwin, 1979.

Como, James T., ed. *Lewis at the Breakfast Table and Other Reminiscences.* New York: Macmillan, 1979.

Gilbert, Douglas, and Clyde S. Kilby. *C. S. Lewis: Images of His World.* Grand Rapids, Mich.: Wm. B. Eerdmans, 1973.

Kilby, Clyde S., and Marjorie Lamp Mead, eds. *Brothers and Friends: The Diaries of Major Warren Hamilton Lewis.* New York: Harper & Row, 1982.

Payne, Leanne. *Real Presence: The Holy Spirit in the Works of C. S. Lewis.* Westchester, Ill.: Cornerstone Books, 1979.

Other Resources

Web site: www.cslewis.org. Web site of the C. S. Lewis Foundation.

Videotape: *The Chronicles of Narnia,* BBC.

Videotape/DVD: *Shadowlands,* directed by Richard Attenborough, dramatized love story of Lewis and his wife, Joy Davidman Gresham, 1993.

"Next to the Blessed Sacrament itself your neighbour is the holiest object presented to your senses."

HUSTON SMITH
(1919–)

A lifelong Christian despite wide religious experimentation, Huston Smith is a pioneer among religion scholars who has popularized the commonalities among what he calls the world's wisdom traditions—Hinduism, Buddhism, Judaism, Christianity, Confucianism, Sikhism, Taoism, Jainism, and Islam—by taking their study out of the classroom and into people's homes via television and popular books.

Born to Methodist missionaries in China in 1919, Smith came to the United States at age seventeen with the intention of becoming a missionary himself. But after two years in a church pulpit, he returned to school and received a Ph.D. in philosophy of religion at the University of Chicago. In 1955 his undergraduate course on world religions at Washington University in St. Louis was so popular that a local television station asked him to create a series of programs on the subject. When that station evolved into what is now the Public Broadcasting System, it carried Smith's shows to millions of viewers unfamiliar with non-Christian religions. Smith's book based on the series, *The Religions of Man* (later retitled *The World's Religions*), sold millions of copies and became a mainstay of living-room coffee tables and college bookshelves.

Smith has consistently taught that all the world's major religious traditions are imbued with the divine, and are therefore worthy of study, respect, and understanding.

Smith differs from many religion scholars in his habit of dispensing with the observational study of religions in favor of firsthand experience. He has whirled with Islamic dervishes, practiced yoga with Hindu holy men, meditated with Tibetan

Buddhists, ingested peyote with Huichol Indian medicine men, and celebrated the Sabbath with Jewish families. He has consistently sought out the mystical in each religion and has taught that all the world's major religious traditions are imbued with the Divine and are therefore worthy of study, respect, and understanding.

In 1996 Smith was the subject of the five-part Bill Moyers television series *The Wisdom of Faith with Huston Smith.* After retiring from his professorship at the University of California, Berkeley, he jumped into the debate between science and religion, calling for recognition of traditional religious wisdom alongside the modern achievements of science. He lives in Berkeley and continues to write and lecture widely.

His Words

From a purely human standpoint the wisdom traditions are the species' most prolonged and serious attempts to infer from the maze on this side of the tapestry the pattern which, on its right side, gives meaning to the whole. As the beauty and the harmony of the design derive from the way its parts are related, the design confers on those parts a significance that we, seeing only scraps of the design, do not normally perceive. We could almost say that this belonging to the whole, in something of the way the parts of a painting suggest, is what religion is all about.
—*The World's Religions,* p. 387

The community today can be no single tradition; it is the planet. Daily the world grows smaller, leaving understanding the only place where peace can find a home. We are not prepared for the annihilation of distance that science has effected. Who today stands ready to accept the solemn equality of peoples? Who does not have to fight an unconscious tendency to equate foreign with inferior? Some of us have survived this bloodiest of centuries; but if its ordeals are to be birth pangs rather than death throes, the century's scientific advances must be matched by comparable advances in human relations.
—*The World's Religions,* p. 390

Books by Huston Smith

Beyond the Post-Modern Mind. Wheaton, Ill.: Crossroads, 1982.

Cleansing the Doors of Perception: The Religious Significance of Entheogenic Plants and Chemicals. New York: Jeremy P. Tarcher, 2000.

Forgotten Truth: The Common Vision of the World's Religions. San Francisco: HarperSanFrancisco, 1992.

Huston Smith: Essays on World Religion. Edited by M. Darrol Bryant. New York: Paragon House, 1992.

One Nation under God: The Triumph of the Native American Church. Editor, with Reuben Snake. Santa Fe, N.M.: Clear Light Publishers, 1996.

Why Religion Matters: The Fate of the Human Spirit in an Age of Disbelief. San Francisco: HarperSanFrancisco, 2001.

The World's Religions. San Francisco: HarperSanFrancisco, 1991. Revised and updated edition of *The Religions of Man.* New York: Harper & Row, 1958.

Other Resources

Videotapes: *The Wisdom of Faith with Huston Smith.* Directed by Pamela Mason Wagner. 1996. *The Mystic's Journey,* with Huston Smith, 1997; three classic films: *India and the Infinite: The Soul of a People; Islamic Mysticism: The Sufi Way;* and *Requiem for a Faith: Tibetan Buddhism.*

"Some of us have survived this bloodiest of centuries; but if its ordeals are to be birth pangs rather than death throes, the century's scientific advances must be matched by comparable advances in human relations."

D. T. SUZUKI
(1870–1966)

One of the most famous interpreters of Zen Buddhism in the Western world, D. T. Suzuki was also among the first Japanese spokespersons to popularize the practice of Zen in the United States.

Born into a no-longer-privileged samurai family, Daisetsu Teitaro Suzuki grew up in genteel poverty in northern Japan. His zeal for self-education, which included learning English, eventually led him to take classes at the Imperial University in Tokyo. He did not earn a degree there, but he did develop an interest in Zen training. He eventually became a lay student of Shaku Soen.

In 1893 Suzuki traveled with Shaku Soen to the Parliament of the World's Religions in Chicago. He translated into English Shaku Soen's written speech and read it to the general assembly, thus indirectly becoming the first official voice of Zen on American soil. Four years later Suzuki returned to the United States to work with the Illinois-based publisher Paul Carus in translating Buddhist texts and writing his own commentaries. In 1906 he joined Shaku Soen in a nationwide tour during which both men gave talks on Zen.

Suzuki returned to Japan immediately after this tour but came back to the United States in 1950 to teach Zen at Columbia University, an assignment that continued intermittently over the next eight years. Like Thich Nhat Hanh decades later, Suzuki was never confirmed as a Zen master—or teacher—in any formal lineage, but he made a life for himself in the West by teaching and writing

D. T. Suzuki taught and wrote about Zen Buddhism for the benefit of Western students, among them writer Jack Kerouac and composer John Cage.

about Zen for the benefit of Western lay practitioners. Among his more well-known students were the writer Jack Kerouac and the composer John Cage, both of whom reflected the influence of Zen in their works. Suzuki also evolved into a celebrated public figure, frequently interviewed by the media and much admired for his character, charm, and erudition.

His Words

An intuitive mind has its weaknesses, it is true, but its strongest point is demonstrated when it deals with things most fundamental in life, that is, things related to religion, art, and metaphysics. And it is Zen that has particularly established this fact—in *satori* [the experience of enlightenment]. The idea that the ultimate truth of life and of things generally is to be intuitively and not conceptually grasped, and that this intuitive prehension is the foundation not only of philosophy but of all other cultural activities, is what the Zen form of Buddhism has contributed to the cultivation of artistic appreciation among the Japanese people.
—*Zen and Japanese Culture,* p. 219

Let us first realize the fact that we thrive only when we are cooperative by being alive to the truth of the interrelationship of all things in existence. Let us then die to the notion of power and conquest and be resurrected to the eternal creativity of love, which is all-embracing and all-forgiving. As love flows out of rightly seeing reality as it is, it is also love that makes us feel that we—each of us individually and all of us collectively—are responsible for whatever things, good or evil, go on in our human community, and we must therefore strive to ameliorate or remove whatever conditions are inimical to the universal advancement of human welfare and wisdom.
—*The Awakening of Zen,* p. 70

Books by D. T. Suzuki

The Awakening of Zen. Boston: Shambhala Publications, 1987.
Essays in Zen Buddhism. 1st ser. New York: Grove Press, 1961.
Essays in Zen Buddhism. 2d ser. York Beach, Maine: Samuel Weiser, 1971.

An Introduction to Zen Buddhism. New York: Grove Press, 1960.

Manual of Zen Buddhism. New York: Grove Press, 1960.

Mysticism, Christian and Buddhist. New York: Harper & Row, 1957.

Shin Buddhism. New York: Harper & Row, 1970.

Zen and Japanese Culture. Princeton: Princeton University Press, 1959.

"Let us then die to the notion of power and conquest and be resurrected to the eternal creativity of love, which is all-embracing and all-forgiving."

SIMONE WEIL
(1909–1943)

Although only a few of Simone Weil's articles appeared in her lifetime, her posthumously published writing has made her one of the most influential philosophers of the twentieth century, and a kind of patron saint to those who strive for the spiritual life outside organized religion.

Weil was born in Paris, into an intellectual, nonobservant Jewish family. From early childhood she exhibited the two passions that would guide her life: her thirst for knowledge and her concern for and identification with the oppressed and suffering—at the age of five she refused to eat sugar when she learned that French soldiers in World War I were not rationed it. She attended the most prestigious French schools, where she excelled, graduating at the head of her class at the École Normale Supérièure, one place ahead of her classmate Simone de Beauvoir.

Weil spent the first years after her graduation as a secondary school philosophy teacher and, increasingly, as a left-leaning political activist, although she never aligned herself with any particular political philosophy. She felt an imperative to experience the plight of the worker firsthand. To that end, in the midst of generally frail health, she harvested grapes, worked in a Renault factory, and fought with the Republican army in the Spanish Civil War, all the while pouring herself into the philosophical essays and fragments for which she is now known.

Weil gained a profound love for Jesus and the Christian faith—yet she felt it her special calling to remain a believer outside the church, as a witness to its history of oppression and abuse of power.

In 1938, while visiting the Benedictine Abbey at Solesmes, France,

Weil had the first of several overwhelming mystical experiences, in which she gained a profound love for Jesus and the Christian faith—yet she felt it her special calling to remain a believer outside the church, as a witness to its history of oppression and abuse of power. Never baptized, she remained an odd kind of Christian-outside-the-church for the rest of her brief life, and her writings began to focus on her newfound faith and to reflect on her struggle to express the unusual position to which she found herself called. Written in the language of philosophy rather than in standard Christian jargon, her work exhibits a striking freshness and integrity. Weil stands as a role model for everyone who has struggled honestly with faith in the face of mistrust of organized religion, showing how a profound faith can be experienced outside religious institutions.

In 1942 she fled France for England, where she worked in Charles de Gaulle's Free French movement. In 1943 she contracted tuberculosis, from which she died. Throughout the course of her illness Weil refused food and medical treatment as an act of solidarity with her countrymen in occupied France.

Her Words

We experience good only by doing it.

We experience evil only by refusing to allow ourselves to do it, or, if we do it, by repenting of it.

When we do evil we do not know it, because evil flies from the light.

—"The Great Beast," in *The Simone Weil Reader*, p. 393

Religion, insofar as it is a sense of consolation, is a hindrance to true faith; and in this sense atheism is a purification.

—"Contemplation of the Divine," in *The Simone Weil Reader*, p. 412

Not only does the love of God have attention for its substance; the love of our neighbor, which we know to be the same love, is made of this same substance. Those who are unhappy have no need for anything in this world but people capable of giving them their attention. The capacity to give one's attention to a sufferer is a very rare and difficult thing; it is almost a miracle; it is a miracle. Nearly all those who think

they have this capacity do not possess it. Warmth of heart, impulsiveness, pity are not enough.
—"Reflections on the Right Use of School Studies with a View to the Love of God," in *The Simone Weil Reader,* p. 51

Books by Simone Weil

Gravity and Grace. New York: Routledge, 1992.
The Simone Weil Reader. Edited by George Panichas. New York: Schocken Books, 1987.
Waiting for God. New York: Ballantine Books, 1970.

Books about Simone Weil

Coles, Robert. *Simone Weil: A Modern Pilgrimage.* Woodstock, Vt.: SkyLight Paths, 2000.
Petrement, Simone. *Simone Weil: A Life.* Translated by Raymond Rosenthal. New York: Schocken Books, 1976.

"Not only does the love of God have attention for its substance; the love of our neighbor, which we know to be the same love, is made of this same substance."

6

THEY SHOWED US LOVE IN **ACTION**

Is there a spiritual path worthy of the term that does not include among its most precious beliefs a call for justice? "Justice, justice shall you pursue," Moses demands of the ancient Israelites. "The Word of the Lord doth find its fulfillment in truth and in justice," says the Qur'an. For Hindus, Lord Rama, the warrior king of India's epic Ramayana, is the embodiment of justice. The traditions also link justice with love of the Creation and all that is in it. From that, it is easy to conclude that striving for justice is incumbent upon the Creation's human offspring.

The Social Gospel movement is one such reading of Christian Scripture. It first stirred in Walter Rauschenbusch, the movement's icon, through his turn-of-the-century experience as a Baptist minister in Hell's Kitchen, an aptly named New York City neighborhood replete with crime, exploitation, and poverty. After witnessing similar deprivation in Europe, he began to write widely that Christians must work for social betterment, that the Kingdom of God requires personal *and* societal salvation.

Albert Schweitzer also responded to the inner call to act on behalf of others. A biblical scholar, theologian, philosopher, and musicologist as well as a physician, Schweitzer became world famous for his decades of medical work in Gabon (formerly French Equatorial Africa), where he treated thousands suffering from leprosy, sleeping sickness, and other ailments. The Nobel Peace Prize winner, a Christian, summed up his religious philosophy as a "reverence for life."

Three women, all touched by Roman Catholic sensibilities, are included here. The best known is Mother Teresa of Calcutta, a uniquely twentieth-century religious celebrity. Diminutive, stooped, and garbed in her familiar blue-trimmed white sari habit, Mother Teresa jetted around the globe, meeting with all manner of people, her focus set on raising funds for her worldwide network of charitable programs, starting with Calcutta's Nirmal Hriday Home for Dying Destitutes. Today the Missionaries of Charity, the order she founded, serves the "poorest of the poor" in more than one hundred nations. She lives on in death as her era's ultimate example of selfless, loving service to others.

Dorothy Day, founder of the Catholic Worker movement and newspaper, epitomized lay social activism within the church. Like Mother Teresa, Day was grounded in a firm belief in the God-given dignity of every individual, voluntary poverty, prayer, and hospitality for the homeless, hungry, and forgotten. But she also challenged the political and religious establishment, staunchly defending pacifism in times of war and criticizing her church's financial priorities. The Vatican has moved to canonize Mother Teresa. Ironically, it has also moved to canonize Day, a prospect that many of her supporters find odd.

Catherine de Hueck Doherty started out as an Eastern Orthodox Christian but became a Roman Catholic at age twenty. She began life in an aristocratic family in czarist Russia, yet it became her passion to serve God by caring for the poor and suffering. She founded Madonna House, which now has more than twenty facilities around the world where those in need are cared for. "A love that is not incarnate," she said, "is not real love."

Two Buddhist monks—both from Southeast Asia, both dissenters to war—are also included. Thich Nhat Hanh is from Vietnam; Maha Ghosananda is from Cambodia. Both threw themselves into the peace movements that sought to end the carnage resulting from decades of war in their countries.

Thich Nhat Hanh, in exile from Vietnam since 1966, pioneered the engaged Buddhism movement, which links social action and civil disobedience with meditative and other spiritual practices. The founder of France's Plum Village Retreat Center, he continues to oppose oppression in his homeland. Maha Ghosananda, called

Cambodia's Gandhi, worked tirelessly to aid Cambodian refugees fleeing the Khmer Rouge and, after the 1991 peace accord, to effect reconciliation among his people.

Mawlana Muhammad Ilyas's love was of a different sort. A Sufi, he had as his passion guiding Muslims back to Islamic tradition by training volunteers to go door to door to teach the faith, first in his native India and more recently across much of the Muslim world. Finally, we include Robert Holbrook Smith, cofounder of Alcoholics Anonymous (AA), the organization that revolutionized recovery by making spiritual surrender to a Higher Power, however conceived, central to its program. In doing so AA exposed many to a pragmatic spirituality that often was also a lifesaver.

DOROTHY DAY
(1897–1980)

• • • • • • •

Founder of the Catholic Worker movement, Dorothy Day was among the great Catholic lay activists of the twentieth century and an inspiration to faith-based social- and political-change movements worldwide.

Day's youth in Chicago tenements gave her a taste of life at the bottom rung of society, as well as her first positive impressions of Catholic piety, from her friends' parents. When her father found a decent job, the family moved into more comfortable surroundings. But, inspired by the books of Upton Sinclair and other social reformers, Day continued visiting low-income areas, finding beauty amid what most considered squalor.

She won a scholarship to the University of Illinois in 1914. There she tended toward radical and socialist thought and dropped out after two years. She moved to New York and worked as a reporter for the *Call,* a Socialist newspaper, and later for the *Masses,* a magazine opposing America's involvement in World War I. Day was imprisoned in 1917 for rallying outside the White House for women's right to vote and was freed by presidential order along with the forty other protesters. Back in New York, she worked briefly as a nurse before returning to journalism in Chicago and then New Orleans.

Dorothy Day with Peter Maurin started the Catholic Worker, *a monthly newspaper that took bold stands on many issues. Day made the newspaper's ideals realities for many people.*

Day's upbringing was largely irreligious, but as an adult she was drawn to the Roman Catholic Church. In New York she started making late-night visits to a Catholic church where she was fascinated by the worship and by the church's embrace of immigrants. In 1922 she lived with three young women in Chicago who attended Mass regularly and made time for prayer every day, which deeply impressed Day. She called prayer and thanksgiving the "noblest acts we are capable of." When she had a daughter, Tamar Theresa Day, with her then common-law husband, Forster Batterham, Day had the baby baptized. After breaking with Batterham, she formally joined the Catholic Church, a move that briefly estranged her from some radical friends.

In 1932 Day met Peter Maurin, a Catholic social reformer who had embraced poverty and envisioned a social order based on the Gospels that would unite intellectual and worker. The two started the *Catholic Worker*, a monthly newspaper that took bold stands on many issues, advocating pacifism during World War II and support for conscientious objectors. Within three years the paper counted 150,000 subscribers. Day made the newspaper's ideals realities for many people. She rented an apartment for ten homeless women and later rented another for men. Soon after, she moved the community to two buildings in New York's Chinatown. The idea spread, and by 1936 there were thirty-three Catholic Worker homes throughout the country.

Day would maintain her pacifism—her most controversial stance—her whole life, virulently protesting the Vietnam war in her later years. Since her death in 1980, the church has taken steps to name her a saint, a move that has sparked controversy even among her supporters: some believe it is a fitting affirmation of what she stood for; others say her message will be diluted or claim that Day would have wanted money spent on her canonization to go to the poor instead.

Her Words

This work of ours toward a new heaven and a new earth shows a correlation between the material and the spiritual, and, of course, recognizes the primacy of the spiritual. Food for the body is not enough. There must be food for the soul. Hence the leaders of the work, and as many as we can induce to join us, must go daily to Mass, to receive food for the soul. And as our perceptions are quickened, and as we pray that our faith be increased, we will see Christ in each other, and we will

not lose faith in those around us, no matter how stumbling their progress is.
—*Catholic Worker,* February 1940, p. 7

The great need of the human heart is for love, and especially do women's lives seem empty if they are deprived of their own to love. Indeed, we know that the first commandment is to love, and we show our love, as St. Teresa said, for our God by our love for our fellows. And that is why a great emphasis must be placed on the works of mercy.
—*Catholic Worker,* November 1945, p. 1

Books by Dorothy Day

Dorothy Day: Selected Writings. Edited by Robert Ellsberg. Maryknoll, N.Y.: Orbis Books, 1992.

Loaves and Fishes. Foreword by Thomas Merton. Introduction by Robert Coles. Maryknoll, N.Y.: Orbis Books, 1997.

The Long Loneliness. Chicago: St. Thomas More Press, 1993.

On Pilgrimage. Foreword by Michael O. Garvey. Introduction by Louise Zwick. Grand Rapids, Mich.: Wm. B. Eerdmans, 1999.

Books about Dorothy Day

Coles, Robert. *Dorothy Day: A Radical Devotion.* Reading, Mass.: Addison-Wesley, 1987.

Connor, Charles. *Classic Catholic Converts.* San Francisco: Ignatius Press, 2001.

Forest, Jim. *Love Is the Measure: A Biography of Dorothy Day.* Maryknoll, N.Y.: Orbis Books, 1994.

Miller, William D. *Dorothy Day: A Biography.* New York: Harper & Row, 1982.

Roberts, Nancy L. *Dorothy Day and the Catholic Worker.* Albany, N.Y.: State University of New York Press, 1994.

For a more complete list of books by and about Dorothy Day, see Coles, *Dorothy Day,* pp. 171–174.

Organization

Catholic Worker communities: 175 independent organizations around the world. Contact information at www.catholicworker.org/communities/commstates.cfm.

Other Resources

Newspaper: *Catholic Worker*, 36 East First St., New York, NY 10003; phone: 212-777-9617.

Web site: www.catholicworker.org. Official web site of the Catholic Worker movement.

Film/Videotape: *Entertaining Angels: The Dorothy Day Story*, Paulist Pictures, 1996.

"This work of ours toward a new heaven and a new earth shows a correlation between the material and the spiritual, and, of course, recognizes the primacy of the spiritual. Food for the body is not enough. There must be food for the soul."

CATHERINE DE HUECK DOHERTY
(1896–1985)

• • • • • • •

A pioneer in Christian social justice work in Canada and the United States, Catherine de Hueck Doherty established the philanthropic religious community Madonna House, which now maintains twenty-three field houses throughout the world where the needy are fed and cared for.

De Hueck Doherty grew up in an aristocratic family in prerevolutionary Russia. She was baptized and received her early religious training in the Eastern Orthodox Church, but she also had considerable formative contact with Roman Catholicism, attending a Catholic school for much of her childhood in Alexandria, Egypt, where her father held a diplomatic post. She became a Catholic at the age of twenty but remained in many ways devoted to the Orthodox faith and its spirituality throughout her life.

From an early age de Hueck Doherty became convinced that the sufferings of Jesus—a common object of meditation in Catholic piety—are to be seen today in the suffering of the people around us and that by ministering to the needs of the suffering, one is literally in touch with God. It became her lifelong passion to serve God by caring for the poor and suffering.

She fled Russia with her husband, Baron de Hueck, after the Bolshevik Revolution and eventually settled in Canada. The couple divorced in the 1930s—around the same time Catherine was inspired by the words of Jesus in the Gospels: "Sell all you possess, give it to the poor, and come—follow me!" She decided to follow the command literally and went to live and work with the poor in the slums of Toronto, where she founded Friendship House. She

De Hueck Doherty never saw her actions as "social work" but rather as simply living the truth of Christ's words: "What you do to the least of my brethren, you do to me."

established Friendship Houses in New York's Harlem section, Chicago, and other cities in the 1930s and 1940s. In 1943 she married Edward Doherty, who became her partner in her work, and who with her founded Madonna House, a religious community of men and women devoted to serving God by serving others.

She never saw her actions as "social work" but rather as simply living the truth of Christ's words: "What you do to the least of my brethren, you do to me." For de Hueck Doherty, love was not abstract: love was giving clothes, or a cup of coffee, or a listening ear. "A love that is not incarnate is not real love," she often said.

Her Words

Christ emptied himself for love of us. Consider the Almighty, and stop at the word Almighty, which encompasses everything that God is: beauty, truth, all His attributes. Jesus Christ, the second person of the Holy Trinity, descended into the womb of a woman as a seed. Do not try to apprehend or comprehend, but prostrate yourself before the most incomprehensible mystery of the tremendous love that God has shown.
—*For This I Have Laid Down My Life*

Books by Catherine de Hueck Doherty

Poustinia: Encountering God in Silence, Solitude, and Prayer. Combermere, Ont.: Madonna House, 2000.

Sobornost: Eastern Unity of Mind and Heart for Western Man. Combermere, Ont.: Madonna House, 1992.

Soul of My Soul: Reflections from a Life of Prayer. Notre Dame, Ind.: Ave Maria Press, 1985.

Organization

Madonna House Apostolate, 2888 Dafoe Rd., Combermere, ON K0J 1L0, Canada; phone: 613-756-3713; fax: 613-756-0211.

Other Resources

Web sites: www.madonnahouse.org. Web site of the Madonna House communities.

www.catherinedoherty.org. Official web site promoting de Hueck Doherty's canonization in the Roman Catholic Church.

"A love that is not incarnate is not real love."

MAHA GHOSANANDA
(1929–)

The supreme leader of Cambodian Buddhism, Maha Ghosananda is a radiant monk who has been called Cambodia's Gandhi. Samdech Preah Maha Ghosananda, whose name means "Great Joyful Proclaimer," has worked tirelessly for peace and healing in Southeast Asia, directing compassion indiscriminately toward both the oppressed and their oppressors.

Maha Ghosananda was born in a farming village of Takeo Province, Cambodia, in the Mekong River Delta. Inclined to meditation and the monastic life from his youth, he was ordained a monk, with his parents' blessing, at the age of fourteen. The first two decades of his life as a monk included rigorous academic study and earned him a Ph.D. in Buddhist studies at Nalanda University in Bihar, India. To complement his university training, he visited Buddhist centers throughout Asia, studying with some of the greatest contemporary masters from a range of traditions and schools.

In 1965, at the age of thirty-six, Maha Ghosananda moved to Thailand and became a disciple of the great meditation master Achaan Dhammadaro. During his years in Thailand, Cambodia was bombed by the United States, with a ground war following. Then came years of holocaust under the tyrant Pol Pot's Khmer Rouge regime, during which Maha Ghosananda's entire family was killed.

Maha Ghosananda has continued to promote nonviolent means, not only for peace but also for solutions to a wide range of peace-threatening issues, such as deforestation and the use of land mines.

Maha Ghosananda threw himself with vigor into the nonviolent peace movement, doing all he could for his fellow Cambodians. He established temples in all the Cambodian refugee camps on the Cambodia-Thailand border and traveled from camp to camp to teach and encourage his people. The sight of him in his saffron robes is said to have stirred the Cambodian refugees to tears—by 1978 he was one of the last Cambodian monks left alive.

After the signing of the 1991 peace accord, Maha Ghosananda led the first of the Dhammayietra Walks for Peace and Reconciliation across Cambodia. When his nonviolent procession passed through villages, hundreds and sometimes thousands of people joined in the peaceful demonstration. He has continued to promote nonviolent means, not only for peace but also for solutions to a wide range of peace-threatening issues, such as deforestation and the use of land mines. He has been nominated four times for the Nobel Peace Prize.

His Words

I do not question that loving one's oppressors—Cambodians loving the Khmer Rouge—may be the most difficult attitude to achieve. But it is a law of the universe that retaliation, hatred, and revenge only continue the cycle and never stop it. Reconciliation does not mean that we surrender rights and conditions, but rather that we use love in all of our negotiations. It means that we see ourselves in the opponent—for what is the opponent but a being in ignorance, and we ourselves are also ignorant of many things. Therefore, only loving kindness and right mindfulness can free us.

—*Step by Step*

Book by Maha Ghosananda

Step by Step: Meditations on Wisdom and Compassion. Berkeley: Parallax Press, 1992.

"Reconciliation does not mean that we surrender rights and conditions, but rather that we use love in all of our negotiations."

MAWLANA MUHAMMAD ILYAS
(1885–1944)

One of the twentieth century's most influential Islamic figures, Mawlana Muhammad Ilyas founded the international revivalist Faith Movement, or Tablighi Jama'at ("missionary society"), with the primary aim of guiding Muslims to adopt or readopt Islamic practices. A religious scholar and a follower of the Naqshbandi Sufi order, he achieved success by sincerity, persistence, and intense devotion to his cause. His movement has had significant impact not only in his native South Asia but also in Africa, Malaysia, Europe, and North America. Its major gathering at Raiwind near Lahore, Pakistan, is said to be the largest annual meeting of Muslims next to the hajj (pilgrimage to Mecca).

Muhammad Ilyas Kandhalawi (the title *Mawlana,* which he acquired later, means "our master") was born into a family of religious scholars in what is now the Indian state of Uttar Pradesh. He was educated at a well-known center of Islamic learning and became a teacher at another major school. He began his missionary activities in the early 1920s among a group known as the Meos in Mewat (southwest of Delhi); they, like many people in premodern India, did not consider exclusive Muslim or Hindu identity to be important. Ilyas discovered that some Muslims there had even adopted the worship of Hindu deities, contrary to Islam's emphasis on divine unity and monotheism. He therefore began,

One of the twentieth century's most influential Muslims, Ilyas's movement has had significant impact not only in his native South Asia but also in Africa, Malaysia, Europe, and North America. Its major gathering at Raiwind near Lahore, Pakistan, is said to be the largest annual meeting of Muslims next to the hajj (pilgrimage to Mecca).

along with some of his disciples, to educate these Muslims in the basic teachings of their faith. Religious outreach, or spreading the truth of Islam, is called *da'wah* in Arabic and is considered an obligation for all Muslims.

Initially Ilyas worked to establish houses of worship and study throughout the region, but he soon determined that it would be more productive to train preachers to go door to door and instruct people in the religious practices of Islam. Resigning from his teaching position, he established the Tablighi movement with headquarters in Nizamuddin, a suburb of Delhi, in 1926. His efforts were so successful that some 25,000 people attended the first Tablighi conference, held in Mewat in 1941. Since the partition of India in 1947, the movement's activities have been centered in Pakistan.

The unique feature of the program is that it depends on teams of ordinary volunteers—not professional educators—who travel from place to place, at their own expense, in order to teach fellow Muslims (conversion of non-Muslims is said not to be a primary aim). Mainly men engage in the itinerant preaching, although women also participate in the movement through educational and other activities.

At Ilyas's death, leadership of the movement passed to his son, Muhammad Yusuf (1917–1965), under whom in 1948 the Tablighi movement began to expand across the Muslim world. By the late 1970s its international influence had become obvious. Since the movement today refuses to make its organizational structure public, some scholars and other observers question whether it is truly non-political, as it claims to be. Ilyas himself—who founded the movement during a time of political turmoil between Muslims and Hindus in India—was said to have kept aloof from politics, concentrating solely on his religious task.

Despite his influence, Ilyas's launching of a major grassroots religious movement has not received much attention from scholars. Undoubtedly that is because the movement is difficult to study, since its leaders do not believe in communicating through the media or writings, preferring communication from person to person, spirit to spirit. Ilyas wrote no books, and the literature on him and his movement consists mainly of inspirational and devotional writings in the Urdu language.

Books about Mawlana Muhammad Ilyas

Anwarul Haq, M. *The Faith Movement of Mawlana Muhammad Ilyas.* London: Allen & Unwin, 1972.

Masud, Muhammad Khalid, ed. *Travellers in Faith: Studies of the Tablighi Jama'at as a Transnational Islamic Movement for Faith Renewal.* Leiden, Netherlands: Brill, 2000.

Ilyas's passion was da'wah, *the obligation to spread Islam's teachings.*

MOTHER TERESA
(1910–1997)

A Roman Catholic nun whose dedication to helping the poor in India earned her the name Saint of the Gutters, Mother Teresa founded the Missionaries of Charity, an order of nuns devoted to serving the poor in Calcutta, India. Today the order has grown from twelve sisters in Calcutta to over three thousand worldwide. For her work she was awarded the Nobel Peace Prize in 1979.

Mother Teresa was an Albanian, born Agnes Gonxha Bojaxhiu in Skopje, in what is now Macedonia. At eighteen she joined the Order of the Sisters of Our Lady of Loreto in Ireland, where she took the name Sister Teresa. She was sent to Calcutta to teach at Saint Mary's High School, where she was beloved by the children, who gave her the nickname Ma. She later became principal of Saint Mary's. During this time she learned Hindi and Bengali and helped in the care of the sick. In 1946, while traveling by train to be treated for tuberculosis, she received an inner "call within a call" and left Saint Mary's to minister to the sick and poor in the slums of Calcutta. Two years later she left the Loreto community, received nursing training, and went to live among the poor.

In 1950 Mother Teresa founded her own order, the Missionaries of Charity. In addition to the vows of poverty, chastity, and obedience, she embraced a fourth vow of service to the poor. Soon after she opened the Nirmal Hriday Home for Dying Destitutes in Calcutta.

In 1950 Mother Teresa founded a new Roman Catholic order, the Missionaries of Charity. In addition to the traditional vows of poverty, chastity, and obedience, she embraced a fourth vow of service to the poor.

In the following years her work spread throughout the world. This small, stooped woman, always dressed in a white traditional Indian sari trimmed with blue, became an international celebrity, willing to go virtually anywhere and meet with anyone to further her work of aiding the poorest of the poor. She initiated programs for the sick, hungry, and homeless, and she opened treatment centers for alcoholics and drug addicts. In her later years she was forced to scale back her activities because of ill health but remained head of her order until 1996, a year before her death. The Roman Catholic Church has begun the process to declare Mother Teresa a saint.

Her Words

It is not enough for us to say: "I love God, but I do not love my neighbor." Saint John says that you are a liar if you say you love God and you don't love your neighbor. How can you love God whom you do not see, if you do not love your neighbor whom you see, whom you touch, with whom you live? And so this is very important for us to realize, that love, to be true, has to hurt.
—Nobel Prize acceptance speech, 1979

The biggest disease today is not leprosy or tuberculosis, but rather the feeling of being unwanted.
—*London Observer,* October 3, 1971

Many people mistake our work for our vocation. Our vocation is the love of Jesus.
—Documentary film *Mother Teresa,* quoted in *New York Times,* November 28, 1986

Books by Mother Teresa

Heart of Joy: The Transforming Power of Self-Giving. Ann Arbor, Mich.: Servant Books, 1987.
Mother Teresa: In My Own Words. New York: Gramercy Books, 1997.
A Simple Path. New York: Ballantine Books, 1995.

Books about Mother Teresa

Chawla, Navin. *Mother Teresa.* London: HarperCollins, 1996.

Muggeridge, Malcolm. *Something Beautiful for God: Mother Teresa of Calcutta.* San Francisco: HarperSanFrancisco, 1986.

Spink, Kathryn. *Mother Teresa: A Complete Authorized Biography.* San Francisco: HarperSanFrancisco, 1998.

For a more complete listing of books by and about Mother Teresa, see www.tisv.be/mt/book.htm.

Organizations

Missionaries of Charity, 45 A. J. C. Bose Rd., Calcutta WB 700016, West-Bengal, India; phone: 033-2447115.

Missionaries of Charity, 335 East 145th St., Bronx, N.Y. 10451; phone: 718-292-0019.

Other Resources

Web site: www.tisv.be/mt/indmt.htm. Mother Teresa's official web site.

Films/Videotapes: *Biography: Mother Teresa—a Life of Devotion,* A & E Biography Series, 1997; *Intimate Portrait: Mother Teresa,* Lifetime Home Video, 1999; *Mother Teresa,* by Ann and Jeanette Petrie, Petrie Productions, available at www.petrieproductions.com; *Mother Teresa: In the Name of God's Poor,* dramatization starring Geraldine Chaplin, Hallmark/Family Channel; *Something Beautiful for God,* by Malcolm Muggeridge, BBC.

Audiotape: *Mother Teresa,* a musical tribute by Jeanne Hardt, recorded in English and Spanish, Songtek Productions, 1997.

"The poor are very wonderful people. One evening we went out and we picked up four people from the street. And one of them was in a most terrible condition. And I told the sisters: 'You take care of the other three; I will take care of this one that looks worse.' So I did for her all that my love can do. I put her in bed, and there was such a beautiful smile on her face. She took hold of my hand, as she said one word only: 'thank you'—and she died."

WALTER RAUSCHENBUSCH
(1861–1918)

• • • • • • •

Born in Rochester, New York, the son of a German-born Lutheran missionary, Walter Rauschenbusch became a leading spokesman in the United States for the Social Gospel movement, which seeks to rectify social and economic injustice in the name of Christianity's prophetic tradition.

In 1886 Rauschenbusch was ordained a minister of the Second German Baptist Church in Hell's Kitchen, a downtrodden New York City neighborhood. There, he saw firsthand an array of social ills, from disease and poverty to ignorance and drunkenness. While many in America blamed the poor for their situation, Rauschenbusch called upon Christians to take responsibility for the disadvantaged by instituting sweeping social changes. In 1891 he studied in Germany for a year and then traveled across Europe. He encountered conditions afflicting the working classes everywhere he went, reinforcing his belief that social reform is a Christian duty. In 1897 he became a professor at Rochester Theological Seminary and later taught church history there.

In 1907 Rauschenbusch published *Christianity and the Social Crisis,* in which he said entry into the Kingdom of God requires not only personal and individual salvation but also efforts toward the betterment of society. He became an icon of the Social Gospel movement, whose platform included the abolition of child labor and better working conditions for adults. Many of these ideas made their way into the organized labor movement of the early twentieth century and were eventually encompassed in the New Deal legislation of the 1930s. Rauschenbusch died in 1918.

Rauschenbusch called upon Christians to take responsibility for the poor and disadvantaged by instituting sweeping social changes.

His Words

Love creates an enjoyment of contact and a desire for more of it, a sense of the worth and human beauty of those we love, pride in their advancement, joy in their happiness, pain in their suffering, a consciousness of unity. . . . This is the wide sense in which we must use the word love if we are to realize the incomparable power and value of love in human life. Our understanding of life depends on our comprehension of the universal power of love. Our capacity to build society depends on our power of calling out love. Our faith in God and Christ is measured by our faith in the value and workableness of love.
—*Dare We Be Christians?* pp. 25–26

If love is the greatest thing in the world and if it is the prime condition of social progress, what of the Christian religion, which has identified itself with faith in love? . . . It clearly needs active personal agents who will incarnate its vitalities, propagate its principles, liberate its undeveloped forces, purify its doctrine, and extend the sway of its faith in love over new realms of social life. Dare we be such men? Dare we be Christians? Those who take up the propaganda of love and substitute freedom and fraternity for coercion and class differences in social life are the pioneers of the Kingdom of God; for the reign of the God of love will be fulfilled in a life of humanity organized on the basis of solidarity and love.
—*Dare We Be Christians?* pp. 46–47

Books by Walter Rauschenbusch

Christianity and the Social Crisis. Nashville, Tenn.: Westminster John Knox Press, 1995.
Christianizing the Social Order. New York: Macmillan, 1912.
Dare We Be Christians? Reprint, Cleveland, Ohio: Pilgrim Press, 1993.
For God and the People: Prayer of the Social Awakening. Boston: Pilgrim Press, 1910.
The Social Principles of Jesus. New York: Grosset & Dunlap, 1916.
A Theology for the Social Gospel. n.p.: Wipf and Stock, 1996.

Books about Walter Rauschenbusch

Fishburn, Janet Forsythe. *The Fatherhood of God and the Victorian Family: The Social Gospel in America.* Philadelphia: Fortress Press, 1982.

Minus, Paul M. *Walter Rauschenbusch: American Reformer.* New York: Macmillan, 1988.

Ramsey, William M. *Four Modern Prophets: Walter Rauschenbusch, Martin Luther King, Jr., Gustavo Gutiérrez, Rosemary Radford Ruether.* Louisville, Ky.: Westminster John Knox Press, 1986.

Sharpe, Dolores Robinson. *Walter Rauschenbusch.* New York: Macmillan, 1942.

"Our understanding of life depends on our comprehension of the universal power of love. Our capacity to build society depends on our power of calling out love. Our faith in God and Christ is measured by our faith in the value and workableness of love."

ALBERT SCHWEITZER
(1875–1965)

One of the world's most famous humanitarians, Albert Schweitzer was a physician, philosopher, theologian, and musicologist. Although Schweitzer was a true citizen of the world whose philanthropy knew no national, racial, or ideological boundaries, it was his missionary work in Africa that won him the 1952 Nobel Peace Prize. His religious philosophy is summed up in his famous phrase "reverence for life," which implies love and compassion toward all living things. He made a significant contribution to biblical scholarship by demonstrating that any search for the "historical Jesus" is inherently subjective and scientifically insufficient, because of the lack of nonbiblical sources, while affirming the mystical spirit of Jesus and emphasizing the eschatological aspects of his teaching. Schweitzer gained renown as an organist and wrote a major study of Johann Sebastian Bach, which stressed the religious nature of his music.

The son of a Lutheran pastor, Albert Schweitzer was born in Kaysersberg, Upper Alsace, which was then in Germany and is now in France. In 1899 he received a doctorate in philosophy from the University of Strasbourg; in 1900 he earned a doctorate in theology as well and was ordained as the curate of the Church of Saint Nicholas in Strasbourg. Out of compassion for human suffering, he began to study medicine in 1905 and earned his M.D. from the University of Strasbourg in 1913.

Schweitzer's religious philosophy is summed up in his famous phrase "reverence for life," which implies love and compassion toward all living things. One of Europe's most renowned musicians and thinkers, he gave it up to study medicine and become a doctor to the disadvantaged in Africa.

Moved by the sight of the Bartholdi statue of a dejected African slave in an Alsatian town square, Schweitzer chose to work in Africa. In 1913 he established a missionary hospital in Lambaréné, Gabon (then in French Equatorial Africa), where he treated thousands of Africans, especially for leprosy and sleeping sickness. Along with his wife, Hélène Bresslau, who worked with him as a nurse, he spent most of the rest of his life there, traveling occasionally to Europe for fund-raising and visiting the United States once, in 1949, to address the Goethe Festival in Colorado. He used his Nobel Prize money to expand his hospital and build a leper colony. Queen Elizabeth II awarded Schweitzer Britain's Order of Merit in 1955.

His Words

Only when we are able to attribute a real meaning to the world and to life shall we be able also to give ourselves to such action as will produce results of real value. As long as we look on our existence in the world as meaningless, there is no point whatever in desiring to effect anything in the world.
—*The Philosophy of Civilization*, p. xiii

Nothing of value in the world is ever accomplished without enthusiasm and self-sacrifice.
—*The Philosophy of Civilization*, p. xiii

Those who regard the decay of civilization as something quite normal and natural console themselves with the thought that it is not civilization, but *a* civilization, which is falling a prey to dissolution; that there will be a new age and a new race in which there will blossom a new civilization. But that is a mistake. The earth no longer has in reserve, as it had once, gifted people as yet unused, who can relieve us and take our place in some distant future as leaders of the spiritual life.
—*The Philosophy of Civilization*, p. 39

Books by Albert Schweitzer

The Animal World of Albert Schweitzer: Jungle Insights into Reverence for Life. Edited by Charles R. Joy. Boston: Beacon Press, 1950.
J. S. Bach. 2 vols. Reprint, New York: Dover, 1988.
The Mysticism of Paul the Apostle. Reprint, Baltimore: Johns Hopkins University Press, 1998.

Out of My Life and Thought: An Autobiography. Reprint, Baltimore: Johns Hopkins University Press, 1998.

The Philosophy of Civilization. Reprint, Buffalo, N.Y.: Prometheus Books, 1987.

The Primeval Forest: Including on the Edge of the Primeval Forest; And, More from the Primeval Forest (The Albert Schweitzer Library). Reprint, Baltimore: Johns Hopkins University Press, 1998.

The Quest of the Historical Jesus: A Critical Study of Its Progress from Reimarus to Wrede. 1906. Reprint, Baltimore: Johns Hopkins University Press, 1998.

Reverence for Life: The Words of Albert Schweitzer. Edited by Harold Robles. San Francisco: HarperSanFrancisco, 1993.

Books about Albert Schweitzer

Brabazon, James. *Albert Schweitzer: A Biography.* Syracuse, N.Y.: Syracuse University Press, 2000.

Marshall, George N., and David Poling. *Schweitzer: A Biography.* Baltimore: Johns Hopkins University Press, 2000.

Organizations

Albert Schweitzer Fellowship, 330 Brookline Ave., Boston, MA 02215; phone: 617-667-5111; web site: www.schweitzerfellowship.org.

Schweitzer Institute, P.O. Box 550, Wallingford, CT 06492; phone: 203-697-3933; e-mail: info@schweitzerinstitute.org; web site: www.schweitzerinstitute.org.

Other Resources

Videotapes: *Albert Schweitzer,* 1958; *The Light in the Jungle,* starring Malcolm McDowell, 1992; *Le Grand Blanc de Lambaréné* (The Great White Man of Lambaréné), French-language movie, by the Cameroonian filmmaker Bassek ba Kobhio, presents an unfavorable view of Schweitzer and the colonial era in Africa, 1994.

CD: *Albert Schweitzer Plays Bach,* organ music, 2 vols.

"Only when we are able to attribute a real meaning to the world and to life shall we be able also to give ourselves to such action as will produce results of real value."

ROBERT HOLBROOK SMITH
(1879–1950)

Known to many today simply as Dr. Bob, Robert Holbrook Smith cofounded Alcoholics Anonymous (AA) with William Griffith Wilson and revolutionized the field of recovery by making spirituality—surrender to a Higher Power—a foundational element. Although some still debate the organization's position that alcoholism is a disease, AA remains the largest organization of its kind in the world, helping millions of alcoholics and inspiring the formation of other Twelve Step addiction recovery programs.

Born to a prominent family in St. Johnsbury, Vermont, Smith became a serious drinker while attending Dartmouth University. His drinking continued while he was a premed student at the University of Michigan. Smith settled in Akron, Ohio, and established a practice after completing his surgical residency at City Hospital.

Unlike many other Prohibition-era drinkers, who had to make do with "bathtub gin," Smith was able to obtain pure grain alcohol, which was available at pharmacies with a doctor's prescription. He managed to maintain his medical practice despite his addiction and began to use large doses of tranquilizers to calm his tremors.

In 1933, prodded by his wife, he attended a meeting of the Oxford Group, a Christian fellowship that advocated the Four Absolutes: honesty, purity, unselfishness, and love. The group practiced the principles of self-survey, confession, restitution, and service to others—concepts that later grew into the Twelve Steps of AA.

Robert Holbrook Smith (Dr. Bob) revolutionized the field of recovery by making spirituality—surrender to a higher power—a foundational element.

In 1935 Smith met Bill Wilson, a fellow alcoholic who had already quit drinking. Wilson moved into his home with the encouragement of

Smith's wife and members of the Oxford Group. On June 10, Smith took his last drink. This date is generally acknowledged as the founding of Alcoholics Anonymous, although in the early days AA was still a part of the Oxford Group. Smith and Wilson began working with patients in Akron who were hospitalized for alcoholism, using a combination of medication and prayer. Anonymity became a foundation of the group, and Smith and Wilson became known as Bob S. and Bill W.

His Words

Our Twelve Steps, when simmered down to the last, resolve themselves into the words *love* and *service.* We understand what love is and we understand what service is. So let's bear those two things in mind.
—Address at the first international conference of Alcoholics Anonymous, Cleveland, Ohio, 1950

It's about accountability. If we are helping others, then we must stay focused on our sobriety and we are constantly being reminded of the tools we learn in our recovery groups for living "substance free."

Just like our walk with God. We must stay in His word, pray and meditate on His word, and surround ourselves with people who are also believers of God. Yes for accountability and for growth and knowledge in God's precepts.

The two go hand in hand—accountability to God first and to other addicts by helping them in their recovery walk.
—*Dr. Bob and the Good Oldtimers,* pp. 76–77

Books about Robert Holbrook Smith

Dr. Bob and the Good Oldtimers. New York: Alcoholics Anonymous World Services, 1980.

Robertson, Nan. *Getting Better: Inside Alcoholics Anonymous.* New York: William Morrow, 1988.

Organization

Alcoholics Anonymous, Grand Central Station, P.O. Box 459, New York, NY 10163; web site: www.aa.org.

"Our Twelve Steps, when simmered down to the last, resolve themselves into the words love *and* service. *We understand what love is and we understand what service is. So let's bear those two things in mind."*

THICH NHAT HANH
(1926–)

• • • • • • • •

In exile from his native Vietnam since 1966, the Buddhist monk, scholar, and author Thich Nhat Hanh is a politically and spiritually inspirational figure to many. Pioneer of the concept of engaged Buddhism, he combines social action and civil disobedience with traditional Buddhist meditation practice and spirituality.

Thich Nhat Hanh, or Thây ("teacher" in Vietnamese), as his followers call him, was born in central Vietnam. He became a Buddhist monk at the age of sixteen and by twenty-four had founded the An Quang Buddhist Institute, a center of Buddhist learning in South Vietnam. In the early 1960s Thich Nhat Hanh came to the United States for two years to study and teach comparative religion at Columbia and Princeton Universities. When the war broke out in Vietnam, he returned to his homeland and undertook a program of social action that included founding a peace magazine, lobbying world leaders to stop the war, and launching the School of Youth for Social Service, which brought Buddhist peace workers to the region.

In 1966, when he was forty, Thich Nhat Hanh's peace activism caused him to be banished from Vietnam by the governments of both the Communist north and the non-Communist south for his role in undermining the war effort and opposing the violence that he saw as destructive and meaningless. Even though the region is no longer unstable, he has not been allowed to return home.

Thich Nhat Hanh has traveled the world with the mission of spreading Buddhist thought and a message of mindfulness, respect for life, generosity, and reconciliation.

After his exile Thich Nhat Hanh traveled the world spreading Buddhist thought and a message of mindfulness, respect for life, generosity, and reconciliation. He also continued his advocacy of nonviolence, addressing college audiences and political leaders alike. In 1967 the nonviolent peace activist Martin Luther King, Jr., nominated Thich Nhat Hanh for the Nobel Peace Prize.

Well into the 1970s, Thich Nhat Hanh orchestrated rescue missions for Vietnamese trying to escape political oppression. He also led a Buddhist delegation to the Paris peace talks that helped broker an accord between Vietnam and the United States. In 1982 he founded a retreat center and Buddhist community in France called Plum Village, where he offers spiritual lessons in mindfulness, the practice of existing wholly in the present moment. He also continues to travel, drawing crowds from all races, religions, and nationalities.

His Words

On the altar in my hermitage in France are images of Buddha and Jesus, and every time I light incense, I touch both of them as my spiritual ancestors. I can do this because of contact with these real Christians. When you touch someone who authentically represents a tradition, you not only touch his or her tradition, you also touch your own. This quality is essential for dialogue.
—*Living Buddha, Living Christ*, pp. 6–7

Meditation is not to get out of society, to escape from society, but to prepare for a re-entry into society. We call this "engaged Buddhism." When we go to a meditation center, we may have the impression that we leave everything behind—family, society, and all the complications involved in them—and come as an individual in order to practice and search for peace. This is already an illusion, because in Buddhism, there is no such thing as an individual.
—*Being Peace*, p. 47

Books by Thich Nhat Hanh

Anger: Wisdom for Cooling the Flames. New York: Riverhead Books, 2001.
Being Peace. Edited by Arnold Kotler. Illustrated by Mayumi Oda. Berkeley: Parallax Press, 1987.
Fragrant Palm Leaves: Journals, 1962–1966. Translated by Mobi Warren. Berkeley: Parallax Press, 1998.

The Heart of the Buddha's Teaching: Transforming Suffering into Peace, Joy, and Liberation. Berkeley: Parallax Press, 1998.

Living Buddha, Living Christ. New York: Riverhead Books, 1995.

The Miracle of Mindfulness: A Manual on Meditation. Translated by Mobi Ho. Boston: Beacon Press, 1987.

Zen Keys. Translated by Albert and Jean Low. Garden City, N.Y.: Anchor Books, 1974.

Organizations

Plum Village: Upper Hamlet (for men): Le Pey, 24240, Thenac, France; phone: 33-5-53-58-48-58; fax: 33-5-53-57-34-43; e-mail: UH-office@plumvillage.org.

Plum Village: Lower Hamlet (for women): Meyrac, 47120 Loubes-Bernac, France; phone: 33-5-53-94-75-40; fax: 33-5-53-94-75-90; e-mail: LH-office@plumvillage.org.

Green Mountain Dharma Center (for men): P.O. Box 354, South Woodstock, Vermont 05071; phone: 802-457-2786/9442; fax: 802-457-8170; e-mail: stoneboy@vermontel.net.

Green Mountain Dharma Center (for women): P.O. Box 182, Ayres Lane, Hartland-Four-Corners, VT 05049; phone: 802-436-1103/1102; fax: 802-436-1101; e-mail: MF-office@plumvillage.org.

Deer Park Monastery: 2499 Melru Lane, Escondido, CA 92026; phone: 760-291-1003; fax: 760-291-1172; e-mail: deerpark@plumvillage.org

Other Resources

Web site: www.plumvillage.org. Official web site of Plum Village.

"Meditation is not to get out of society, to escape from society, but to prepare for a re-entry into society. We call this 'engaged Buddhism.'"

7

THEY BROUGHT THE **TRADITIONS** TOGETHER

The twentieth century saw unprecedented levels of interfaith mixing and matching. Surely advances in communications and travel facilitated this spiritual cross-pollination. But so did a growing view that the great religious paths, whatever their apparent contradictions, all lead to the same ultimate source.

Some groups recoiled at the displays of universal acceptance, such as those witnessed at the 1993 and 1999 Parliaments of the World's Religions, giving rise to a traditionalist backlash that turned increasingly sharp, and even violent, as the century drew to a close. By contrast, many progressives—particularly in the West—embraced this multiculturalism, seeing in it the dawn of a golden, almost messianic, age during which millennia of ignorance and prejudice might be overcome, and shamanist and monotheist might embrace respectfully.

The spiritual universalist regards all life as one. That was the message of the Oglala Sioux shaman and healer known to his people as Hehaka Sapa and to the world at large as Black Elk. After centuries of colonial powers' trying to stamp them out, tribal traditions such as his gained renewed respect in the multicultural spirit. *Black Elk Speaks,* Hehaka Sapa's life story as told to the poet John Neihardt, is the century's classic account of one tradition. As such, it became a stand-in for all tribal paths.

Colonialism, trade, migration, and adventurism spread religious traditions around the globe. Meher Baba, who declared himself Avatar of our age, was born of a Zoroastrian family in India but taught in universal terms appealing to Muslims, Hindus, Christians, and Jews as well, epitomizing the religious mingling of East and West. However, it was not until the twentieth century that the spiritual traditions of the East, from Arabia to Southeast Asia, traveled to the West in a big way. The pioneers included Paramahansa Yogananda, author of the classic *Autobiography of a Yogi;* Hazrat Inayat Khan, among the first Sufi mystics to affect the West; Bawa Muhaiyaddeen, another Sufi; and J. Krishnamurti, the reluctant guru who advocated a spiritual life free of all "isms." Each of them established organizations in the West that attracted spiritual seekers willing to step beyond their cultural and theological roots.

Seyyed Hossein Nasr's efforts to bring traditions together are of another sort. True, he is also a teacher. But his is a traditional academic path. His task has been to explain traditional Islamic values to Westerners—no small feat given the conflict between the West and some who espouse a political Islam.

Then there were those such as Bede Griffiths. He traveled the other way, from West to East, but not as a missionary. Griffiths was a British-born Benedictine monk who exuded gentleness and who embraced the Hindu form. In 1955 he went to India to establish a Hindu-style ashram for the pursuit of Christian contemplation. His journey became a well-worn path for many Westerners as the century progressed.

By the century's end spiritual multiculturalism had advanced to a degree that in some cases it was difficult to separate East from West, the spiritual from the temporal, science from faith. This is especially true for Deepak Chopra and Andrew Weil.

Chopra was born in New Delhi but was thoroughly Western in his scientific outlook until, while practicing medicine in New England, he turned to the most Western of Eastern contemplative disciplines, Transcendental Meditation. Making radical changes in his life, he returned to his cultural roots and Ayurvedic medicine, India's ancient and holistic system for healthy living. He then proceeded to package his mind-body paradigm for Western audiences, who made him a highly popular seminar leader and best-selling author.

Weil, from Philadelphia, is also a Western-trained physician. He moved away from that model with the help, at least in part, of Amerindian tribal shamans and healers skilled in the spiritual-psychological-medicinal use of consciousness-altering drugs. Weil also became a highly popular speaker and writer spreading the gospel of spiritually supported, holistic, natural living as the antidote for the end of the century's many lifestyle- and chemically induced ailments. His contributions to the fields of ethnomycology, ethnobotany, and ethnopharmacology were recognized when a psychedelic mushroom, *Psilocybe weilii,* was named after him. Appropriately, the mushroom was discovered in Georgia's Cherokee County, named after a tribal group struggling to maintain traditional beliefs while living in the staunchly monotheistic subculture of the American South.

BAWA MUHAIYADDEEN
(c. 1885–1986)

Among the first to bring Sufism to the West, Bawa Muhaiyaddeen has written some of the most translated and disseminated words of any teacher of Islamic mysticism. With only a halting command of English, he built a following that meticulously recorded and cataloged his speeches, continuing even today to compile books of his teachings.

Little is known of Bawa Muhaiyaddeen's early years. Believed to have been born at least fifteen years before the turn of the century, he spent most of his life in his native Sri Lanka. In the early 1900s word started to spread of a mystic living in the Sri Lankan jungle, and his home became a frequent pilgrimage stop. One pilgrim invited him to speak in the nearby village of Jaffna, and his public ministry was born. His talks soon attracted an eclectic mix of spiritual seekers, despite his use of a difficult-to-understand form of classical Tamil.

He spent several years teaching a small band of followers in predominantly Hindu Jaffna before answering an invitation to teach in Colombo, the Sri Lankan capital. There the Serenedib Sufi Study Circle was formed around his teachings and began to transcribe and publish his talks. In response to yet another invitation, he came to Philadelphia in 1971 and established the Bawa Muhaiyaddeen Fellowship. He spent the remainder of his life teaching at the fellowship's center, on college campuses, and elsewhere. He appealed to seekers from a broad spectrum of religious traditions, with his emphasis on love for all beings and

Bawa Muhaiyaddeen taught a Sufism that appealed to seekers from a broad spectrum of religious traditions, with his emphasis on love for all beings and the potential for a personal experience of the divine.

the potential for a personal experience of the divine. He taught simple, emotionally evocative rituals, such as *dhikr*—chanting the ninety-nine Islamic names for God—and the practice of repeating a mantra in one's head with every breath. Although many of his followers adopted traditional Muslim lifestyles, he never insisted they do so.

Upon his death, Bawa Muhaiyaddeen was buried in the United States' first *mazar,* or Muslim shrine. His presence remains palpable at the fellowship's center, where his bedroom is kept intact, videos and audiotapes of his speeches are frequently played, and his followers maintain a schedule of classes, early-morning *dhikr,* free vegetarian meals, and Muslim prayer services at the center and its adjacent mosque.

His Words

When a prospector searches for gold, he must sift the earth in order to extract this precious metal. He takes what is valuable and discards the rest. Similarly, wherever you search, whether it be in the east, west, north, or south, whether it be in Hinduism, Zoroastrianism, Christianity, Judaism, or Islam, you must search for and extract only that one valuable thing, the gold, the treasure of God, the truth. As you search through all the scriptures, you must discard everything else, just as the prospectors discard the dirt and stones. God's wealth is all you need for your life and for the resplendence of your soul.
—*Islam and World Peace,* p. 40

Say, "*La ilaha, ill-Allahu.*" Do not waste your breath. With every breath say, "*La ilaha ill-Allahu.*" Whatever time it is, you should never remain idle. Whether you are staying here or elsewhere, these words have to be said. They must be said with your breath. You do not have to make a sound. Your tongue should gently form the words within your mouth. You should say, "*La ilaha ill-Allahu.*" The outgoing breath, *La ilaha:* Other than You nothing exists, should be drawn along with awareness.
—*With Every Breath Say, "La ilaha ill-Allahu,"* pamphlet published by Bawa Muhaiyaddeen Fellowship, p.1

Books by Bawa Muhaiyaddeen

Dhikr: The Remembrance of God. Philadelphia: Fellowship Press, 1999.

Four Steps to Pure Iman. Philadelphia: Fellowship Press, 1979.
Islam and World Peace: Explanations of a Sufi. Philadelphia: Fellowship Press, 1987.
My Love, You My Children: One Hundred and One Stories for Children of All Ages. Philadelphia: Fellowship Press, 1979.
To Die before Death: The Sufi Way of Life. Philadelphia: Fellowship Press, 1997.

For a more complete list of books by Bawa Muhaiyaddeen, see *Islam and World Peace,* p. 165.

Organization

Bawa Muhaiyaddeen Fellowship, 5820 Overbrook Ave., Philadelphia, PA 19131-1221; phone: 215-879-6300; fax: 215-879-6307; e-mail: info@bmf.org; web site: www.bmf.org.

Other Resources

Mazar: The tomb of Bawa Muhaiyaddeen in rural Chester County, Pennsylvania, has become a popular pilgrimage site.

"God's wealth is all you need for your life and for the resplendence of your soul."

BLACK ELK
(c. 1863–1950)

Known to his people as Hehaka Sapa, Black Elk was a shaman and healer who witnessed the near-destruction of traditional Native American tribal life by the European industrial culture. Pivotal to his spiritual mission was a powerful childhood vision that he recounted in the book *Black Elk Speaks.* Its publication was instrumental in helping the world understand the American Indian perspective on religion, culture, and way of life.

An Oglala Lakota Sioux, Black Elk was born at Little Powder River, Wyoming. At age nine, while seriously ill, he had what might be described as a vision or a near-death experience. He saw descend from the sky two men who told him, "Hurry up, your grandfather is calling you." He was then raised into the clouds, where he met six old men, whom he understood to be the Powers of the World. Each of these Grandfathers bestowed upon Black Elk a special power: healing, cleansing, awakening and peace, growth, transcendent vision, and regeneration.

From atop a high mountain, he was shown the hoop of the world and how all life is one. He was then sent back to his body in his parents' tipi, where they informed him that he had lain unconscious for twelve days. He didn't speak about his vision until eight years later, when he finally told a medicine man, who helped him transform the vision into a ritual.

The publication of Black Elk Speaks *was instrumental in helping the world understand the American Indian perspective on religion, culture, and way of life.*

At age thirteen Black Elk was a warrior in the Battle of Little Bighorn. He later became a medicine man, and from 1887 to 1889 he performed with the Buffalo Bill Wild West Show, traveling to New York, England, France, and Italy. In 1890 he witnessed the massacre of the Sioux at Wounded Knee. He converted to Christianity in 1904 and took the name Nicholas Black Elk, saying, "My children have to live in this world." In 1931 he told his life story to the poet John Neihardt; it was published as *Black Elk Speaks.* He gave annual medicine-man performances to educate non-Indians about Native American culture and religion.

His Words

Then I was standing on the highest mountain of them all, and round about beneath me was the whole hoop of the world. And while I stood there I saw more than I can tell and I understood more than I saw; for I was seeing in a sacred manner the shapes of all things in the spirit, and the shape of all shapes as they must live together like one being. And I saw that the sacred hoop of my people was one of many hoops that made one circle, wide as daylight and as starlight, and in the center grew one mighty flowering tree to shelter all the children of one mother and one father. And I saw that it was holy.
—*Black Elk Speaks,* p. 33

There was once a Lakota holy man, called Drinks Water, who dreamed what was to be; and this was long before the coming of the Wasichus (white man). He dreamed that the four-leggeds were going back into the earth and that a strange race had woven a spider's web all around the Lakotas. And he said: "When this happens, you shall live in square gray houses, in a barren land, and beside those square gray houses you shall starve." . . . Sometimes dreams are wiser than waking.
—*Black Elk Speaks,* p. 8

Book by Black Elk

Black Elk Speaks: Being the Life Story of a Holy Man of the Oglala Sioux. Edited by John G. Neihardt. 1961. Reprint, Lincoln: University of Nebraska Press, 2000.

Books about Black Elk

Brown, Joseph E., ed. *The Sacred Pipe: Black Elk's Account of the Seven Rites of the Oglala Sioux.* Civilization of the American Indian Series, vol. 36. Norman: University of Oklahoma Press, 1989.

Demallie, Raymond J., ed. *The Sixth Grandfather: Black Elk's Teachings Given to John G. Neihardt.* Lincoln: University of Nebraska Press, 1985.

Desersa, Esther Black Elk, Hilda Neihardt Petri, et al., eds. *Black Elk Lives: Conversations with the Black Elk Family.* Lincoln: University of Nebraska Press, 2000.

Steltenkamp, Michael F. *Black Elk: Holy Man of the Oglala.* Norman: University of Oklahoma Press, 1993.

Other Resources

Videotape: *Black Elk,* Charlotte Black Elk speaks about her great-grandfather, C-SPAN.

"Grandfather, Great Spirit, once more behold me on earth and lean to hear my feeble voice. You lived first, and you are older than all need, older than all prayer. All things belong to you—the two-leggeds, the four-leggeds, the wings of the air and all green things that live."

DEEPAK CHOPRA
(1947–)

A physician who is a leader in integrative medicine, Deepak Chopra has brought Western science together with Eastern wisdom to create new approaches to health emphasizing the connection between body, mind, and spirit, and using meditation, herbal remedies, yoga, and massage. He has popularized the healing methods of Ayurveda, the traditional medicine of India, and presented a view of holistic well-being that encompasses both personal success and spiritual advancement.

Chopra was born in New Delhi, the eldest son of a British-trained Indian cardiologist. Following his father's footsteps, he graduated from the All India Institute of Medical Sciences in 1968. Chopra came to the United States in 1970 and became chief of staff at New England Memorial Hospital in the early 1980s. He began practicing Transcendental Meditation (TM) and made radical changes in his habits and way of life. In 1985 he met the TM movement's founder, Maharishi Mahesh Yogi, who suggested that he study Ayurveda. Subsequently Chopra became the founding president of the American Association for Ayurvedic Medicine. He was later named medical director of the Maharishi Ayur-Veda Health Center in Massachusetts. Several of Chopra's early books, inspired by the Maharishi's work, promoted the value of meditation and other practices drawn from the teachings of the Vedas (ancient scriptures of India) as an aid to combating disease and the effects of aging.

Chopra has made a lasting impact with his contributions to alternative medicine and his message of "infinite possibilities" through living in harmony with spiritual laws.

Chopra broke with TM in 1993 and went on to develop his own programs. No longer a clinical practitioner, he became a prominent motivational speaker and a leader of public seminars and workshops. He also conducts professional training around the world. He has published numerous best-selling books, audiotapes and videotapes, and CDs. Despite criticism from medical colleagues who question his approach, Chopra has made a lasting impact with his contributions to alternative medicine and his message of "infinite possibilities" through living in harmony with spiritual laws.

His Words

Life at its source is creation. When you get in touch with your own inner intelligence, you get in touch with the creative core of life. In the old paradigm, control of life was assigned to DNA, an enormously complex molecule that has revealed less than 1 percent of its secrets to geneticists. In the new paradigm, control of life belongs to awareness. All the examples . . . of children who can curtail the secretion of growth hormone, medical students who alter their output of interleukins when they feel anxious, yogis who can manipulate their heartbeat at will, indicate that the most basic bodily processes respond to our state of mind.
—*Ageless Body, Timeless Mind,* p. 36

Intention combined with detachment leads to life-centered, present-moment awareness. And when an action is performed in present-moment awareness, it is most effective. Your intent is for the future, but your attention is in the present. As long as your attention is in the present, then your intent for the future will manifest, because the future is created in the present. You must accept the present as is. Accept the present and intend the future.
—*The Seven Spiritual Laws of Success,* p. 73

Books by Deepak Chopra

Ageless Body, Timeless Mind. New York: Harmony Books, 1993.
Boundless Energy: The Complete Mind/Body Program for Overcoming Chronic Fatigue. New York: Three Rivers Press, 1997.
How to Know God: The Soul's Journey into the Mystery of Mysteries. New York: Random House, 2000.

Journey into Healing: Awakening the Wisdom within You. New York: Harmony Books, 1999.

The Path to Love: Renewing the Power of Spirit in Your Life. New York: Harmony Books, 1997.

Quantum Healing: Exploring the Frontiers of Mind/Body Medicine and Creating Health. New York: Bantam Books, 1990.

The Return of the Rishi: A Doctor's Search for the Ultimate Healer. 1988. Reprint, Boston: Houghton Mifflin, 1991.

The Seven Spiritual Laws of Success. San Rafael, Calif.: New World Library, Amber Allen, 1994.

Organizations

Chopra Center for Well Being, 7630 Fay Ave., La Jolla, CA 92037; phone: 888-424-6772; e-mail: info@chopra.com. Mind-body healing retreat center and spa.

Quantum Publications, P.O. Box 1088, Sudbury, MA 01776; phone: 800-858-1808. Books, audiotapes and videotapes, workshops.

Other Resources

Web site: www.chopra.com.

Videotapes/DVDs: *Body, Mind, and Soul: The Mystery and the Magic; The Seven Spiritual Laws of Success/Crystal Cave,* 2000; *The Way of the Wizard/Alchemy: The Art of Spiritual Transformation,* 1999.

"As long as your attention is in the present, then your intent for the future will manifest, because the future is created in the present."

BEDE GRIFFITHS
(1906–1993)

A leading figure in interfaith dialogue, the Benedictine monk Bede Griffiths lived in a Christian ashram (hermitage) in India and wore the robes of a Hindu holy man. He was not only learned in both Christian theology and Indian philosophy but also accomplished in mystical contemplation. Father Bede conveyed the unity of the two traditions through his many books and articles as well as daily teachings at his ashram and lectures around the world.

Born Alan Richard Griffiths to a middle-class Anglican family in Walton-on-Thames, England, he studied English literature, philosophy, and journalism at Oxford, where C. S. Lewis became his tutor and friend. Initially an atheist, Griffiths was drawn into Christian spirituality following a yearlong experiment in simple, communal living in the countryside. After a period of intense prayer, fasting, and introspection, he converted to Roman Catholicism in 1931 and the next year became a Benedictine novice at Prinknash Abbey, receiving the name Bede, which means "prayer." He was ordained in 1940.

Father Bede received permission to go to India in 1955 to found a monastery. Eventually he became the leader of the Saccidananda Ashram (also known as Shantivanam), established by two French monks in the South Indian state of Tamil Nadu. In pursuing a life of Christian contemplation in a Hindu context, Father Bede discovered what he called "the other half of my soul." In emulation of the Indian monastic tradition, he took the Sanskrit name Dhayananda, meaning "bliss of prayer"; still later he took the name Dayananda, "bliss of compassion." While ever faithful to his Christian identity, Father Bede embodied a genuine universality of spirit. Along with Thomas Merton

In pursuing a life of Christian contemplation in a Hindu context, Bede Griffiths discovered what he called "the other half of my soul."

and Henry La Saux, he showed the way to a Christian spirituality that is transformed by the ancient spiritual traditions of Asia. He traveled widely to spread his message of unity, lecturing in the United States, Europe, and Australia, and participating in many East-West dialogues in monastic communities.

His Words

There is a final transcendent state of Being and Consciousness, in which alone perfect bliss is to be found, to which every religion bears witness. This state transcends all concepts of the mind and images of the senses, and is known only when the Divine Being chooses to reveal himself to man. This is the ultimate mystery, the ultimate truth, to which everything in nature aspires, but which so transcends the whole order of nature that it appears as darkness rather than light, as something unreal and illusory, as a Void, a Silence, a Negation of Being. And yet such is the witness of every great religious tradition: in this Void, in this Darkness, in this Silence, all fullness, all light, all truth, all goodness, all love, all joy, all peace, all happiness is to be found.
—*Vedanta and Christian Faith,* p. 163

Books by Bede Griffiths

Christ in India: Essays towards a Christian-Hindu Dialogue. Springfield, Ill.: Templegate Publishers, 1994.

The Cosmic Revelation: The Hindu Way to God. Springfield, Ill.: Templegate Publishers, 1994.

The Golden String: An Autobiography. 1954. Springfield, Ill.: Templegate Publishers, 1992.

The Marriage of East and West: A Sequal to the Golden String. Springfield, Ill.: Templegate Publishers, 1992.

The One Light: Bede Griffiths' Principal Writings. Edited by Bruno Barnhart. Springfield, Ill.: Templegate Publishers, 2001.

Return to the Center. Springfield, Ill.: Templegate Publishers, 1994.

River of Compassion: A Christian Commentary on the Bhagavad Gita. Springfield, Ill.: Templegate Publishers, 2001.

Vedanta and Christian Faith. Clearlake, Calif.: Dawn Horse Press, 1991.

Universal Wisdom: A Journey through the Sacred Wisdom of the World. Selected and introduced by Bede Griffiths. San Francisco: HarperSanFrancisco, 1994.

Books about Bede Griffiths

Bruteau, Beatrice, ed. *The Other Half of My Soul: Bede Griffiths and the Hindu-Christian Dialogue.* Wheaton, Ill.: Quest Books, 1996.

Du Boulay, Shirley. *Beyond the Darkness: A Biography of Bede Griffiths.* New York: Doubleday, 1998.

Swindells, John, ed. *A Human Search: Bede Griffiths Reflects on His Life: An Oral History.* Interview by Andrew Harvey and John Swindells. Liguori, Mo.: Triumph Books, 1997.

Organizations

Saccidananda Ashram, Shantivanam, Tannirpalli 639 107, Kulittalai-Trichy District, Tamil Nadu, India; e-mail: saccidananda@hotmail.com.

The Bede Griffiths Sangha, Beech Tree Cottage, Gushmere, Kent ME13 9RH United Kingdom; phone: +44 (0) 1227-1227-752871; e-mail: bg.sangha@btinternet.com.

New Camaldoli Hermitage, Big Sur, CA 93920; phone: 831-667-2456.

Osage Monastery, 18701 W. Monastery Rd., Sand Springs, OK 74063; phone: 918-245-2734.

Other Resources

Web site: www.bedegriffiths.com.

Videotapes: *Discovering the Feminine; The History and Interpretation of the Bible; A Human Search: The Life of Father Bede Griffiths; The Space in the Heart of the Lotus: Bede Griffiths and the Hindu-Christian Contemplative Experience;* Carlsbad, Calif.: available from Inner Directions Foundation; phone: 760-599-4075. *The Wisdom of a Prophet;* New York: available from Parabola; phone: 800-783-4903.

Audiotapes: *East and West: The Mystical Connection; Return to the Sacred; Sacred Music: Gateway to the Infinite with Father Bede Griffiths and Russill and Asha Paul;* Ukiah, Calif.: available from New Dimensions Tapes; phone: 800-935-8273.

"[The meeting between East and West] must take place at the deepest level of the human consciousness. It is an encounter ultimately between the two fundamental dimensions of human nature: the male and female—the masculine, rational, active, dominating power of the mind, and the feminine, intuitive, passive and receptive power.

—*The Marriage of East and West*, p. 151

HAZRAT INAYAT KHAN
(1882–1927)

The Indian teacher Pir-o-Murshid Hazrat Inayat Khan was the first person to bring Sufism—the mystical tradition of Islam—to the Western world; thus, he was the forerunner of the many Sufi groups that have since flourished here. He founded the Sufi Order International, a unique organization that emphasizes the wisdom found in all religious traditions.

Born into a musical, intellectual Muslim family in Baroda, India, Inayat Khan grew up in a household where discussions of religious, philosophic, and artistic matters were part of daily life and where non-Muslim religious traditions were treated with respect and honor. The young Inayat Khan received training in classical Indian music and by his late teens had become a renowned concert artist as a master of the vina, an Indian stringed instrument.

At the height of his fame as a performer, Inayat Khan met the renowned Sufi teacher Mohammed Abu Hasana, a member of the Chishti Sufi Order. He immediately became Hasana's disciple. In his four years of close contact with Hasana, Inayat Khan experienced a level of realization that made God a reality in his life and made him into a natural teacher of the Sufi way of life. As his master lay dying, he instructed Inayat Khan to go to the Western world and teach. In September 1910, Inayat Khan sailed for America to fulfill his teacher's direction. He spoke, taught, and performed on the vina among small groups of Americans and Europeans—at first not even identifying his teaching with the word *Sufism*—

Hazrat Inayat Khan experienced a level of realization that made God a reality in his life and that made him into a natural teacher of the Sufi way of life.

and emphasizing, as his teacher had before him, the essential unity of truth that can be found through all religions. A movement grew around him.

Around 1920 he settled in a suburb of Paris, where he established a school, wrote many volumes, and developed the Universal Worship Service of his Sufi Order International, which includes reading from the texts of many religions. He died in India in 1927, on his first trip there since his departure.

His son, Pir Vilayat Khan, has continued to spread his father's message of nonsectarian Sufism in the West.

His Words

Sympathy breaks the congestion of the heart.
—*The Complete Sayings of Hazrat Inayat Khan,* no. 381

The nature of love is as the nature of water in the depth of the earth. If we do not dig deep enough, we find mud, not water; but when we dig deep, we find pure water.
—*The Complete Sayings of Hazrat Inayat Khan,* no. 1728

The Sufi sees the one truth in all its forms. If anyone asks a Sufi to come and offer prayer in the Christian church, he is ready to do so. If someone would like to take him to the synagogue and pray as the Jews do, he would be quite willing; and among Muslims, he will offer *nimaz* [prayers] as they do. In the Hindu temple he sees the same God, the living God, in the place of the idol; the temple of the Buddha inspires him instead of blinding him with idolatry. Yet his true mosque will be his heart in which the Beloved lives, who is worshiped by both Muslim and Kufr [unbeliever] alike.
—*The Heart of Sufism,* p. 4

Books by Hazrat Inayat Khan

The Complete Sayings of Hazrat Inayat Khan. New Lebanon, N.Y.: Omega Press, 1991.

The Heart of Sufism: Essential Writings of Hazrat Inayat Khan. Boston: Shambhala Publications, 1999.

The Inner Life. Boston: Shambhala Publications, 1997.

The Sufi Message of Hazrat Inayat Khan. 14 vols. New Lebanon, N.Y.: Omega Press, 1961–1967.

Books about Hazrat Inayat Khan

De Jong-Keesing, Elizabeth. *Inayat Khan: A Biography.* The Hague: East West Publications, 1974.

Khan, Pir Vilayat Inayat. *The Message in Our Time: The Life and Teaching of the Sufi Master Pir-o-Murshid Inayat Khan.* San Francisco: Harper & Row, 1978.

Khan, Pirzade Zia Inayat. *A Pearl in Wine: Essays on the Life, Music, and Sufism of Hazrat Inayat Khan.* New Lebanon, N.Y.: Omega Publications, 2001.

Organization

Sufi Order International North American Secretariat, P.O. Box 30065, Seattle, WA 98103; phone: 206-525-6992; fax: 206-525-7013.

Other Resources

Web site: www.sufiorder.org. Official web site of the Sufi Order International.

"The nature of love is as the nature of water in the depth of the earth. If we do not dig deep enough, we find mud, not water; but when we dig deep, we find pure water."

J. KRISHNAMURTI
(1895–1986)

Proclaimed a great world teacher by the leaders of the Theosophical Society, Jiddu Krishnamurti went on to renounce the role thrust upon him and to advocate pursuit of the spiritual life outside organized religion and free from "isms" of any kind.

Krishnamurti was born in a small village in South India and moved with his family to the city of Madras when he was a young boy. It was there that he met Annie Besant, an Englishwoman who was head of the esoteric Theosophical Society; she became convinced that he was destined to be the great spiritual teacher of the modern age. She adopted him and took him with her to England, where he was educated and prepared for his anticipated role. But in 1929, after years of questioning himself and his destiny, Krishnamurti broke with the Theosophical Society, proclaiming famously that "truth is a pathless land."

His fame as a spiritual teacher became even greater after his departure from the society. He preached a spirituality free from dogma, ritual, and authority figures—a message for which there was, and remains, a large and enthusiastic audience. Krishnamurti evolved his unique teaching from his own being and living, for he had read no religious or philosophical literature. His aim was to set people psychologically free so that they might be in harmony with themselves, with nature, and with others. He taught that humankind has created the environment in which we live and that nothing can ever put a stop to violence and suffering except a transformation in the human psyche.

Krishnamurti preached a spirituality free from dogma, ritual, and authority figures—a message for which there was, and remains, a large and enthusiastic audience.

From 1929 until his death in 1986, Krishnamurti continued to travel and teach; his talks were recorded and compiled into a large number of books.

His Words

Truth is a pathless land. Man cannot come to it through any organization, through any creed, through any dogma, priest or ritual, nor through any philosophic technique. He has to find it through the mirror of relationship, through the understanding of the contents of his own mind, through observation and not through intellectual analysis or introspective dissection. Man has built in himself images as a fence of security—religious, political, personal. These manifest as symbols, ideas, beliefs. The burden of these images dominates man's thinking, his relationships, and his daily life. These images are the cause of our problems, for they divide man from man.
—Speech on leaving the Theosophical Society, 1929

Books by J. Krishnamurti

The Awakening of Intelligence. San Francisco: HarperSanFrancisco, 1987.
Freedom from the Known. San Francisco: HarperSanFrancisco, 1979.
Think on These Things. New York: HarperCollins, 1989.
Total Freedom: The Essential Krishnamurti. San Francisco: HarperSanFrancisco, 1996.

Books about J. Krishnamurti

Fields, Sydney. *Krishnamurti: The Reluctant Messiah.* New York: Paragon House, 1989.
Jayakar, Pupul. *Krishnamurti: A Biography.* San Francisco: Harper & Row, 1986.
Lutyens, Mary. *Krishnamurti: His Life and Death.* New York: St. Martin's Press, 1991.
———. *Krishnamurti: The Early Years.* Boston: Shambhala Publications, 1997.

Organizations

Krishnamurti Foundation of America, Ojai, CA.; phone: 805-646-2726; e-mail: kfa@kfa.org.

Krishnamurti Foundation Trust, Brockwood Park, Bramdean, Hampshire SO24 0LQ, England; phone: 44-1962-771-525.

Other Resources

Web site: www.kfa.org. Official web site of the Krishnamurti Foundation of America.

Videotapes: *The Transformation of Man,* five videotapes of Krishnamurti in dialogue with the physicist David Bohm and the psychiatrist David Shainberg, 1976.

"Truth is a pathless land. Man . . . has to find it through the mirror of relationship, through the understanding of the contents of his own mind, through observation and not through intellectual analysis or introspective dissection."

MEHER BABA
(1894–1969)

• • • • • • •

Meher Baba declared himself the Avatar of our age—God in human form, whose most recent advents were as Muhammad, Jesus, Buddha, Krishna, Rama, and Zoroaster. The Avatar's message, he said, is always essentially the same—"Love God and serve God in others"—adapted to the needs of humanity during each advent. His aim was not to bring a new message but to breathe life into the old by revitalizing the major spiritual paths.

Born Merwan Sheriar Irani to a Zoroastrian family in Pune, India, he was awakened to his divinity in 1913 when kissed on the forehead by Hazrat Babajan, a Muslim woman revered as a perfect master. Four other masters—Shirdi Sai Baba, Upasni Maharaj, Tajuddin Baba, and Narayan Maharaj—also played a role in his "unveiling," after which Merwan became known as Meher Baba ("Compassionate Father"). Saying he had come not to teach but to awaken, he observed silence for forty-four years (1925–1969), communicating first with an alphabet board and later through gestures. His silence was undertaken not as a spiritual discipline, he said, but as a necessary condition for his work.

His mission included work with the poor, lepers, untouchables, children, and the *masts*, people who are "God-intoxicated," or spiritually dazed. Periods of intense activity, including world travel, alternated with times of seclusion, during which Meher Baba said he was doing his "universal work" of giving a "spiritual push" to the entire Creation. The result, he stated, would be a "new humanity" based on love, with all religions brought together. The impact of his work would be felt through his mani-

Periods of intense activity, including world travel, alternated with prolonged times of seclusion and complete silence, during which Meher Baba said he was doing his "universal work" of giving a "spiritual push" to the entire Creation.

festation as Avatar, a world-transforming process he linked to the breaking of his silence by speaking the divine "word."

His book *God Speaks* describes Creation as the quest of the infinite Reality for conscious experience of itself. Consciousness develops through the evolution of the soul as it assumes successive forms of stones, plants, and animals, culminating in the human form, Meher Baba said. It is then integrated through a phase of human reincarnations and perfected through a process of "involution" (the spiritual path), finally to unite consciously with the Infinite. Everyone is destined for this supreme goal of God-realization.

Meher Baba gave no importance to religious rituals, dogmas, or miracles but emphasized internal renunciation of desires, remembrance of God with love in the midst of daily life, and selfless service. In the 1960s he actively warned against the dangers of drugs, especially LSD and marijuana. Today his tomb-shrine in Meherabad, near Ahmednagar, India, is a place of pilgrimage for people of all faiths.

His Words

True love is unconquerable and irresistible. It goes on gathering power and spreading itself until eventually it transforms everyone it touches. Humanity will attain a new mode of being and life through the free and unhampered interplay of pure love from heart to heart.
—*Discourses,* pp. 8–9

To penetrate into the essence of all being and significance, and to release the fragrance of that inner attainment for the guidance and benefit of others, by expressing in the world of forms *truth, love, purity,* and *beauty*—this is the sole game which has any intrinsic and absolute worth. All other happenings, incidents, and attainments in themselves can have no lasting importance.
—*Discourses,* p. 200

Books by Meher Baba

Discourses. 7th rev. ed. Myrtle Beach, S.C.: Sheriar Foundation, 1987.
The Everything and the Nothing. Myrtle Beach, S.C.: Sheriar Foundation, 1995.
God Speaks: The Theme of Creation and Its Purpose. 2d ed., revised and enlarged. Walnut Creek, Calif.: Sufism Reoriented, 1973.
Listen, Humanity. Edited by D. E. Stevens. New York: Crossroad, 1998.

Books about Meher Baba

Anzar, Naosherwan. *The Beloved: The Life and Work of Meher Baba.* Myrtle Beach, S.C.: Sheriar Press, 1974. Illustrated with photographs.

Donkin, William. *The Wayfarers: Meher Baba with the God-Intoxicated.* Myrtle Beach, S.C.: Sheriar Foundation, 2000.

Purdom, Charles. *The God-Man: The Life, Journeys, and Work of Meher Baba with an Interpretation of His Silence and Spiritual Teaching.* Myrtle Beach, S.C.: Sheriar Press, 1964.

Organizations

Avatar Meher Baba Trust, King's Rd., Post Bag 31, Ahmednagar, M.S. 414 001, India; web site: www.ambppct.org.

Avatar's Abode, P.O. Box 184, Woombye, QLD 4559, Australia; phone: 61-07-5442-1544; web site: www.avatarsabode.com.au.

Meher Spiritual Center, 10200 Highway 17 N., Myrtle Beach, SC 29577; phone: 843-272-5777; e-mail: MeherGate@aol.com.

Sheriar Foundation, North Myrtle Beach, SC; phone: 843-272-1767; e-mail: books@sheriarfoundation.org; web site: www.sheriarfoundation.org.

Other Resources

Web site: www.avatarmeherbaba.org. Official web site of the Avatar Meher Baba Trust. Lists writings, relevant web sites, activities, photos, and organizations.

Periodical: *Glow International,* published quarterly by Beloved Archives, East Windsor, NJ; phone: 609-426-4345; e-mail: meherbaba@aol.com.

Film: *Meher Baba, Avatar of the Age: The Human Side of God;* Myrtle Beach, SC: available from Oceanpower Film Distributor; phone: 843-272-8524; web site: www.AvatarOfTheAge.com.

Videotapes: *Meher Baba: The Awakener;* documentary by Tim Thelen; *O Parvardigar;* film montage with music performed by Pete Townshend of the Who.

"True love is unconquerable and irresistible. It goes on gathering power and spreading itself until eventually it transforms everyone it touches."

SEYYED HOSSEIN NASR
(1933–)

A preeminent Muslim philosopher, Seyyed Hossein Nasr is also a highly respected teacher and spokesman for traditional Islamic values in a modern world. Influenced by the work of writers such as René Guénon, Frithjof Schuon, Titus Burckhardt, and Martin Lings, his lectures, writings, and speeches span a wide variety of subjects, including comparative religion and philosophy, science, nature, the arts, architecture, and literature. An advocate of the perennial philosophy at the core of the major world religions, he has been an important contributor to comparative religious studies and interfaith dialogue, setting forth his own model for the transcendent unity of world religions. He is an outspoken critic of both Islamic fundamentalism and Western secular science and culture. A central focus of his work has been the role of the intellect in the quest for Truth, although Nasr also emphasizes the need for spiritual practice along with theoretical knowledge.

Born in Tehran, Nasr was educated in Iran and the United States, where he graduated from the Massachusetts Institute of Technology with a bachelor's degree in physics and mathematics, and from Harvard University with a master's in geology and geophysics and a doctorate in the history of science and philosophy. He subsequently returned to his homeland and became a professor at Tehran University in 1958. While in Iran he also studied with several eminent masters of Islamic philosophy and law. With the onset of the Iranian revolution in 1979, he returned to the West. Since

A central focus of Nasr's work has been the role of the intellect in the quest for Truth, although he also emphasizes the need for spiritual practice along with theoretical knowledge.

1984 Nasr has been University Professor of Islamic Studies at George Washington University in Washington, D.C., and president of the Foundation for Traditional Studies. He is the author of numerous books and hundreds of articles in English, Farsi, Arabic, and French.

His Words

Despite both modernism and latter-day "fundamentalism," traditional Islam still survives, not only in its past artistic and intellectual movements, but in the present-day lives of those scholars and saints who still follow the path of the Prophet, in those craftsmen and artists who continue to recreate those visual and audible forms that are vehicles for the grace of the Quranic revelation, and in that vast majority of Muslims whose hearts, minds, and bodies still reverberate to the traditional teachings of Islam. One can even say that there has been a certain revival of traditional Islam in the spiritual, intellectual, and artistic domains during the past few decades: a revival that has gone largely unnoticed because of the sensationalism of most of the news media and the lack of comprehension of many scholars concerned with the contemporary Islamic world. Traditional Islam will in fact endure to the end of history, for it is none other than that tree whose roots are sunk in the Quranic revelation and whose trunk and branches have constituted all that Islam has been over the centuries, before the aberrations and deviations of modern times came to cause many to confuse this authentic tradition with, not only the anti-traditional, but also the counter-traditional, whose nature is more difficult to detect precisely because "Satan is the ape of God."
—*Traditional Islam in the Modern World,* p. 22

Books by Seyyed Hossein Nasr

Islamic Art and Spirituality. Albany: State University of New York Press, 1987.

Knowledge and the Sacred. Albany: State University of New York Press, 1989.

Man and Nature: The Spiritual Crisis of Modern Man. Chicago: Kazi Publications, 1998.

Religion and the Order of Nature. New York: Oxford University Press, 1996.

Science and Civilization in Islam. New York: New American Library, 1970.
Sufi Essays. 2d ed. Albany: State University of New York Press, 1991.
Traditional Islam in the Modern World. London: Kegan Paul International, 1990.
A Young Muslim's Guide to the Modern World. Chicago: Kazi Publications, 1994.

Books about Seyyed Hossein Nasr

Hahn, Lewis E., ed. *The Philosophy of Seyyed Hossein Nasr.* Library of Living Philosophers, vol. 28. Chicago: Open Court Publishing, 2000.
Hewitt, Hugh. *Searching for God in America.* Dallas: Word Publishing, 1996. Companion volume to video of the same title, with a chapter on Nasr.

For a more complete list of books by and about Seyyed Hossein Nasr, see Hahn, *The Philosophy of Seyyed Hossein Nasr.*

Organizations

Foundation for Traditional Studies, P.O. Box 370, Oakton, VA 22124; phone: 703-476-8837; e-mail: ftsdc@erols.com; web site: www.traditional-studies.org.

Nasr Foundation, c/o Kazi Publications, 3023 W. Belmont Ave., Chicago, IL 60618; e-mail: info@nasrfoundation.org; web site: www.nasr.org.

Other Resources

Audiotapes: Courses, lectures, and interviews are available from the Nasr Foundation.

Videotapes: *God: The Reality to Serve, Love, and Know,* "God at 2000" series, no. 6, 2000; *The Islamic Mind with Seyyed Hossein Nasr,* interview by Bill Moyers, 1990; *Searching for God in America,* PBS-TV series of conversations with religious leaders, no. 6, 1996.

Periodical: *Sophia: The Journal of Traditional Studies,* published semiannually by the Foundation for Traditional Studies; web site: www.sophiajournal.com.

> *"Traditional Islam will in fact endure to the end of history, for it is none other than that tree whose roots are sunk in the Quranic revelation and whose trunk and branches have constituted all that Islam has been over the centuries."*

PARAMAHANSA YOGANANDA
(1893–1952)

One of the first major yoga teachers in the West, Paramahansa Yogananda wrote *Autobiography of a Yogi,* which is considered a twentieth-century classic of spiritual writing. The Self-Realization Fellowship, which he founded, continues to disseminate his teachings in a variety of forms. Packaging Hindu-derivative messages for a multifaith audience, Paramahansa Yogananda helped spur Americans' interest in Eastern religions and predated today's wide attraction to spirituality free from traditional denominational boundaries.

Born Mukunda Lal Ghosh to a well-to-do Bengali family, he met and became a disciple of Swami Sri Yukteswar Giri when he was seventeen. In 1915 he graduated from the University of Calcutta and soon took formal vows as a monk of India's monastic Swami Order, receiving the new name Yogananda (signifying bliss, *ananda,* through divine union, *yoga*). Two years later he founded a school for boys that combined modern educational and yoga training.

In 1920, Yogananda served as India's delegate to the International Congress of Religious Liberals in Boston, where he delivered a talk titled "The Science of Religion." He remained in the United States to found the Self-Realization Fellowship (SRF), which aimed to spread yoga and Indian teachings in the West. He spent the next several years lecturing around the country and in 1925 established the SRF headquarters in Los Angeles. Yogananda's teachings focused on the unity of all religions and the ability of all to attain a direct connection to the

Yogananda's teachings focused on the unity of all religions and the ability of all to attain a direct connection to the divine.

divine. His method of meditation and yoga was based on techniques he said were scientific, reviving the ancient practice of Kriyayoga.

In 1935, Yogananda returned to India on a speaking tour and met several times with Mahatma Gandhi. While he was there, Yogananda's guru bestowed on him the spiritual title *paramahansa,* which means "supreme swan" and signifies that its bearer has attained an unbroken communion with God. In his later years, Yogananda focused on his writing, including his autobiography and his still-popular translation and explanation of the Bhagavad Gita. He also supervised publication of a series of Self-Realization Fellowship Lessons for home study.

His Words

To be constantly at the mercies of nature—that is surely not freedom. Our enthusiastic minds are rudely seized by a sense of helplessness when we are victimized by floods, tornadoes, or earthquakes; or when, apparently without rhyme or reason, illness or accident snatches our dear ones from our bosom. It is then we know we haven't conquered much. In spite of all our efforts to make life what we want it to be, there will always remain certain conditions introduced on this planet—infinite and guided by an unknown Intelligence, operating without our initiative—which preclude our control.
—*Inner Peace,* p. 104

Realizing that a man's body is like an electric battery, I reasoned that it could be recharged with energy through the direct agency of the human will. As no action of any kind is possible without *willing,* man may avail himself of the prime mover, will, to renew his strength without burdensome apparatus or mechanical exercises. By the simple Yogoda techniques, one may consciously and instantly recharge his life force (centered in the medulla oblongata) from the unlimited supply of cosmic energy.
—*Autobiography of a Yogi,* p. 289

Books by Paramahansa Yogananda

Autobiography of a Yogi. Los Angeles: Self-Realization Fellowship, 1993.
The Bhagavad Gita: Royal Science of God-Realization: The Immortal Dialogue Between Soul and Spirit: A New Translation and Commentary. Los Angeles: Self-Realization Fellowship, 1995.

Inner Peace. Los Angeles: Self-Realization Fellowship, 1999.

The Science of Religion. Los Angeles: Self-Realization Fellowship, 1974.

For a more complete list of books by Yogananda Paramahansa, see *Autobiography,* p. 574.

Organization

Self-Realization Fellowship International Headquarters, 3880 San Rafael Ave., Dept. 9W, Los Angeles, CA 90065-3298; phone: 323-225-2471.

Other Resources

Web site: www.selfrealization.org. Official web site of the Self-Realization Fellowship.

"By the simple Yogoda techniques, one may consciously and instantly recharge his life force . . . from the unlimited supply of cosmic energy."

ANDREW WEIL
(1942–)

As a leading authority on integrative medicine, mind-body interactions, and medical botany, Andrew Weil has expanded the way people view alternative healing methods and the notion of a holistic lifestyle based on the body-mind-spirit connection. His investigations into mind-altering substances led to his classic work, *The Natural Mind,* in which he offered a revolutionary view of drug addiction as rooted in the longing for higher consciousness—which, he suggested, could be better found through meditation.

Born in Philadelphia, Weil acquired a degree in botanical biology from Harvard College in 1964 and an M.D. from Harvard Medical School in 1968. He is now clinical professor of medicine and public health at the University of Arizona in Tucson, directing its Program in Integrative Medicine. He is also the founder of the Foundation for Integrative Medicine and editor in chief of the professional journal *Integrative Medicine.* The web site he sponsors (www.askdrweil.com) is a widely popular interactive resource for information on a holistic lifestyle.

In the 1970s, as a fellow of the Institute of Current World Affairs, Weil traveled the world to amass information about medicinal plants and healing, including several trips to the Amazon jungle. In Mexico, under the guidance of a *curandera* (traditional healer), he participated in a ceremony at which he consumed a hallucinogenic mushroom considered a cure-all. He subsequently began to write about healing plants, drugs and addiction, altered states of consciousness, and related topics. As a tribute to his contributions to ethnomycology, ethnobotany, and ethnopharmacology, a psychedelic

This Harvard-trained doctor has expanded the way people view alternative healing methods and the notion of a holistic lifestyle based on the body-mind-spirit connection.

mushroom *(Psilocybe weilii)* discovered in 1995 in Cherokee County, Georgia, was named after him.

His Words

Health is wholeness—wholeness in its most profound sense, with nothing left out and everything in just the right order to manifest the mystery of balance. Far from being simply the absence of disease, health is a dynamic and harmonious equilibrium of all the elements and forces making up and surrounding a human being.
—*Health and Healing,* p. 51

Books by Andrew Weil

Eating Well for Optimum Health: The Essential Guide to Food, Diet, and Nutrition. New York: Alfred A. Knopf, 2000.
Eight Weeks to Optimum Health. New York: Alfred A. Knopf, 1997.
Health and Healing: Understanding Conventional and Alternative Medicine. 1983. Reprint, Boston: Houghton Mifflin, 1986.
The Marriage of the Sun and the Moon: A Quest for Unity in Consciousness. Boston: Houghton Mifflin, 1980.
Natural Health, Natural Medicine: A Comprehensive Manual for Wellness and Self-Care. Boston: Houghton Mifflin, 1990.
The Natural Mind: An Investigation of Drugs and the Higher Consciousness. Rev. ed. Boston: Houghton Mifflin, 1986.
Spontaneous Healing: How to Discover and Enhance Your Body's Natural Ability to Maintain and Heal Itself. New York: Alfred A. Knopf, 1995.

Other Resources

Web site: "Ask Dr. Weil," www.askdrweil.com.
CDs: *Breathing: The Master Key to Self Healing,* 2000; *Meditation for Optimum Health,* 1997; *Sound Body, Sound Mind,* healing music; 1997.
Videotapes/DVDs: *Eating Well for Optimum Health; Eight Weeks to Optimum Health; Spontaneous Healing,* 1996.
Periodical: *Self-Healing Newsletter,* published monthly, P.O. Box 2057, Marion, OH 43305; phone: 800-523-3296.

"The achievement of balance adds an extra quality to a whole. It makes the perfect whole greater than the sum of its parts, makes it beautiful and holy, and so connects it to a higher reality."

8

THEY SPOKE FROM THE POWER OF **SILENCE**

To be silent is to listen: to the still small voice within, to the emptiness, to the monkey of the mind, to Creation, to the language of God. To be silent in spiritual repose is to listen to eternity. "Man does not put silence to the test," said the Roman Catholic theologian Max Picard, "silence puts man to the test."

The history of religion is replete with stories of prophets and saints going off to deserts, forests, mountains, and monasteries to be silent, to meditate, to contemplate. Moses on the mountain, Jesus in the garden, the Buddha at the base of a tree, Muhammad in the desert. Modernity's onslaught did much to undo this tradition in the West. Monastic orders diminished, and organized silent spirituality receded from public consciousness. In the East the tradition remained stronger, but even there it came under assault from a global utilitarianism concerned more with worldly production than with inner process.

The wholesale adoption in the West of Eastern techniques for cultivating silence altered the contemplative landscape during the twentieth century. In some cases this alteration was accompanied by the divorce of many forms from their cultural and monastic roots to accommodate Westerners juggling family life with the contemplative urge.

Ramana Maharshi, one of the earliest Eastern silent saints to become known in the West, is a twentieth-century example of his tradition's enduring roots. Born in a South Indian Hindu village, he left home as a teenager and went into seclusion at the base of a mountain. After several years seekers began to flock to him for *darshan,* simply being in his radiant presence, since he hardly spoke. Eventually an ashram grew around him, he attracted his first Western followers, and he became an international phenomenon through the translation of his teachings into a variety of languages.

Ajahn Chah exemplifies another Asian meditative tradition that traveled to the West. His is the Theravadan Buddhist forest tradition of Thailand, brought out of the jungle by adventurous American seekers who reshaped it and transplanted it in the hills of Massachusetts and California. Illness largely incapacitated Ajahn Chah during his final years, but it did not stop students from flocking to his silent but always inspirational presence.

In 1968 Shunryu Suzuki established the first Soto Zen monastery in the West in California, following his earlier founding of the San Francisco Zen Center, where he began accepting non-Asian students. He taught *zazen,* sitting meditation, the classic technique for bringing together body, breath, and mind to achieve deepening stillness, and his 1970 classic *Zen Mind, Beginner's Mind* was an immediate best-seller that remains a basic introductory text to the subject. Another Zen school is the Korean tradition, represented here by Seung Sahn, who was told to remain silent for three years upon receiving dharma transmission (becoming a patriarch in his teaching lineage) when he was just twenty-two.

On the windswept coast of Nova Scotia's Cape Breton Island, Pema Chödrön, the first American woman to become a full *bhikshuni,* or Buddhist nun, presided until recently over Gampo Abbey, which follows the Tibetan Karma Kagyü tradition. The abbey's daily schedule is an endless round of rigorous work, meditation, and silence. Chödrön writes and travels widely to lecture and teach, making her a leading exponent of Tibetan-style meditation and a personification of East-West spiritual unification.

The teachers of silence named here so far either retained or adopted traditional Eastern forms. Maharishi Mahesh Yogi did it another way. He jettisoned tradition. His Transcendental Meditation is silent mantra meditation stripped of its Indian cultural veneer and given a Western scientific packaging. By this means, the Maharishi, as he is called, achieved unsurpassed pop cultural success, while establishing a series of educational, health-care, governmental, and other initiatives designed to showcase meditation's benefits and to gain for it mainstream Western acceptance.

Eastern techniques came to dominate meditative and contemplative practice during the latter years of the twentieth century. But that is not to say that prominent Western tradition contemplatives were entirely absent. Two of the best known are Thomas Merton, who despite his twenty-seven years as a Trappist monk became famous as a writer and public figure, and Thomas Keating, a leader in the Christian contemplative prayer movement who likens quiet prayer to "resting in God." They and others helped restore silence to an honored, if still minor, place in Western religious life.

AJAHN CHAH
(1917–1992)

• • • • • • •

As the foremost modern exemplar of the Thai forest tradition of Theravadan Buddhism, the Venerable Ajahn (sometimes spelled *Achaan*) Chah exerted spiritual influence over an entire generation of Western students who traveled to the East in search of wisdom in the 1960s. His teaching has been foundational for the American Vipassana or Insight Meditation community, whose most influential teachers—Jack Kornfield, Joseph Goldstein, Sharon Salzberg, and others—were among his students.

The man who became Venerable Ajahn Chah was born Pra Bhodinyana Thera into a farming family in the village of Baan Gor, in Thailand's northeast. At the age of twenty he took ordination as a *bhikkhu,* or Buddhist monk. After spending several years traveling around Thailand studying with meditation masters of the forest tradition, he was invited to establish a monastery near his home village. From this forest monastery, Wat Pah Pong, his fame as a teacher began to spread.

Ajahn Chah's teaching was remarkably simple and direct, unrelenting yet compassionate, and spiced with humor. He presented the heart of Buddhist practice in terms suitable for anyone, regardless of background, and trained his students in methods of calming the mind and heart in order to cultivate true insight. He taught that the path of patience, wisdom, and selfless compassion is accessible to anyone and because of that was sought out by people from all corners of society.

Ajahn Chah's teaching was remarkably simple and direct, unrelenting yet compassionate, and spiced with humor. He presented the heart of Buddhist practice in terms suitable for anyone, regardless of background.

In 1966 the first Westerner came to study with Ajahn Chah; he was an American who became the monk Ajahn Sumedho. From that time on the number of foreigners increased steadily until, in 1975, a branch monastery for Westerners was established nearby. Ajahn Chah went on to establish monasteries in England, Switzerland, Australia, New Zealand, Italy, and the United States.

Although he was incapacitated by poor health in his later years and had to abandon formal teaching, people still flocked to his monastery, finding inspiration simply by being in his compassionate presence.

His Words

One day a famous lecturer on Buddhist metaphysics came to see Achaan Chah. This woman gave periodic teachings in Bangkok on the *abidharma* and complex Buddhist psychology. In talking to Achaan Chah, she detailed how important it was for people to understand Buddhist psychology and how much her students benefited from their study with her. She asked him if he agreed with the importance of such understanding.

"Yes, very important," he agreed.

Delighted, she further questioned whether he had his own students learn abidharma.

"Oh yes, of course."

And where, she asked, did he recommend they start—which books and studies were best?

"Only here," he said, pointing to his heart. "Only here."
—*A Still Forest Pool,* p. 12

Books by Ajahn Chah

Being Darma: The Essence of the Buddha's Teachings. With Paul Breiter and Jack Kornfield. Boston: Shambhala Publications, 2001.

Bodhinyana. Redwood Valley, Calif.: Abhayagiri Monastery, 2000.

Food for the Heart. Ubol Rajathanai, Thailand: Wat Pah Nanachat, 1992.

Living Dahmma. Ubol Rajathanai, Thailand: Wat Pah Nanachat, 1992.

A Still Forest Pool: The Insight Meditation of Achaan Chah. Compiled and edited by Jack Kornfield and Paul Breiter. Wheaton, Ill.: Theosophical Publishing House, 1985.

A Taste of Freedom. Ubol Rajathanai, Thailand: Wat Pah Nanachat, 1991.

Organization

Abhayagiri Monastery, 16201 Tomki Rd., Redwood Valley, CA 95470. An American Theravadan Buddhist monastery whose coabbots were both direct disciples of Ajahn Chah.

Other Resources

Web site: ksc15.th.com/petsei. Devoted to Ajahn Chah and his teaching; maintained by Bodhinyanarama, a Theravadan monastery in New Zealand.

When asked by a teacher where it was best for a student to begin, Ajahn Chah pointed to his heart. "Only here," he said.

THOMAS KEATING
(1923–)

Born in New York, Thomas Keating is one of the leaders of the worldwide movement in Christianity to return to the church's contemplative roots. While a student at Yale University in the 1940s, he experienced what he called a "profound conversion" that led him to enter a cloistered Roman Catholic monastery of the Cistercian Order of the Strict Observance. He served his religious order, one of the most disciplined within Christianity, at monasteries in Massachusetts (he was abbot of Saint Joseph's Abbey in Spencer) and Colorado, where he became interested in popularizing the form of wordless meditation that is the heart of monastic practice.

A prolific and respected author of books on contemplative prayer, Keating is a founder with M. Basil Pennington and others of the modern Centering Prayer movement and of Contemplative Outreach, a worldwide nonprofit organization dedicated to encouraging the practice of Centering Prayer, a Christian form of meditation. It is this network of individuals and small faith communities that is the focus of his work today.

Keating believes Centering Prayer is one among many forms of Christian prayer, which also include the rosary, devotional practices, and vocal prayers such as the Our Father and Hail Mary. However, it differs from these approaches in that it is a silent practice, not associated with words, thoughts, or ideas. He believes God speaks in the language of silence, which requires one to listen quietly and attentively—"resting in God," as it is described in the classic texts of contemplation. His work draws on the teachings of the

A prolific and respected author of books on contemplative prayer, Keating is a Trappist monk and a founder of the modern Centering Prayer movement.

early desert fathers and mothers of the church, as well as on the writings of mystics such as St. John of the Cross, St. Teresa of Ávila, St. Thérèse of Lisieux, and the author of *The Cloud of Unknowing*.

Keating's book *Open Mind, Open Heart* is his best-known work and lays the foundation for his philosophy of prayer. His writings reflect his belief that Christianity is essentially contemplative. In addition to writing, he travels throughout the world to lecture on Christian prayer and meditation and to learn more about the practices of world religions. He is a cofounder of the Snowmass Interfaith Conference and former chair of Monastic Interreligious Dialogue.

His Words

Centering Prayer is a method of refining one's intuitive faculties so that one can enter more easily into contemplative prayer. It is not the only path to contemplation, but it is a good one. As a method, it is a kind of extract of monastic spirituality. . . . You have to keep up a certain level of silence in the psyche and nervous system if you want to obtain the benefits of contemplative prayer.
—*Open Mind, Open Heart,* p. 34

Centering Prayer is . . . a journey into the unknown. It is a call to follow Jesus out of all the structures, security blankets, and even spiritual practices that serve as props. They are all left behind insofar as they are part of the false self system. . . . The false self is an illusion. Humility is the forgetfulness of self.
—*Open Mind, Open Heart,* p. 72

[In contemplative prayer] our private, self-made worlds come to an end; a new world appears within and around us and the impossible becomes an everyday experience. Yet the world that prayer reveals is barely noticeable in the ordinary course of events.
—*Open Mind, Open Heart,* p. 13

Books by Thomas Keating

Awakenings. New York: Crossroad, 1990.
The Better Part: Stages of Contemplative Living. New York: Continuum, 2000.

The Divine Indwelling: Centering Prayer and Its Development. New York: Lantern Books, 2001.

Finding Grace at the Center: The Beginning of Centering Prayer. With M. Basil Pennington and Thomas E. Clarke. Woodstock, Vt.: SkyLight Paths, 2002.

Open Mind, Open Heart: The Contemplative Dimension of the Gospel. Rockport, Mass.: Element Books, 1992.

Reawakenings. New York: Crossroad, 1992.

Organization

Contemplative Outreach Ltd., P.O. Box 737, 10 Park Pl., Ste. 2B, Butler, NJ 07405; phone: 973-838-3384; fax: 973-492-5795; e-mail: office@coutreach.org; web site: www.contemplativeoutreach.org. Publishes *Contemplative Outreach Newsletter.*

"[In contemplative prayer] our private, self-made worlds come to an end; a new world appears within and around us and the impossible becomes an everyday experience."

MAHARISHI MAHESH YOGI
(c. 1918–)

Best known for making meditation not only a household word but also a daily practice for millions, Maharishi Mahesh Yogi spread the Transcendental Meditation program, popularly known as TM, around the world.

Born Mahesh Prasad Varma, he graduated from the University of Allahabad and immediately joined his guru, Swami Brahmananda Saraswati, known to devotees as Guru Dev. He became a devoted disciple and personal secretary, and at the end of Guru Dev's life the swami reportedly directed Mahesh to spread the ancient Vedic wisdom. As a consequence, he established the Spiritual Regeneration Movement in 1958, to bring a universal meditation practice to people living in the world. He held that a practice suitable for householders must be simple, natural, and effortless, requiring no belief or change in lifestyle other than sitting comfortably in meditation for about twenty minutes twice a day.

His teaching of meditation and its principles was immediately recognized as simple yet profound, and he was acknowledged as a modern-day maharishi (great seer). First traveling the world to teach TM himself, he later established a program to train meditation teachers. Thereafter he became known as the Maharishi Mahesh Yogi.

Correlating ancient wisdom and modern science, he elaborated his theoretical system, which he called the Science of Creative Intelligence, in 1972 and instituted the TM-Sidhis Program, which added advanced practices such as levitation, or "yogic flying," in 1976. He encouraged scientific research into the effects of meditation, and findings showed that in addition to individual benefits,

Maharishi Mahesh Yogi's teaching of meditation and its principles was immediately recognized as simple yet profound, correlating ancient wisdom and modern science.

regular TM practice by 1 percent of a population resulted in positive changes for society as a whole (such as reduced crime rates). This unprecedented scientific discovery of the influence of collective consciousness was called the Maharishi Effect.

In 1975 the Maharishi inaugurated the Dawn of the Age of Enlightenment, announcing a "reversal in the trends of the time" from a downward to an upward spiral. From then on, he turned his attention principally toward developing an ideal society, to creating, as he put it, "heaven on earth." Chief among these contributions have been programs in enlightened education, government, defense, health care, music, and architecture. Schools, universities, and other institutions have been established to make the Maharishi's revitalization of ancient wisdom for modern times available globally.

His Words

The [TM] technique may be defined as turning the attention inwards towards the subtler levels of a thought [the TM mantra] until the mind transcends the subtlest state of the thought and arrives at the source of thought.
—*Maharishi Mahesh Yogi on the Bhagavad-Gita,* p. 330

To go to a field of greater happiness is the natural tendency of the mind. Because in the practice of transcendental meditation the conscious mind is set on the way to experiencing transcendental, absolute Being, whose nature is bliss-consciousness, the mind finds the way increasingly attractive as it advances in the direction of bliss. . . .

This practice is pleasant for every mind. Whatever the stage of evolution of the aspirant, whether he is emotionally developed or intellectually advanced, his mind, by its very tendency to go to a field of greater happiness, finds a way to transcend the subtlest state of thinking and arrive at the bliss of absolute Being. This practice is, therefore, not only simple but also automatic.
—*The Science of Being and the Art of Living,* pp. 55–56

Books by Maharishi Mahesh Yogi

Love and God. Washington, D.C.: Age of Enlightenment Press, 1973.

Maharishi Mahesh Yogi on the Bhagavad-Gita: A New Translation and Commentary. Vol. 1. New York: Viking Penguin, 1990.

The Science of Being and Art of Living: Transcendental Meditation. New York: Dutton/Plume, 2001.

Books about Maharishi Mahesh Yogi

Oates, Robert. *Creating Heaven on Earth.* Fairfield, Iowa: Heaven on Earth Publications, 1990.

Olson, Helena E., and Roland O. Olson. *His Holiness Maharishi Mahesh Yogi: A Living Saint for the New Millennium, Stories of His First Visit to the USA.* Edited by Theresa Olson. Schenectady, N.Y.: Samhita Productions, 2001.

Simon, Paul. *The Maharishi: The Biography of the Man Who Gave Transcendental Meditation to the World.* Rockport, Mass.: Element Books, 1994.

Organization

Maharishi University of Management Press, 1000 North 4th St., Fairfield, IA 52557; phone: 800-369-6480, 641-472-1110; web site: mum.edu/press/welcome.html. Books, tapes, and other resources by Mahesh and information about the activities of his worldwide movement.

Other Resources

Web sites: www.alltm.org/Maharishi.html. Chronological summary of Mahesh's accomplishments along with links to principal web sites. www.maharishi.org. Contact information for Maharishi Vedic Universities and related sites. www.maharishi-india.org. Official web site of Maharishi's programs in India.

www.tm.org. Official U.S. web site of the Transcendental Meditation (TM) program.

Schools: Maharishi Open University, Station 24, 6063 NP Vlodrop, Netherlands; e-mail: mou@Maharishi.net; web site: www.mou.org. For global distance learning.

Maharishi University of Management, 1000 North 4th St., Fairfield, IA 52557; phone: 800-369-6480 or 641-472-1110; web site: mum.edu.

"[The] mind, by its very tendency to go to a field of greater happiness, finds a way to transcend the subtlest state of thinking and arrive at the bliss of absolute Being."

THOMAS MERTON
(1915–1968)

Thomas Merton lived twenty-seven years as a Trappist monk of the Cistercian Abbey of Gethsemani, a cloistered monastery in central Kentucky, yet he had gained a wide reputation as a writer, social critic, and progressive religious thinker by the time of his death at fifty-two. With more than seventy books (diaries, biographies, poetry, meditative writing, and political essays) to his credit as well as hundreds of articles published in both religious and secular magazines and journals, he was an accessible, engaging writer who spoke passionately against racism, militarism, bigotry, religious prejudice, and political oppression. His works, sometimes censored by his superiors, have had a profound impact on contemporary religious and philosophical thought. His 1949 best-selling autobiographical classic, *The Seven Storey Mountain,* appears on lists of the most influential books of the last century. His uncensored journals, published in seven volumes, are the latest of his major works to appear in print.

Born in Prades, France, the son of artists who died when he was young, Merton lived in Bermuda and Britain before enrolling briefly at Cambridge University in England. In 1934 he entered Columbia University in New York City, where he earned a master's degree in English, studying under Mark Van Doren. It was at this time that he went from agnostic to Roman Catholic. In 1941, after teaching English and working in a Harlem settlement house, he entered Gethsemani, where he eventually made his

Generations of readers of varying faiths have found solace as well as challenge in Merton's words and life. His complete journals—uncensored, unlike many of his books published during Merton's lifetime—honestly chronicle his spiritual struggles.

final vows and served as master of students and novices. Taking the name Father Louis, he chose the Cistercian tradition for its rigorous silence and solitude. Despite his years as a hermit at Gethsemani, he carried on lively friendships through the mail and in person with many of his generation's most respected writers and religious leaders, including the noted Jewish scholar Abraham Joshua Heschel; the Zen writer D. T. Suzuki; the social critic W. H. Ferry; and the author John Howard Griffin. In his writings, Merton urged greater cooperation between Eastern and Western monastics and people of differing faith traditions. He died in Bangkok, Thailand, while attending a monastic conference, on the twenty-seventh anniversary of his entering Gethsemani. He was electrocuted when a fan in his hotel room fell on him.

Generations of readers of varying faiths have found solace as well as challenge in Merton's words and life. His journals honestly chronicle his spiritual struggles. All his work reflects an ability to distill and synthesize the complex ideas of the most thoughtful theologians, poets, and philosophers of the past and present, and to analyze their contributions in the context of the Christian perspective.

His Words

If I affirm myself as a Catholic merely by denying all that is Muslim, Jewish, Protestant, Hindu, Buddhist, etc., in the end I will find that there is not much left for me to affirm as a Catholic: and certainly no breath of the Spirit with which to affirm it.
—*Conjectures of A Guilty Bystander,* p. 144

My Lord God, I have no idea where I am going. I do not see the road ahead of me. I cannot know for certain where it will end. Nor do I really know myself, and the fact that I think I am following your will does not mean that I am actually doing so. But I believe that the desire to please you does in fact please you. And I hope I have that desire in all that I am doing. I hope that I will never do anything apart from that desire. And I know that if I do this you will lead me by the right road, though I may know nothing about it. Therefore I will trust you always though I may seem to be lost and in the shadow of death. I will not fear, for you are ever with me, and you will never leave me to face my perils alone.
—*Thoughts in Solitude,* p. 103

Books by Thomas Merton

The Collected Poems of Thomas Merton. New York: New Directions 1987.

Conjectures of a Guilty Bystander. New York: Doubleday, 1976.

Contemplation in a World of Action. Notre Dame, Ind.: University of Notre Dame Press, 1999.

The Journals of Thomas Merton. 7 vols. Edited by Patrick Hart. San Francisco: HarperSanFrancisco, 1994–1998.

Mystics and Zen Masters. New York: Farrar, Straus, & Giroux, 1987.

New Seeds of Contemplation. New York: New Directions, 1972.

Raids on the Unspeakable. New York: W. W. Norton, 1972.

The Seven Storey Mountain: An Autobiography of Faith. Orlando, Fla.: Harcourt, 1999.

Thoughts in Solitude. New York: Farrar, Straus, & Giroux, 1998.

The Way of Chuang Tzu. New York: New Directions, 1976.

Books about Thomas Merton

Hart, Patrick, ed. *Thomas Merton, Monk: A Monastic Tribute.* Kalamazoo, Mich.: Cistercian Publications, 1983.

Mott, Michael. *The Seven Mountains of Thomas Merton.* Orlando, Fla.: Harcourt, 1993.

For a more complete listing of books by and about Thomas Merton, see Mott, *The Seven Mountains of Thomas Merton.*

Organizations

Abbey of Gethsemani, Trappist, KY 40051; phone: 502-549-4113; web site: www.monks.org.

International Thomas Merton Society, Thomas Merton Center, Bellarmine University, 2001 Newburg Rd., Louisville, KY 40205-0671; phone 502-452-8187; fax: 502-452-8038; e-mail: pmpearson@bellarmine.edu; web site: www.merton.org.

Thomas Merton Foundation, 2117 Payne St., Louisville, KY 40206-2011; phone: 502-899-1991; fax 502-899-1907; e-mail: ttaylor@mertonfoundation.org; web site: www.mertonfoundation.org.

Other Resources

Periodicals: *Merton Annual* and *Merton Seasonal: A Quarterly Review*, Thomas Merton Center, Bellarmine University.

Research Center: Papers of Thomas Merton Collection, Columbia University; web site: www.columbia.edu.

"A true personal encounter brings us not only knowledge of another, fellowship with another, but also a deeper comprehension of our own inner self."

PEMA CHÖDRÖN
(1936–)

The first American woman to undergo full ordination as a *bhikshuni,* or Buddhist nun, in the Tibetan tradition, Pema Chödrön is a leading author and teacher of Buddhism in the West.

She was born Deidre Blomfield-Brown in New York City. After attending Miss Porter's School in Connecticut and graduating from the University of California, Berkeley, she taught elementary school for many years, both in New Mexico and in California. During this period she married and had two children.

A trip to the French Alps in the late 1960s brought her in contact with Lama Chime Rinpoche, a renowned Tibetan Buddhist monk, who became her teacher. In 1974, while studying with Lama Chime in London, she received her novice (first stage) ordination as a nun from Karmapa Rigpe Dorje, sixteenth head of the Karmapa Kagyü lineage of Tibetan Buddhism. Since then she has been known as Pema Chödrön.

At the urging of Lama Chime, she began studying with Chögyam Trungpa Rinpoche, one of the most active early disseminators of Tibetan Buddhism throughout Europe and America. She developed an especially strong bond with Chögyam Trungpa and studied with him until his death in 1987. She now considers him her root guru (the first major teacher in her current line of teaching).

As a popular spokesperson for Buddhism in general and, more specifically, for women in Buddhism, Pema Chödrön has emerged as a prominent teacher of Buddhist texts and practices to laypeople throughout North America.

In 1981, at the invitation of the Karmapa, Pema Chödrön journeyed to Hong Kong to receive full ordination as a Buddhist nun. She subsequently directed the Tibetan Buddhist center Karma Dzong in Boulder, Colorado, for three years, after which she assumed directorship of Gampo Abbey on the northeastern coast of Cape Breton Island in Nova Scotia.

Pema Chödrön's first two books, *The Wisdom of No Escape* and *Start Where You Are,* continue to assist a wide Western audience of Buddhists and non-Buddhists to apply the teachings of the Buddha more dynamically to their everyday lives. They also launched her career as a popular spokesperson for Buddhism in general and, more specifically, for women in Buddhism. Meanwhile, she also emerged as a prominent teacher of Buddhist texts and practices to laypeople throughout North America.

Since the mid-1990s health problems have limited Pema Chödrön's ability to travel and have put an end to her administrative duties at Gampo Abbey. Nevertheless, she continues to write and to conduct small teaching programs at the abbey and at several other Canadian and U.S. locations each year.

Her Words

Holding on to beliefs limits our experience of life. That doesn't mean that beliefs or ideas or thinking are problems; the stubborn attitude of having to have things be a particular way, grasping on to our beliefs and thoughts, all these cause the problems. To put it simply, using your belief systems this way creates a situation in which you choose to be blind instead of being able to see, to be deaf instead of being able to hear, to be dead rather than alive, asleep rather than awake.
—*The Wisdom of No Escape,* pp. 70–71

The Buddha said that we are never separated from enlightenment. Even at the times we feel most stuck, we are never alienated from the awakened state. This is a revolutionary assertion. Even ordinary people like us with hang-ups and confusion have this mind of enlightenment called *bodhichitta.* The openness and warmth of *bodhichitta* are in fact our true nature and condition. Even when our neurosis feels far more basic than our wisdom, even when we're feeling most confused and hopeless, *bodhichitta*—like the open sky—is always

here, undiminished by the clouds that temporarily cover it.
—*The Places That Scare You,* p. 32

Books by Pema Chödrön

The Places That Scare You: A Guide to Fearlessness in Difficult Times. Boston: Shambhala Publications, 2001.
Start Where You Are: A Guide to Compassionate Living. Boston: Shambhala Publications, 1994.
When Things Fall Apart: Heart Advice for Difficult Times. Boston: Shambhala Publications, 1998.
The Wisdom of No Escape: And the Path of Loving-Kindness. Boston: Shambhala Publications, 1991.

Organization

Gampo Abbey, Pleasant Bay, Cape Breton, NS B0E 2P0, Canada; phone: 902-224-2752; fax: 902-224-1521; e-mail: gampo@shambhala.org.

Other Resources

Audiotapes: *Good Medicine: How to Turn Pain into Compassion with Tonglen Meditation,* 1999; *Pure Meditation: The Tibetan Buddhist Practice of Inner Peace,* 2000.
Videotapes: *Pema Chödrön and Alice Walker in Conversation,* 1999; *Pema Chödrön: Good Medicine,* 1999.

"The Buddha said that we are never separated from enlightenment. Even at the times we feel most stuck, we are never alienated from the awakened state. This is a revolutionary assertion."

RAMANA MAHARSHI
(1879–1950)

• • • • • • • •

An Indian sage and exemplar of the Hindu nondualist school of Advaita Vedanta, Ramana Maharshi spoke little other than periodically to answer questions about the spiritual life posed to him by his disciples. But those answers, gathered into published form, have made him one of the twentieth century's most influential teachers of Hindu philosophy in both the East and the West.

Ramana Maharshi was born in a village of southern India and lived a very ordinary life until the age of seventeen, when he suddenly—without any formal training, teacher, or practice—underwent a profound experience of the nature of the self and of the Absolute, an experience that overwhelmed him and never left him.

Following this experience he left his home and found his way to a temple at the foot of the holy mountain Arunachala, where he remained secluded for several years. Word spread that a particularly holy *sannyasin* (renunciate) was living at the temple, and people began to gather around him, simply to be in his luminous and consoling presence—since for several years he hardly spoke. He did at last break his silence, however, and began to respond to the questions put to him by the growing number of spiritual seekers.

People journeyed to Ramanashram to ask Ramana Maharshi questions about the spiritual life and to take darshan*—that is, to benefit from simply being in the presence of a spiritual master. His teaching, his principal instruction to all his devotees, was always to meditate on the question "Who am I?"*

A group of disciples grew up around him, and this group became an ashram, or community, called Ramanashram, which continues to exist. For the rest of his life, people journeyed to Ramanashram to ask Ramana Maharshi questions about the spiritual life and to take *darshan*—that is, to benefit from simply being in the presence of a spiritual master. His teaching, his principal instruction to all his devotees, was always to meditate on the question "Who am I?"

In 1911 Ramana Maharshi gained his first Western disciple, an Englishman, and soon after he became an international phenomenon through his published talks. The Ramanashram community came to include people of many nationalities, and Ramana Maharshi's answers to questions were written down and published in many languages.

His Words

As all living beings desire to be happy always, without misery, as in the case of everyone there is observed supreme love for one's self, and as happiness alone is the cause for love, in order to gain that happiness which is one's nature and which is experienced in the state of deep sleep where there is no mind, one should know one's self. For that, the path of knowledge, the inquiry of the form "Who am I?", is the principal means.
—*The Spiritual Teaching of Ramana Maharshi*

You cannot love God without knowing Him nor know Him without loving Him. Love manifests itself in everything you do, and that is Karma. The development of mental perception is the necessary preliminary before you can know or love God in the proper way.
—quoted in Swarnagiri, *Crumbs from His Table,* p. 31

Books by Ramana Maharshi

Be as You Are: The Teachings of Sri Ramana Maharshi. Edited by David Godman. London: Penguin Arkana, 1991.

The Collected Works of Ramana Maharshi. Edited by Arthur Osborne. York Beach, Maine: Samuel Weiser, 1997.

The Spiritual Teaching of Ramana Maharshi. Boston: Shambhala Publications, 1988.

Books about Ramana Maharshi

Osborne, Arthur. *Ramana Maharshi and the Path to Self-Knowledge.* York Beach, Maine: Samuel Weiser, 1995.

Swarnagiri, Ramanananda. *Crumbs from His Table.* Tiruvannamalai, India: Sri Ramanashram, 1995.

Organization

Arunachala Ashrama, Bhagavan Sri Ramana Maharshi Center, 66–12 Clyde St., Rego Park, NY 11374; phone: 718-575-3215; e-mail: Ashrama@aol.com; web site: www.arunachala.org.

Other Resources

Web site: www.ramana-maharshi.org. Official web site of Ramanashram.

"You cannot love God without knowing Him nor know Him without loving Him."

SEUNG SAHN
(1927–)

Zen Master Seung Sahn is the person most responsible for bringing Korean Zen Buddhism to the West, which he did by establishing a network of Zen centers and monasteries throughout North America, Europe, Africa, and Australia.

Seung Sahn was born in Seun Choen, North Korea, into a Protestant Christian family during the time of Japanese military rule; as a young man he was heavily involved in the Korean independence movement. After the end of World War II, while studying at Korea's Dong Guk University, he became increasingly convinced of his inability to help people through either political activities or academic studies. He became a Buddhist monk in 1948—his first encounter with Buddhism was reading the Heart Sutra—beginning his monastic life with an intensive solitary mountain retreat. When he came down from the mountain, the renowned Zen Master Ko Bong confirmed his enlightenment and gave him official transmission, making him a Zen master and seventy-eighth patriarch in his lineage at the extraordinarily young age of twenty-two.

Known to his students as Dae Soen Sa Nim, Seung Sahn taught in Korea and Japan throughout the 1950s and 1960s and became widely known for his wise, challenging, and often humorous teaching style, which seems effortlessly to transcend language and cultural barriers.

In 1972 he was invited to visit the United States, and he settled in the Providence, Rhode Island, area with the intention of introducing his style of Zen teaching to Americans. His

Seung Sahn's small apartment turned into a Zen center, and the group of Brown University students who first sought him out became the nucleus of an international organization.

small apartment turned into a Zen center, and the group of Brown University students who first sought him out became the nucleus of an international organization that, thirty years later, has grown to include centers throughout the United States as well as in France, Poland, South Africa, Hong Kong, Australia, and, of course, Korea.

His Words

Don't worry—just try. Trying is better than a Zen Master, better than Buddha, better than God. It is already great love, great compassion, and the great *bodhisattva* way. Don't check your feelings; don't check your mind; don't check your understanding; don't check outside. Then there is no inside, no outside, no I, no you, no they: you are one with your situation. That is very important.
—*Only Don't Know,* p. 15

Books by Seung Sahn

The Compass of Zen. Boston: Shambhala Publications, 1988.
Dropping Ashes on the Buddha: The Teaching of Zen Master Seung Sahn. Edited by Stephen Mitchell. New York: Grove Press, 1976.
Only Don't Know: Selected Teaching Letters of Zen Master Seung Sahn. Edited by Hyon Gak Sunim. Boston: Shambhala Publications, 1999.

Other Resources

Web site: www.kwanumzen.com. Official web site of the Kwan Um School of Zen, with much information about its founder and centers, and links to other sites of interest.
Periodical: *Primary Point,* 99 Pound Rd., Cumberland, RI 02864; phone: 401-658-1188. Quarterly magazine of the Kwan Um School of Zen.
Videotape: *Wake Up! On the Road with Zen Master Seung Sahn,* entertaining documentary by Brad Anderson that follows Seung Sahn on a teaching trip through Europe; available from *Primary Point* magazine.

"Don't worry—just try. Trying is better than a Zen Master, better than Buddha, better than God. It is already great love, great compassion, and the great bodhisattva *way."*

SHUNRYU SUZUKI
(1905–1971)

By founding several important Zen Buddhist centers in the United States, including San Francisco Zen Center and Tassajara Zen Mountain Center in California (the first Soto Zen monastery in the West), Shunryu Suzuki became one of America's most influential Zen pioneers.

Suzuki was born the son of a Japanese Zen Buddhist priest directing an obscure rural temple and became a monk at the age of thirteen. After graduating from Komazawa University, he went on to study at Eiheiji, the supreme monastery of the Soto school of Zen Buddhism, which emphasizes seated meditation *(zazen)* over all other forms of practice. During his twenties Suzuki longed to bring Zen practice to America but, bowing to tradition and the advice of his teacher, he went home to assume leadership of his ailing father's temple. He married and had three children, but his relatively tranquil life was soon interrupted by a series of upheavals: first World War II, then the occupation by American troops, and, in 1952, the brutal murder of his wife by a mentally disturbed boarder.

In addition to tending the temple's traditional members—Buddhists from Asian backgrounds—Shunryu Suzuki began conducting classes, services, and sitting meditation sessions for people of non-Asian descent, most of whom had no prior contact with any Buddhist institution.

Finally, in 1959, Suzuki journeyed to San Francisco, where he remained for the rest of his life. His first assignment from the Soto school was to take over supervision of the Soto temple in that city. Already a Zen master, having received formal recognition by his teacher, Suzuki became an abbot of this temple in 1962. In addition to tending the temple's traditional members—Buddhists from Asian backgrounds—he began conducting classes, services, and sitting meditation sessions for people of non-Asian descent, most of whom had no prior contact with any Buddhist institution.

In time the rapid growth in the size of the latter group led to a split in the temple's *sangha* (congregation). Suzuki left with the non-traditional group to found San Francisco Zen Center at a separate location in 1961. Seven years later he established the Zen Mountain Center in Tassajara. His book *Zen Mind, Beginner's Mind,* published in 1970, became an immediate bestseller and continues to enjoy wide popularity as an introduction to Zen for Westerners.

His Words

In Japan we have the phrase *soshin,* which means "beginner's mind." The goal of [Zen] practice is always to keep our beginner's mind. . . . In the beginner's mind there is no thought, "I have attained something." All self-centered thoughts limit our vast mind. When we have no thought of achievement, no thought of self, we are true beginners. Then we can really learn something. The beginner's mind is the mind of compassion. When our mind is compassionate, it is boundless.
—*Zen Mind, Beginner's Mind,* p. 22

So you may ask, "What is the real teaching of Buddha?" If you don't understand it you will keep asking, "What is it? What is it? What does it mean?" You are just seeking for something you can understand. This is a mistake. We don't exist in that way. [The thirteenth-century Zen master and founder of the Soto school] Dogen Zenji says, "There is no bird who flies knowing the limit of the sky. There is no fish who swims knowing the end of the ocean."
—*Branching Streams Flow in the Darkness,* pp. 58–59

Books by Shunryu Suzuki

Branching Streams Flow in the Darkness. Berkeley: University of California Press, 1999.
Zen Mind, Beginner's Mind. New York: Weatherhill, 1970.

Books about Shunryu Suzuki

Chadwick, David. *Crooked Cucumber: The Life and Zen Teaching of Shunryu Suzuki.* New York: Broadway Books, 1999.

———. *To Shine One Corner of the World: Moments with Shunryu Suzuki.* New York: Broadway Books, 2001.

Organizations

San Francisco Zen Center, 300 Page St., San Francisco, CA 94102; phone: 415-863-3136; fax: 415-431-9220.

Tassajara Zen Mountain Center, 39171 Tassajara Rd., Carmel Valley, CA 93924; phone: 415-431-3771.

"When we have no thought of achievement, no thought of self, we are true beginners. Then we can really learn something."

About the Photographs

Page 1—from left to right

Chögyam Trungpa at Karmê Chöling Buddhist Meditation Center (Barnet, Vermont) in the early 1970s. Courtesy of the Shambhala Archives. Used by permission.

Starhawk drumming. Courtesy of Lisa Sithian/Reclaiming Quarterly. Used by permission.

Aimee Semple McPherson preaching in the 1920s. Courtesy of the Heritage Department of the International Church of the Foursquare Gospel. Used by permission.

Page 47—from left to right

Daniel Berrigan. Used by permission.

Mahatma Gandhi making his own clothes. Courtesy of the Gandhi Institute for Nonviolence. Used by permission.

Page 75—from left to right

Vivekananda at the first Parliament of the World's Religions in Chicago, 1893. Courtesy of the Ramakrishna-Vivekananda Center, New York City. Used by permission.

Rabindranath Tagore with a young child in the late 1930s. Courtesy of the Tagore Centre UK. Used by permission.

Page 103—from left to right

Alexander Schmemann (center) with Alexander Solzhenitsyn, and his spouse, Juliana Schmemann. Used by permission.

Reinhold Niebuhr. Courtesy of the Archives of the Burke Library at Union Theological Seminary in the City of New York. Used by permission.

Page 135—from left to right

SIMONE WEIL. Used by permission.

MARTIN BUBER at his desk. Courtesy of the Estate of Martin Buber. Used by permission.

Page 167—from left to right

DOROTHY DAY and Ammon Hennacy during a protest in New York. Courtesy of the Department of Special Collections and University Archives, Marquette University. Used by permission.

ROBERT "DR. BOB" HOLBROOK SMITH. Courtesy of Dr. Bob's Home. Used by permission.

Page 197—from left to right

BLACK ELK. Photo taken by J. E. Brown, courtesy of Elenita Brown. Used by permission.

BEDE GRIFFITHS handing out cake at his birthday celebration. Courtesy of Bede Griffiths Trust web site. Used by permission.

Page 231—from left to right

THOMAS MERTON with H. H. THE DALAI LAMA on Merton's visit to Dharamsala, India, November 1968. From the collection of the Abbey of Gethsemani, Trappist, Kentucky. Used by permission.

SHUNRYU SUZUKI at Rinso-in, his temple in Japan in the mid-1960s. From the collection of the San Francisco Zen Center. Used by permission.

About the Contributors

DIANNE APRILE is an award-winning journalist and author of four books, including *Making a Heart for God: A Week Inside a Catholic Monastery* (Woodstock, Vt.: SkyLight Paths, 2001) and *The Abbey of Gethsemani: Place of Peace and Paradox.* She is on the faculty of the MFA in Writing program at Spalding University (Louisville, Kentucky). *[Thomas Merton; Evelyn Underhill; Thomas Keating]*

CAROLE ANN CAMP is a United Church of Christ pastor. Her latest book, *Labyrinths from the Outside In* (Woodstock, Vt.: SkyLight Paths, 2000), is coauthored with Donna Schaper. She has also written several biographies for young adults, including *Sally Ride; American Astronomers;* and *American Women Scientists. [Mary Daly; Carl Gustav Jung; C. S. Lewis; Oscar Romero]*

KENDRA CROSSEN BURROUGHS is a writer and editor specializing in religion and philosophy. She is the annotator of *Bhagavad Gita: Annotated and Explained* (Woodstock, Vt.: SkyLight Paths, 2001) and *The Gospel of Sri Ramakrishna: Annotated and Explained* (Woodstock, Vt.: SkyLight Paths, 2002) and is the compiler and editor of *The Essential Ken Wilber* and *Entering the Tao. [Thomas Berry; Black Elk; Joseph Campbell; Chögyam Trungpa; Deepak Chopra; Bede Griffiths; G. I. Gurdjieff; Gustavo Gutiérrez; Mawlana Muhammad Ilyas; Hazrat Inayat Kahn; Abraham Isaac Kook; J. Krishnamurti; Hans Küng; Maharishi Mahesh Yogi; Abraham Maslow; Meher Baba; Mother Teresa; Sayyed Hossein Nasr; Albert Schweitzer; William J. Seymour; Shirdi Sai Baba; Robert Holbrook Smith; Starhawk; Rabindranath Tagore; Desmond Tutu; Andrew Weil; Ken Wilber]*

MICHAEL KRESS is the editor of a Jewish educational web site and a former editor at Beliefnet.com. A graduate of Harvard Divinity School, he has written on religion and spirituality for *Newsweek,* the *Boston Globe,* the *Philadelphia Inquirer,* Salon.com, and *Publishers Weekly. [Dietrich Bonhoeffer; Martin Buber; Dorothy Day; Mary Baker Eddy; Robert Funk; Mahatma*

Gandhi; Billy Graham; Abraham Joshua Heschel; Pope John XXIII; Martin Luther King, Jr.; Bawa Muhaiyaddeen; Bhaktivedanta Prabuphada; Joseph Soloveitchik; Paramahansa Yogananda]

HOLLY J. LEBOWITZ is a freelance writer specializing in religion and spirituality. A graduate of Harvard Divinity School, she has contributed regularly to *Sojourners* magazine, Beliefnet.com, Religion News Service, and Spirituality.com. She is also the coeditor of *Religion, Race, and Justice in a Changing America. [Daniel Berrigan; Reinhold Niebuhr; Bertrand Russell; Zalman Schachter-Shalomi; Thich Nhat Hanh; Paul Tillich]*

JACK MAGUIRE is an award-winning author and storyteller. He is the annotator of *Dhammapada: Annotated and Explained* (Woodstock, Vt.: SkyLight Paths, 2002) and the author of *Waking Up: A Week Inside a Zen Monastery* (Woodstock, Vt.: SkyLight Paths, 2000). His other books include *The Power of Personal Storytelling* and *Essential Buddhism. [Dalai Lama; Pema Chödrön; D. T. Suzuki; Shunryu Suzuki]*

DAVID O'NEAL is a writer and editor with a special interest in interfaith dialogue, particularly among Christians, Buddhists, and Muslims. He is the compiler and editor of the book *Meister Eckhart, from Whom God Hid Nothing: Sermons, Writings, and Sayings.* He is a graduate of Saint Vladimir's Orthodox Theological Seminary in Crestwood, New York. *['Abdu'l Bahá; Ajahn Chah; Catherine de Hueck Doherty; Mircea Eliade; Maha Ghosananda; Ramana Maharshi; Alexander Schmemann; Seung Sahn; Vivekananda; Simone Weil]*

IRA RIFKIN is an award-winning journalist specializing in religion issues. He has been news director for Beliefnet.com and a national correspondent for Religion News Service. He has written for the *Washington Post, Los Angeles Times,* MSNBC.com, *New Age Journal,* and many other publications. He has contributed to three journalism textbooks. *[General editor; introduction; chapter introductions]*

KIMBERLY WINSTON is a freelance religion reporter. She is the 1996 recipient of the Religion Newswriters Association's Cassells Award for reporting excellence at smaller publications. She is the author of *Faith beyond Faith Healing. [Ram Dass; Pope John Paul II; Aimee Semple McPherson; Malcolm X; Elijah Muhammad; Walter Rauschenbusch; Huston Smith]*

Index

About SKYLIGHT PATHS Publishing

SkyLight Paths Publishing is creating a place where people of different spiritual traditions come together for challenge and inspiration, a place where we can help each other understand the mystery that lies at the heart of our existence.

Through spirituality, our religious beliefs are increasingly becoming a part of our lives—rather than *apart* from our lives. While many of us may be more interested than ever in spiritual growth, we may be less firmly planted in traditional religion. Yet, we do want to deepen our relationship to the sacred, to learn from our own as well as from other faith traditions, and to practice in new ways.

SkyLight Paths sees both believers and seekers as a community that increasingly transcends traditional boundaries of religion and denomination—people wanting to learn from each other, *walking together, finding the way.*

We at SkyLight Paths take great care to produce beautiful books that present meaningful spiritual content in a form that reflects the art of making high quality books. Therefore, we want to acknowledge those who contributed to the production of this book.

PRODUCTION
Tim Holtz, Martha McKinney & Bridgett Taylor

EDITORIAL
Amanda Dupuis, Polly Short Mahoney,
Lauren Seidman & Emily Wichland

COVER DESIGN
Stacey Hood, Big Eyedea, Waitsfield, Vermont

TEXT DESIGN
Susan Ramundo, SR Desktop Services, Ridge, New York

PRINTING & BINDING
Friesens Corporation, Manitoba, Canada

Spirituality

Who Is My God?

An Innovative Guide to Finding Your Spiritual Identity

Created by *the Editors at SkyLight Paths*

Spiritual Type™ + Tradition Indicator = Spiritual Identity

Your Spiritual Identity is an undeniable part of who you are—whether you've thought much about it or not. This dynamic resource provides a helpful framework to begin or deepen your spiritual growth. Start by taking the unique Spiritual Identity Self-Test™; tabulate your results; then explore one, two, or more of twenty-eight faiths/spiritual paths followed in America today. "An innovative and entertaining way to think—and rethink—about your own spiritual path, or perhaps even to find one." —Dan Wakefield, author of *How Do We Know When It's God?*
6 x 9, 160 pp, Quality PB Original, ISBN 1-893361-08-X **$15.95**

Spiritual Manifestos: *Visions for Renewed Religious Life in America from Young Spiritual Leaders of Many Faiths*

Edited by *Niles Elliot Goldstein;* Preface by *Martin E. Marty*

Discover the reasons why so many people have kept organized religion at arm's length.

Here, ten young spiritual leaders, most in their mid-thirties, representing the spectrum of religious traditions—Protestant, Catholic, Jewish, Buddhist, Unitarian Universalist—present the innovative ways they are transforming our spiritual communities and our lives. "These ten articulate young spiritual leaders engender hope for the vitality of 21st-century religion." —Forrest Church, Minister of All Souls Church in New York City
6 x 9, 256 pp, HC, ISBN 1-893361-09-8 **$21.95**

Jewish Spirituality: *A Brief Introduction for Christians*

by *Lawrence Kushner*

Lawrence Kushner, whose award-winning books have brought Jewish spirituality to life for countless readers of all faiths and backgrounds, tailors his unique style to address Christian's questions, revealing the essence of Judaism in a way that people whose own tradition traces its roots to Judaism can understand and enjoy.
5½ x 8½, 112 pp, Quality PB Original, ISBN 1-58023-150-0 **$12.95**

The Geography of Faith

Underground Conversations on Religious, Political and Social Change

by *Daniel Berrigan* and *Robert Coles;* Updated introduction and afterword by the authors

A classic of faith-based activism—updated for a new generation.

Listen in on the conversations between these two great teachers—one a renegade priest wanted by the FBI for his protests against the Vietnam war, the other a future Pulitzer Prize-winning journalist—as they struggle with what it means to put your faith to the test. Discover how their story of challenging the status quo during a time of great political, religious, and social change is just as applicable to our lives today. 6 x 9, 224 pp, Quality PB, ISBN 1-893361-40-3 **$16.95**

Spirituality

Inspired Lives: *Exploring the Role of Faith and Spirituality in the Lives of Extraordinary People*

by *Joanna Laufer* and *Kenneth S. Lewis*
Contributors include *Ang Lee, Wynton Marsalis, Kathleen Norris,* and many more

How faith transforms the lives and work of the creative and innovative people in our world.

In this moving book, soul-searching conversations unearth the importance of spirituality and personal faith for more than forty artists and innovators who have made a real difference in our world through their work. 6 x 9, 256 pp, Quality PB, ISBN 1-893361-33-0 **$16.95**

Women Pray
Voices through the Ages, from Many Faiths, Cultures, and Traditions

Edited and with introductions by *Monica Furlong*

Many ways—new and old—to communicate with the Divine.

This beautiful gift book celebrates the rich variety of ways women around the world have called out to the Divine—with words of joy, praise, gratitude, wonder, petition, longing, and even anger—from the ancient world up to our own time. Prayers from women of nearly every religious or spiritual background give us an eloquent expression of what it means to communicate with God. 5 x 7¼, 256 pp, Deluxe HC with ribbon marker, ISBN 1-893361-25-X **$19.95**

Zen Effects: *The Life of Alan Watts*

by *Monica Furlong*

The first and only full-length biography of one of the most charismatic spiritual leaders of the twentieth century—now back in print!

Through his widely popular books and lectures, Alan Watts (1915–1973) did more to introduce Eastern philosophy and religion to Western minds than any figure before or since. Here is the only biography of this charismatic figure, who served as Zen teacher, Anglican priest, lecturer, academic, entertainer, a leader of the San Francisco renaissance, and author of more than 30 books, including *The Way of Zen, Psychotherapy East and West* and *The Spirit of Zen.*
6 x 9, 264 pp, Quality PB, ISBN 1-893361-32-2 **$16.95**

Simone Weil: *A Modern Pilgrimage*

by *Robert Coles*

The extraordinary life of the spiritual philosopher who's been called both saint and madwoman.

The French writer and philosopher Simone Weil (1906–1943) devoted her life to a search for God—while avoiding membership in organized religion. Robert Coles' intriguing study of Weil details her short, eventful life, and is an insightful portrait of the beloved and controversial thinker whose life and writings influenced many (from T. S. Eliot to Adrienne Rich to Albert Camus), and continue to inspire seekers everywhere. 6 x 9, 208 pp, Quality PB, ISBN 1-893361-34-9 **$16.95**

Spirituality

Three Gates to Meditation Practice
A Personal Journey into Sufism, Buddhism, and Judaism
by *David A. Cooper*

Shows us how practicing within more than one spiritual tradition can lead us to our true home.

Here are over fifteen years from the journey of "post-denominational rabbi" David A. Cooper, author of *God Is a Verb,* and his wife, Shoshana—years in which the Coopers explored a rich variety of practices, from chanting Sufi *dhikr* to Buddhist Vipassanā meditation, to the study of kabbalah and esoteric Judaism. Their experience demonstrates that the spiritual path is really completely within our reach, whoever we are, whatever we do—as long as we are willing to practice it. 5½ x 8½, 240 pp, Quality PB, ISBN 1-893361-22-5 **$16.95**

Praying with Our Hands: *Twenty-One Practices of Embodied Prayer from the World's Spiritual Traditions*
by *Jon M. Sweeney;* Photographs by *Jennifer J. Wilson;*
Foreword by *Mother Tessa Bielecki;* Afterword by *Taitetsu Unno, Ph.D.*

A spiritual guidebook for bringing prayer into our bodies.

This inspiring book of reflections and accompanying photographs shows us twenty-one simple ways of using our hands to speak to God, to enrich our devotion and ritual. All express the various approaches of the world's religious traditions to bringing the body into worship. Spiritual traditions represented include Anglican, Sufi, Zen, Roman Catholic, Yoga, Shaker, Hindu, Jewish, Pentecostal, Eastern Orthodox, and many others.
8 x 8, 96 pp, 22 duotone photographs, Quality PB Original, ISBN 1-893361-16-0 **$16.95**

The Sacred Art of Listening
Forty Reflections for Cultivating a Spiritual Practice
by *Kay Lindahl;* Illustrations by *Amy Schnapper*

More than ever before, we need to embrace the skills and practice of listening. You will learn to: Speak clearly from your heart • Communicate with courage and compassion • Heighten your awareness for deep listening • Enhance your ability to listen to people with different belief systems. 8 x 8, 160 pp, Illus., Quality PB Original, ISBN 1-893361-44-6 **$16.95**

Labyrinths from the Outside In
Walking to Spiritual Insight—a Beginner's Guide
by *Donna Schaper* and *Carole Ann Camp*

The user-friendly, interfaith guide to making and using labyrinths—for meditation, prayer, and celebration.

Labyrinth walking is a spiritual exercise *anyone* can do. This accessible guide unlocks the mysteries of the labyrinth for all of us, providing ideas for using the labyrinth walk for prayer, meditation, and celebrations to mark the most important moments in life. Includes instructions for making a labyrinth of your own and finding one in your area.
6 x 9, 208 pp, b/w illus. and photographs, Quality PB Original, ISBN 1-893361-18-7 **$16.95**

Spirituality

One God Clapping: *The Spiritual Path of a Zen Rabbi*

by *Alan Lew* with *Sherril Jaffe*

Firsthand account of a spiritual journey from Zen Buddhist practitioner to rabbi.

A fascinating personal story of a Jewish meditation expert's roundabout spiritual journey from Zen Buddhist practitioner to rabbi. An insightful source of inspiration for each of us who is on the journey to find God in today's multi-faceted spiritual world.
5½ x 8½, 336 pp, Quality PB, ISBN 1-58023-115-2 **$16.95**

Aleph-Bet Yoga
Embodying the Hebrew Letters for Physical and Spiritual Well-Being

by *Steven A. Rapp*
Foreword by *Tamar Frankiel* and *Judy Greenfeld;* Preface by *Hart Lazer*

Blends aspects of hatha yoga and the shapes of the Hebrew letters. Connects yoga practice with Jewish spiritual life. Easy-to-follow instructions, b/w photos.
7 x 10, 128 pp, Quality PB, ISBN 1-58023-162-4 **$16.95**

The Way Into Jewish Mystical Tradition

by *Lawrence Kushner*

Explains the principles of Jewish mystical thinking, their religious and spiritual significance, and how they relate to our lives. A book that allows us to experience and understand the Jewish mystical approach to our place in the world.
6 x 9, 224 pp, HC, ISBN 1-58023-029-6 **$21.95**

Prayer for People Who Think Too Much
A Guide to Everyday, Anywhere Prayer from the World's Faith Traditions

by *Mitch Finley*

Helps us make prayer a natural part of daily living.

Takes a thoughtful look at how each major faith tradition incorporates prayer into *daily* life. Explores Christian sacraments, Jewish holy days, Muslim daily prayer, "mindfulness" in Buddhism, and more, to help you better understand and enhance your own prayer practices.
"I love this book." —Caroline Myss, author of *Anatomy of the Spirit*
5½ x 8½, 224 pp, Quality PB, ISBN 1-893361-21-7 **$16.95**; HC, ISBN 1-893361-00-4 **$21.95**

Spirituality

A Heart of Stillness
A Complete Guide to Learning the Art of Meditation
by *David A. Cooper*

The only complete, nonsectarian guide to meditation, from one of our most respected spiritual teachers.

Experience what mystics have experienced for thousands of years. *A Heart of Stillness* helps you acquire on your own, with minimal guidance, the skills of various styles of meditation. Draws upon the wisdom teachings of Christianity, Judaism, Buddhism, Hinduism, and Islam as it teaches you the processes of purification, concentration, and mastery in detail.
5½ x 8½, 272 pp, Quality PB, ISBN 1-893361-03-9 **$16.95**

Silence, Simplicity & Solitude
A Complete Guide to Spiritual Retreat at Home
by *David A. Cooper*

The classic personal spiritual retreat guide that enables readers to create their own self-guided spiritual retreat at home.

Award-winning author David Cooper traces personal mystical retreat in all of the world's major traditions, describing the varieties of spiritual practices for modern spiritual seekers. Cooper shares the techniques and practices that encompass the personal spiritual retreat experience, allowing readers to enhance their meditation practices and create an effective, self-guided spiritual retreat in their own homes—without the instruction of a meditation teacher. 5½ x 8½, 336 pp, Quality PB, ISBN 1-893361-04-7 **$16.95**

God Whispers: *Stories of the Soul, Lessons of the Heart*
by Rabbi Karyn D. Kedar 6 x 9, 176 pp, Quality PB, ISBN 1-58023-088-1 **$15.95**

The Empty Chair: *Finding Hope and Joy—*
Timeless Wisdom from a Hasidic Master, Rebbe Nachman of Breslov **AWARD WINNER!**
Adapted by Moshe Mykoff and the Breslov Research Institute
4 x 6, 128 pp, Deluxe PB, 2-color text, ISBN 1-879045-67-2 **$9.95**

The Gentle Weapon: *Prayers for Everyday and Not-So-Everyday Moments*
Adapted from the Wisdom of Rebbe Nachman of Breslov by Moshe Mykoff and S. C. Mizrahi, with the Breslov Research Institute
4 x 6, 144 pp, Deluxe PB, 2-color text, ISBN 1-58023-022-9 **$9.95**

Children's Spirituality

ENDORSED BY CATHOLIC, PROTESTANT, JEWISH, AND BUDDHIST RELIGIOUS LEADERS

Becoming Me: *A Story of Creation*

by *Martin Boroson*
Full-color illus. by *Christopher Gilvan-Cartwright*

For ages 4 & up

Told in the personal "voice" of the Creator, here is a story about creation and relationship that is about each one of us. In simple words and with radiant illustrations, the Creator tells an intimate story about love, about friendship and playing, about our world—and about ourselves. And with each turn of the page, we're reminded that we just might be closer to our Creator than we think!

8 x 10, 32 pp, Full-color illus., HC, ISBN 1-893361-11-X **$16.95**

A Prayer for the Earth
The Story of Naamah, Noah's Wife

by *Sandy Eisenberg Sasso*
Full-color illus. by *Bethanne Andersen*

For ages 4 & up

This new story, based on an ancient text, opens readers' religious imaginations to new ideas about the well-known story of the Flood. When God tells Noah to bring the animals of the world onto the ark, God also calls on Naamah, Noah's wife, to save each plant on Earth. "A lovely tale.... Children of all ages should be drawn to this parable for our times."
—Tomie de Paola, artist/author of books for children

9 x 12, 32 pp, HC, Full-color illus., ISBN 1-879045-60-5 **$16.95**

In God's Name

For ages 4 & up

by *Sandy Eisenberg Sasso*; Full-color illus. by *Phoebe Stone*

Like an ancient myth in its poetic text and vibrant illustrations, this award-winning modern fable about the search for God's name celebrates the diversity and, at the same time, the unity of all the people of the world.

9 x 12, 32 pp, HC, Full-color illus., ISBN 1-879045-26-5 **$16.95**

The 11th Commandment
Wisdom from Our Children

by *The Children of America*

For ages 4 & up

"If there were an Eleventh Commandment, what would it be?" Children of many religious denominations across America answer this question—in their own drawings and words. "A rare book of spiritual celebration for all people, of all ages, for all time." —*Bookviews*

8 x 10, 48 pp, HC, Full-color illus., ISBN 1-879045-46-X **$16.95**

Children's Spirituality

MULTICULTURAL, NONDENOMINATIONAL, NONSECTARIAN

Where Does God Live?

For ages 3–6

by *August Gold* and *Matthew J. Perlman*

Using simple, everyday examples that children can relate to, this colorful book helps young readers develop a personal understanding of God.

10 x 8½, 32 pp, Quality PB, Full-color photo illus., ISBN 1-893361-39-X **$7.95**

God's Paintbrush

For ages 4 & up

by *Sandy Eisenberg Sasso*; Full-color illus. by *Annette Compton*

Invites children of all faiths and backgrounds to encounter God openly in their own lives. Wonderfully interactive; provides questions adult and child can explore together at the end of each episode. "An excellent way to honor the imaginative breadth and depth of the spiritual life of the young." —Dr. Robert Coles, Harvard University

11 x 8½, 32 pp, HC, Full-color illus., ISBN 1-879045-22-2 **$16.95**

Also available:

A Teacher's Guide 8½ x 11, 32 pp, PB, ISBN 1-879045-57-5 **$8.95**

God's Paintbrush Celebration Kit 9½ x 12, HC, Includes 5 sessions/40 full-color Activity Sheets and Teacher Folder with complete instructions, ISBN 1-58023-050-4 **$21.95**

In God's Name

For ages 4 & up

by *Sandy Eisenberg Sasso*; Full-color illus. by *Phoebe Stone*

Like an ancient myth in its poetic text and vibrant illustrations, this award-winning modern fable about the search for God's name celebrates the diversity and, at the same time, the unity of all the people of the world. "What a lovely, healing book!" —Madeleine L'Engle

9 x 12, 32 pp, HC, Full-color illus., ISBN 1-879045-26-5 **$16.95**

In Our Image: *God's First Creatures*

For ages 4 & up

by *Nancy Sohn Swartz;* Full-color illus. by *Melanie Hall*

A playful new twist on the Creation story—from the perspective of the animals. Celebrates the interconnectedness of nature and the harmony of all living things. "The vibrantly colored illustrations nearly leap off the page in this delightful interpretation." —*School Library Journal*

"A message all children should hear, presented in words and pictures that children will find irresistible." —Rabbi Harold Kushner, author of *When Bad Things Happen to Good People*

9 x 12, 32 pp, HC, Full-color illus., ISBN 1-879045-99-0 **$16.95**

Children's Spirituality

MULTICULTURAL, NONDENOMINATIONAL, NONSECTARIAN

God Said Amen

For ages 4 & up

by *Sandy Eisenberg Sasso*
Full-color illus. by *Avi Katz*

A warm and inspiring tale of two kingdoms: Midnight Kingdom is overflowing with water but has no oil to light its lamps; Desert Kingdom is blessed with oil but has no water to grow its gardens. The kingdoms' rulers ask God for help but are too stubborn to ask each other. It takes a minstrel, a pair of royal riding-birds and their young keepers, and a simple act of kindness to show that they need only reach out to each other to find the answers to their prayers.

9 x 12, 32 pp, HC, Full-color illus., ISBN 1-58023-080-6 **$16.95**

For Heaven's Sake

For ages 4 & up

by *Sandy Eisenberg Sasso*; Full-color illus. by *Kathryn Kunz Finney*

Everyone talked about heaven: "Thank heavens." "Heaven forbid." "For heaven's sake, Isaiah." But no one would say what heaven was or how to find it. So Isaiah decides to find out, by seeking answers from many different people. "This book is a reminder of how well Sandy Sasso knows the minds of children. But it may surprise—and delight—readers to find how well she knows us grown-ups too." —Maria Harris, National Consultant in Religious Education, and author of *Teaching and Religious Imagination*

9 x 12, 32 pp, HC, Full-color illus., ISBN 1-58023-054-7 **$16.95**

But God Remembered
Stories of Women from Creation to the Promised Land

For ages 8 & up

by *Sandy Eisenberg Sasso*; Full-color illus. by *Bethanne Andersen*

A fascinating collection of four different stories of women only briefly mentioned in biblical tradition and religious texts. Award-winning author Sasso vibrantly brings to life courageous and strong women from ancient tradition; all teach important values through their actions and faith. "Exquisite.... A book of beauty, strength and spirituality." —Association of Bible Teachers 9 x 12, 32 pp, HC, Full-color illus., ISBN 1-879045-43-5 **$16.95**

God in Between

For ages 4 & up

by *Sandy Eisenberg Sasso*; Full-color illus. by *Sally Sweetland*

If you wanted to find God, where would you look? A magical, mythical tale that teaches that God can be found where we are: within all of us and the relationships between us. "This happy and wondrous book takes our children on a sweet and holy journey into God's presence." —Rabbi Wayne Dosick, Ph.D., author of *The Business Bible* and *Soul Judaism*

9 x 12, 32 pp, HC, Full-color illus., ISBN 1-879045-86-9 **$16.95**

Spirituality

Honey from the Rock
An Introduction to Jewish Mysticism

by *Lawrence Kushner*

An insightful and absorbing introduction to the ten gates of Jewish mysticism and how it applies to daily life. "The easiest introduction to Jewish mysticism you can read."

6 x 9, 176 pp, Quality PB, ISBN 1-58023-073-3 **$15.95**

Eyes Remade for Wonder
The Way of Jewish Mysticism and Sacred Living

A Lawrence Kushner Reader

Intro. by *Thomas Moore,* author of *Care of the Soul*

Whether you are new to Kushner or a devoted fan, you'll find inspiration here. With samplings from each of Kushner's works, and a generous amount of new material, this book is to be read and reread, each time discovering deeper layers of meaning in our lives.

6 x 9, 240 pp, Quality PB, ISBN 1-58023-042-3 **$16.95**; HC, ISBN 1-58023-014-8 **$23.95**

Invisible Lines of Connection
Sacred Stories of the Ordinary

by *Lawrence Kushner* **AWARD WINNER!**

Through his everyday encounters with family, friends, colleagues and strangers, Kushner takes us deeply into our lives, finding flashes of spiritual insight in the process.

5½ x 8½, 160 pp, Quality PB, ISBN 1-879045-98-2 **$15.95**; HC, ISBN 1-879045-52-4 **$21.95**

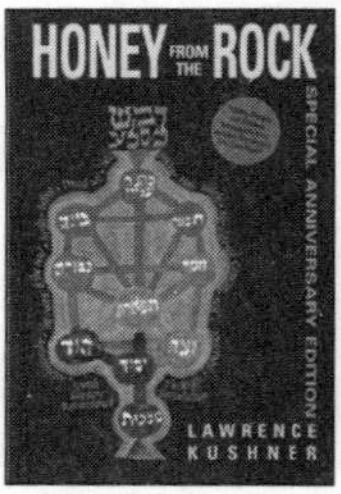

Finding Joy
A Practical Spiritual Guide to Happiness

by *Dannel I. Schwartz* with *Mark Hass* **AWARD WINNER!**

Explains how to find joy through a time honored, creative—and surprisingly practical—approach based on the teachings of Jewish mysticism and Kabbalah.

6 x 9, 192 pp, Quality PB, ISBN 1-58023-009-1 **$14.95**; HC, ISBN 1-879045-53-2 **$19.95**

Ancient Secrets
Using the Stories of the Bible to Improve Our Everyday Lives

by *Rabbi Levi Meier, Ph.D.* **AWARD WINNER!**

Drawing on a broad range of wisdom writings, distinguished rabbi and psychologist Levi Meier takes a thoughtful, wise and fresh approach to showing us how to apply the stories of the Bible to our everyday lives.

5½ x 8½, 288 pp, Quality PB, ISBN 1-58023-064-4 **$16.95**

Books in the "Perfect Stranger" Series

How to Be a Perfect Stranger, In 2 Volumes

A Guide to Etiquette in Other People's Religious Ceremonies

Ed. by *Stuart M. Matlins* and *Arthur J. Magida* **AWARD WINNERS!**

Explains the rituals and celebrations of North America's major religions/denominations, helping an interested guest to feel comfortable, participate to the fullest extent possible, and avoid violating anyone's religious principles. Answers practical questions from the perspective of *any* other faith.

Vol. 1: North America's Largest Faiths

VOL. 1 COVERS: Assemblies of God • Baptist • Buddhist • Christian Church (Disciples of Christ) • Christian Science • Churches of Christ • Episcopalian/Anglican • Greek Orthodox • Hindu • Islam • Jehovah's Witnesses • Jewish • Lutheran • Methodist • Mormon • Presbyterian • Quaker • Roman Catholic • Seventh-day Adventist • United Church of Canada • United Church of Christ 6 x 9, 432 pp, Quality PB, ISBN 1-893361-01-2 **$19.95**

Vol. 2: More Faiths in North America

VOL. 2 COVERS: African American Methodist Churches • Baha'i • Christian and Missionary Alliance • Christian Congregation • Church of the Brethren • Church of the Nazarene • Evangelical Free Church • International Church of the Foursquare Gospel • International Pentecostal Holiness Church • Mennonite/Amish • Native American/First Nations • Orthodox Churches • Pentecostal Church of God • Reformed Church • Sikh • Unitarian Universalist • Wesleyan 6 x 9, 416 pp, Quality PB, ISBN 1-893361-02-0 **$19.95**

The Perfect Stranger's Guide to Funerals and Grieving Practices

A Guide to Etiquette in Other People's Religious Ceremonies

Edited by *Stuart M. Matlins*

6 x 9, 240 pp, Quality PB, ISBN 1-893361-20-9 **$16.95**

The Perfect Stranger's Guide to Wedding Ceremonies

A Guide to Etiquette in Other People's Religious Ceremonies

Edited by *Stuart M. Matlins*

6 x 9, 208 pp, Quality PB, ISBN 1-893361-19-5 **$16.95**